PROCLAIM THE
WONDER

PROCLAIM THE
WONDER

ENGAGING SCIENCE ON SUNDAY

Scott E. Hoezee

Wipf & Stock
PUBLISHERS
Eugene, Oregon

Wipf and Stock Publishers
199 W 8th Ave, Suite 3
Eugene, OR 97401

Proclaim the Wonder
Engaging Science on Sunday
By Hoezee, Scott
Copyright©2003 Baker Publishing Group
ISBN 13: 978-1-5326-8014-4
Publication date 1/28/2019
Previously published by Baker Publishing Group, 2003

This limited edition licensed by special permission of Baker Publishing Group.

For Mom and Dad,
who taught me to be curious
about God's world

Contents

Acknowledgments

A friend likes to tell a joke about the pastor who began and ended every sermon the same way. As he began to preach, this pastor would hold his hands slightly above his head and make a short chopping motion. As he said "Amen" at the end of each sermon, he would repeat this two-handed chop. After witnessing this Sunday after Sunday, someone finally asked the pastor what the motions meant. "Oh," he replied, "those are quotation marks!"

Perhaps one needs to be a preacher to appreciate this, because preachers are keenly aware of how much their sermons are influenced by the work of other thinkers and writers. This book, which is ultimately about preaching, is likewise chock-full of insights from others. This is most obvious in the works that are formally cited, but I wish to acknowledge also those who do not appear in the notes but who helped me tremendously.

This entire project grew out of my three-year involvement in the Pastor-Theologian Program sponsored by the Center of Theological Inquiry (CTI) in Princeton, New Jersey, and generously underwritten by grants from the Lilly Foundation. The bulk of this manuscript was written while I was on sabbatical at CTI in the fall of 2000. I express my profound gratitude to CTI's director, Wallace M. Alston Jr., and to CTI's amazing administrator, Kathi Morley. Bishop William Lazareth was also instrumental in my becoming acquainted with CTI, and the members of the support staff, including Mary Rae Rogers, Marion Gibson, and Maureen Montgomery, were also very helpful in many ways.

The Center of Theological Inquiry is a collegial community, and so I'd like to acknowledge others who were in residence during the fall of 2000. I am grateful to Gabriel Fackre, Beverly Gaventa, Reinhard Hütter, Ann Jervis, Edmondo Lupieri, Kam Weng Ng, Richard Osmer, Sir John Polkinghorne, Philip Rolnick, and Allen Verhey for their many good conversations and comments. I take particular note of the providentially advantageous presence of Sir John Polkinghorne, who occupied the study right next to mine that fall. His world-class expertise in the area of theology and science made his comments nothing short of invaluable. I also thank Robert Jenson, the senior scholar in residence at CTI, for helping to guide and shape my sabbatical period as well as for his suggestions on how to make the manuscript clearer.

The congregation and council of Calvin Christian Reformed Church deserve to be thanked for granting me a period of sabbatical. In particular, I thank council president, Steve Gibson, and my colleague in ministry Rev. Robert Koornneef, for helping to make my sabbatical a reality and for taking on extra responsibilities in my absence.

For my three years in the Pastor-Theologian Program, I was privileged to be part of a group of pastors whom I respect and love. Many of the ideas in these pages were tried out on these people first. So I extend my warmest thanks to Revs. Byron Bangert, Bob Dahlen, Barry Ensign-George, Pam Fickenscher, Shirley Funk, Sonja Hagander, Bob Hausman, Bruce Modahl, Bruce Rigdon, John Rollefson, Sam Speers, Erik Strand, and Chuck Valenti-Hein.

Several people agreed to undertake the quite large task of reading the entire manuscript to correct my errors and provide still more help. I am grateful to Wallace Bratt, James VandenBosch, and also J. Wentzel van Huyssteen, whose specialty in the area of theology and science made his feedback especially encouraging. As authors routinely say, however, if there are errors that persist in these pages, they are wholly my own fault, not that of the people who assisted me.

Thanks is also extended to Dwight Baker, Robert Hosack, and all of the editors and staff at Baker Book House for agreeing to publish this work and for all the effort they put forth to make this book a reality.

Finally, I thank my wife, Rosemary, and my children, Julianna and Graham. Not only did they accompany me to Princeton for four months of sabbatical, they also endured my many absences while I attended pastor-theologian seminars as well as the many, many hours I spent writing, editing, and refining this manuscript. As always, it is to them that I owe perhaps my greatest gratitude for providing the kind of love, nurture, and support that are consistently the very gifts of God in my life.

Scott E. Hoezee
Summer 2002

Introduction

Scottish poet William E. McGonagall may well have been one of the worst poets who ever lived. At least, he has been so ranked by some who are in the know on such matters. But a couplet he once penned succeeds in reflecting the way many Christians, past and present, approach certain aspects of life:

> When faith and reason clash,
> Let reason go to smash.[1]

As the world has now turned the corner into a new millennium, the clashes between faith and reason are nowhere more evident than in the debates that rage along the theology-and-science front. Throughout the church world but particularly in fundamentalist and conservative evangelical circles, a lot of "smashing" goes on. Indeed, the findings and claims of science get discarded so fast in some parts of the wider church world that if we could hear every "smash," the resulting cacophony would sound like a Los Angeles china shop during a 7.0 earthquake!

In his fine book *Duet or Duel?* J. Wentzel van Huyssteen notes that although Darwinism is clearly near the forefront of the theology-and-science debate, often this discussion is no longer centered on Scripture: "Gone are the days when we could still naively ponder how and where evolution might challenge the Bible, how the opening chapters of Genesis should be read, and to what extent our theological understanding of creation and the origin of life should shape our interpretations of the latest, spectacular discoveries of science."[2] Van Huyssteen is correct to point out that in more recent times the challenge of Darwinism to Christian theology has been recognized as being broader than just this or

11

that single point. However, although it may be true that some Christian communities have now moved on from the "naive" biblical questions van Huyssteen mentions, wide swaths of the Christian church world in North America bear witness to the fact that the days of pondering evolution's challenge to the Bible (and even to specific passages of the Bible) are by no means "gone."

In many areas (particularly evolution, but also the overall shape of contemporary cosmology) science is seen as sufficiently threatening to warrant swift smashing and discarding by faithful Christians who seek to remain true to the Bible above all else. But then, many Christians would be quick to point out that they do not have the "smash market" cornered. After all, many scientists in the world operate under the reverse dictum of McGonagall:

> When faith and reason clash,
> 'Tis faith must go to smash.

In a good many laboratories and observatories in the world, it is not even a matter of first examining and then smashing *specific* articles of faith so much as it is a matter of smashing all religion right up front. In his book *The Fifth Miracle*, Paul Davies writes, "Science takes as its starting point the assumption that life wasn't made by a god or a supernatural being; it happened unaided and spontaneously as a natural process. . . . It is the job of science to solve mysteries without recourse to divine intervention."[3] But this comment from Davies is actually very mild compared to other, similar comments we will consider. A number of recent books have contained harsh antireligious diatribes and even wholesale dismissals of the entire notion of theological knowledge. Some science writers today could accurately be described as downright hostile to faith and by extension to the faithful.

Whether or not all or even most scientists agree with such antireligious sentiments does not matter to the many Christians, including some Christian preachers, who catch wind of such words and allow them to serve as global statements on the way *all* scientists think. Many Christian leaders disseminate such statements to the faithful, who in turn receive them as fighting words. And fight they do. A survey of recent book titles reveals the prevalence of warfare and courtroom metaphors employed on both sides of the issue: *The Battle of Beginnings, Darwin on Trial, Darwin Re-Tried, Defeating Darwinism, Bones of Contention, Abusing Science: The Case against Creationism, The Creator in the Courtroom.* Whether or not the books that bear these titles provide lopsided battles or fair trials could be debated, but it is clear which of the two groups feels more threatened: the Christians. In an empirical age, when the facts and fruits of science are on display in everything from microwave ovens to wireless phones that connect to the Internet, from textbooks in public schools to the science pages of the daily newspaper, the people whose core beliefs are *not* matters of scientific proof are the ones who tend to feel the most pressure. Hence, fear runs like a fault line across the evangelical landscape of North America—fear that raises to a fever pitch conversations that otherwise could be thoughtful and calm discussions of the wonderful physical cosmos in which humanity finds itself.

What makes this fear more acute for many Christians is the obvious fact that there is no escaping science, its findings, or its usefulness. The Y2K scare was itself proof of science's grip on our world, including religious communities. Although the fear of global and local computer shutdowns resulted in a number of different behaviors—ranging from sensible precautions like hanging on to recent bank statements to loopy precautions like stocking basement bunkers with Spam and rifles—one of the most clearly discernible results of Y2K was the apocalypticism it unleashed in some Christian communities. Not a few believers around the world concluded that the potentially cataclysmic events the Y2K computer bug would set off would be harbingers of Christ's imminent return. The irony of such expectations, however, is that some of the very Christians who most resist both scientific findings and their influence were themselves so influenced by the pervasive reach of science that they allowed the prospect of a technological glitch to determine their eschatology! In the contemporary industrialized world, there is no escaping science.

Although the Y2K phenomenon was by definition a one-time, non-repeatable event, other behaviors indicate that a broader scientific mentality and method frequently grip the church. For instance, many, especially conservative, churches now routinely quantify congregational life to measure how well things are going in ministry. Statistical analysis and the reduction of everything to hard, cold numbers (How many people attend the services on a Sunday morning? What is the age breakdown? How well does the congregation reflect the demographics of the larger geographic area?) is, however, a very scientific way to treat such matters. Similar comments could be made with regard to the social sciences, the data of which are frequently accepted by outreach-minded congregations as the best tool for ascertaining potential strategies for how the church should be run. But such studies within churches not only make use of science-like forms of data but also reflect the unconscious assimilation of science's overall methodology. As a pastor, I can testify to the tremendous increase of surveys that I have received in the mail from social research institutes hired by my denomination in the last five years. Over and again the current state of the denomination and its future course are in no small measure judged by scientifically designed survey instruments and the analysis of data that pastors send to professionals whose job it is to tell the denomination what the data means. Although this book deals mostly with the physical, not the social, sciences, the pervasiveness of the scientific research method demonstrates how widely science's influence extends.

The twentieth century's preeminent scientist, Albert Einstein, was touted as *Time* magazine's Person of the Century in December 1999. In the accompanying articles various writers pointed out the far-reaching ways Einstein's work has influenced many areas of life, ranging well beyond theoretical physics. "His ideas, like Darwin's, reverberated beyond science, influencing modern culture from painting to poetry."[4] Stephen Hawking went so far as to claim that Einstein changed our very notion of reality.

Meanwhile, on the last day of 1999, two editorials in the *New York Times* hailed the successful rise of a pervasive scientific mentality as the key feature and accomplishment of the last millennium. Anthony Lewis claimed that the biggest transforming change of the last thousand years "is the adoption of the scientific method: the commitment to experiment, to test every hypothesis. But it is broader than science. It is the open mind, the willingness in all aspects of life to consider possibilities other than the received truth. It is openness to reason."[5] Similarly, columnist Bob Herbert asserted that science is changing the definition of what it means to be human. Herbert quotes Dr. Michael Crow who stated simply that "science right now is the most powerful single force in our culture."[6]

In such a time, Christians who fear their faith is under attack by science and its broad-reaching abilities to describe and shape reality may be tempted, therefore, to dart their eyes left and right, up and down, as they cry out (like some pursued victim in a Hitchcock horror film), "It's everywhere!" Indeed it is. And this facet of modern life seems unlikely to change in the twenty-first century. Keith Ward goes so far as to claim, "As the third millennium begins, what will become of Christian belief? . . . My own view is that the third millennium of Christian existence will bring a new integration of scientific and religious thought, the development of a more global spirituality, and a retrieval of some of the deepest spiritual insights of the Christian faith, which have been often under emphasized or overlooked. . . . I aim to show . . . that an informed sci-entific view of the universe is not only compatible with Christian belief, but actually lends quite strong support to the claim of some forms of Christianity. Christian belief in the third millennium can and should be scientifically informed, globally aware, a source of distinctive insights into the human condition, and a great enrichment of human life and welfare. Whether or not it will be is up to Christians themselves."[7] Ward is almost certainly correct. Clearly, however, this prospect of integrating Christianity and the scientific ethos that now surrounds us is a frighten-ing one to some in the Christian community.

For their part, however, although scientists may be annoyed by the claims of Christians, they rarely if ever appear to be threatened by them. Scientists, of course, recognize the tentative nature of the scientific enterprise, leaving themselves open to future revisions should new evi-dence come to light. But a concomitant belief is that if they *are* right, their findings and theories will slowly but surely be corroborated, if not one day vindicated, through subsequent scientific advances. For instance, the first scientists to discover DNA may not have known a tenth of what science now knows about genetics. They may have adhered to a few DNA postulates that have since been largely disproved. But at least the discoverers of DNA knew that if they truly *were* on to something, it would be demonstrated with *greater* certainty, not less, as the biological sciences continued to advance.

Any given scientific model may or may not be correct, but either way, a religious community is unlikely to prove or disprove a scientific theory. Religious fundamentalists may be annoying to some scientists, but they are no threat to science. Of course, some scientists are clearly more vexed by people of faith than are others, which is why some sci-ence writers make a hobby of pooh-poohing faith claims whenever and wherever they can. Still, there is a vast difference between being vexed by certain groups and feeling genuinely threatened by them. Similarly, I may be annoyed by the incessant yapping of the dogs fenced in the yard next door, but they are no threat. A barking Rottweiler who corners me in an alley, however, is a very different matter!

Christians may seem like yapping dogs to scientists, but scientists seem like marauding Rottweilers to at least some Christians. Perhaps this is due in part to the fact that faith does not generally possess the kind of hopeful confidence in future proof or vindication that the realm of science can have regarding its various theories. Of course, Christians do believe that one day God's kingdom will fully come at the return of Christ, providing ultimate vindication for their beliefs. The point here, however, relates to the way theology and science proceed in this world before the final ringing down of history's curtain. The truth of what Christians believe will in the future be as much a matter of having faith as it is now. No advance in theological insight is likely to cinch a doctrine in such a way that faith and trust will no longer be required to believe it. Perhaps it is partly for this reason that Christians sometimes feel as if they are left in the dust vis-à-vis science's sometimes rapid advances.

Science, after all, moves right along, whereas faith seems to stand still, remaining very near the same spot to which it has been anchored for two thousand years. Science makes progress toward the future; theology makes reference to the past (at least so it seems to those on the outside). As Michael Welker has pointed out, it was the acceptance of this post-Enlightenment caricature that led in part to a religious retreat in some parts of the academic world, reducing religious studies in the university to a history of religion, or to a study of comparative religions, or to an internal self-study of the faith without reference to "outside" concerns. In short, religion was pushed into an academic closet, cloistered away from other academic enterprises.

In an age that values movement (notice the message of phrases like "the information superhighway" or Microsoft's advertising slogan, "Where do you want to go today?"), theology appears, even to some Christians, to be relatively passive or even stuck. Worse, some seem to feel that faith is, for this very reason, vulnerable to diminishment and maybe even debunking by areas of inquiry that speed into the future. Whereas scientists do not worry about what will come from the realm of faith, believers *do* often fret that their beliefs are imperiled or at least brought into question by science. The scientific advance whose future prospects provide hope to the scientists who wish to see their theories tested out may serve as a source of anxiety for believers who fear that precisely such future proofs could diminish the faith.

But it's not quite this simple. To the average scientist, religion is not a threat to the nitty-gritty specifics of her physical findings. No matter what Christians believe or the kinds of things they say in church on a Sunday morning, these will have little effect on what will be visible through the eyepiece of an electron microscope come Monday morning. True enough. However, a wider mentality within the scientific community *does* conflict with Christianity (and most other religions, too). Here I'm referring to scientific naturalism. Science as a mode of inquiry investigates the physical world and creates postulates and theories to explain what exists, where it came from, and where it may go next. Scientific naturalism, however, claims that what science can study in the natural, physical world is *all* that exists. If science can't see or detect it, it does not exist. But if that is so, then God, divine providence, and a larger purpose and design for life are invalid because these can be neither investigated nor, therefore, proven. Hence, scientific naturalism makes metaphysical and spiritual claims that conflict with a Christian view of the deeper things of life.

But the boundary line between science proper and the philosophical or religious world-and-life view of scientific naturalism is often blurred. Alan Padgett points out that some scientists profess no more than a "methodological naturalism," claiming that strictly speaking, scientific research always requires a kind of agnosticism where spiritual (and hence nonscientific) matters and questions are concerned. Padgett, however, believes "the term 'methodological naturalism' is always and everywhere a front for full-blown philosophical naturalism. Those who defend this 'mere' methodology always end up resorting to naturalism pure and simple."[8] As will be noted below, Alvin Plantinga has gone so far as to say that the link between methodological naturalism and full-blown naturalism as a religious commitment of the heart is so tight that what Christians really need is an entirely new way to do science. Plantinga has suggested that science for Christians perhaps needs to proceed from a theistic point of view right from the start, correlating as best as possible (and as constantly as possible) the physical world with the claims made by Scripture.

Padgett and Plantinga are perhaps a bit extreme in rejecting science's method of bracketing questions relating to faith and theology in order to pursue its principally empirical and physical task of investigating nature. What cannot be denied, however, is that increasing numbers of scientists do resort to a full-blown naturalism—one that nearly requires a rejection of other forms of knowing about reality, especially theological and faith-based ways of knowing. When some scientists (or laypeople) conflate science and scientific naturalism, religion may be perceived as a threat to science after all, in that these two competing spiritual philosophies do indeed clash. The Christian faith and its belief system are no more compatible with scientific naturalism than they are with, say, New Age beliefs or Shintoism. Further, where some scientists say that science as a field of inquiry *requires* adopting the worldview of scientific naturalism—or that science, of necessity, *leads* to scientific naturalism—then it may mistakenly appear that science and religion are, in and of themselves and by definition, incompatible. This unfortunate confusion leads some scientists to see religion as the enemy, even as it leads at least some Christians to view science as a foe (and not just the philosophical position of scientific naturalism), whose physical findings are always suspect at best and godless at worst.

In what follows I will use the word "science" to refer to the strictly physical field of inquiry into the structures of the universe: biology, physics, astronomy, geology, and the like all represent "science" in that they investigate what a cell looks like, how far away a star is from earth, how old a rock is, and so forth. Science checks into these physical facets of life and then develops various theories or models by which to explain the past and present activity of such things and to project probabilities of how they will work and behave in the future. Occasionally in this book, however, I may conflate science as inquiry with the technological tools that science makes possible. Such tools include everything from medical equipment and treatments to gadgets like computers and cell phones. The term "science," in other words, will refer to the discipline of investigating nature as well as the methods, results, and tools of doing so. I will not use "science" to refer to any philosophical or religious viewpoints.

I will use the phrase "scientific naturalism" to designate the combination of science as inquiry and a particular (usually atheistic) religious and philosophical point of view as espoused by at least some of the people who work in the sciences. I believe "science" and "scientific naturalism" not only can be distinguished from one another but must be. From my vantage point, the difference between these two terms is rather like the difference between politics and communism. Although communism is one form that politics sometimes takes in our world, just being a politician does not necessarily make you a communist. Often very good politicians are highly critical of communist politics. Politics and communism may be related in the grander scheme of things but not in the sense that all politics inevitably or necessarily lead to communism. One could even claim that communism is *bad* politics, a corruption of politics. Politics by itself is the art of leading people via various government institutions—an art that can be defined and practiced without any reference to communism whatsoever. In similar fashion, science can (and probably should) be practiced with perfect legitimacy and accuracy without any necessary reference to the naturalist or atheistic perspective of some who work in the sciences.

This separating of physical science from metaphysical claims *about* science is a vital activity for Christians to pursue if the overarching purpose of this project is going to seem in any sense valid. The goal of this book is to sketch the contours of the larger theological and scientific landscapes to find ways to diminish the fear and hatred of science. If this is possible, the state of the interaction between theology and science may arrive at a saner, more productive place. In recent years any number of books about theology and science have had similar goals. Unlike most of these volumes, however, I wish to suggest that the place to begin such a lowering of the temperature between science and theology is the pulpit. A little pulpit talk about science on Sunday whereby science gets reflected positively in the preacher's sermon could quite possibly be a good way to begin addressing this frequently complex, routinely controversial subject in ways that proffer hope for a constructive relationship between God's Word and a scientific world. What's more, it may proffer this hope on the "popular" lay level of the Christian community and not in academic circles alone.

Why Preaching?

For better or worse in our increasingly audiovisual culture, the Sunday sermon has become a primary locus of learning for most Christians. This is not to diminish or minimize other ways of learning, including adult education forums, study groups, or the reading of thoughtful books and periodicals. However, in most (especially Protestant) congregations, the Sunday sermon remains one of the few focused times in the average week when laypersons have the opportunity to think theologically and biblically about their lives as well as about the issues of the day. It is no accident, for instance, that when President Clinton was enduring the worst of the Monica Lewinsky scandal, replete with multiple moral layers and the president's own spiritual talk of confession and forgiveness, major newspapers around the country used what was said from the nation's pulpits on Sunday mornings for Monday morning assessments of what communities of faith were thinking. The pulpit and the thoughts expressed there are properly seen as a reflection of what congregants may be thinking or at least of what trained spiritual leaders believe should be the shape and outcome of considered theological reflection (which presumably is what good preachers desire to display and disseminate with their preaching in the first place).

Preachers are, therefore, in a prime position either to further the suspicion that some Christians feel in relation to science or to move believers to a better, more secure (and also more productive) place in their thinking. Interestingly, already in the seventeenth century those who opposed Galileo's new, heliocentric view of the cosmos found the pulpits of Italy's churches to be a key place in which to combat Galileo's science. According to Dava Sobel's book *Galileo's Daughter,* some people in Italy urged preachers to denounce Galileo in their Sunday sermons. At least one preacher in Florence did so one Sunday in 1614 when he stretched the meaning of Acts 1:11 ("Men of Galilee, why do ye stand looking up to heaven?") into a critique of Galileo's astronomy![9] My suggestion here is for preachers to allow what is said from contemporary pulpits to do just the opposite of impugning the scientific enterprise by instead helping to move parishioners to a more secure, positive appreciation of what science can teach us. But how can preachers even begin to do this? What strategies might be employed week in and week out to accomplish a soothing of fears and an elevating of dialogue?

Clearly, whichever strategies I suggest will have to range much more broadly than proposing occasional sermons that deal specifically with science and theology. After all, Christians believe that theology encompasses the whole of reality. Dealing faithfully with the broad reaches of both theology and science will require preachers to find equally pervasive ways to weave together the strands of science and theology—threads of thought that currently run independent of one another through the warp and woof of church life in many places. In short, it is not any one sermon or even a sermon series that can achieve the goal of changing the tenor of the discussions between theology and science. Rather, such a change will result from the preacher's overall approach to the life of faith in the modern world of science—an attitude that must weave in and through all sermons. Perhaps then change may slowly come.

Most clergy (and most people in the pews as well) sense that preachers can indeed have such an effect on a congregation. The residue of many years of thoughtful preaching produces a congregation of good and attentive listeners who expect something to happen in the sermon. They expect to learn something to mull over and maybe even wrestle with in the days to come. Conversely, the residue of many years of shallow preaching in which the preacher's illustrations are drawn chiefly from the humor pages of *Reader's Digest* can produce a congregation that is impatient with deeper matters of faith and willing to treat even bad sermons with no more than a shrug. Such congregations have been taught not to expect much from sermons.

Many times even a preacher's personality makes an imprint on a congregation. A particularly ebullient preacher of my acquaintance once took a call to a congregation that for ten years had been led by a very antisocial, painfully shy preacher whose smiles were forced (if they came at all) and whose presence in fellowship hours was never witnessed. The effects showed in a congregation that was likewise unwelcoming of strangers and rather cold in general. But after six years' worth of my friend's joyful élan in the pulpit and narthex, the congregation had a very different timbre. This change did not happen immediately or even in the course of just one year. But slowly preachers can affect a congregation's way of seeing life and perceiving the faith. My suggestion here is that in addition to some very specific themes that a preacher can sprinkle into his preaching from time to time, some overall attitudes toward science and its place within the larger Christian world-and-life view can help a congregation to shape its own attitudes over time. These strategies and attitudes are what I wish to explore.

It needs to be very clear up front that I am *not* suggesting preachers "use" science as some kind of tool or artificial insertion into a sermon. Instead, I want to highlight the fact that there are occasions in preaching (and in the consideration of specific texts in the Bible) when themes related to science arise quite *naturally*. A few obvious examples would be when preaching on Genesis 1 or 2, Psalms 8, 19, and 104, and any other passages that direct our attention to matters related to the physical world.

But the places where science and the Christian faith intersect are not limited to specific passages in the Bible but include broader topics in theology and in the life of the congregation. For instance, the nature of humanity—who we are as creatures, the mysteries of the soul and spirit, how we think and feel—is a broad topic about which both science and the Christian faith have much to say. Preachers who understand at least some of the specific things that science has to say on, for example, the human brain and our sense of self can fruitfully equip members of the congregation to bring together theological claims about the nature of humanity and what they read in the paper about advances and theories in the neurosciences. Advances in genetics and gerontology are bringing increasing numbers of ethical questions to the forefront. How can preachers help to shape the congregation's spiritual and theological reflections on such issues in ways that will carry over to those times during the week when church members are confronted with the views of the media on these same issues, not to mention those times when church members are confronted with the painful ethical decisions involved in a troubled pregnancy, infertility, or an elderly parent's facing end-of-life issues?

Yet another area where faith and science naturally interact is ecology and stewardship of the environment. Christians see the creation as a great gift of God and, hence, as a cause to praise God. But what are believers specifically thankful *for*? Couldn't the new wonders that fields like astronomy and oceanography reveal about the physical creation fruitfully be added to our burgeoning list of the Creator's gifts for which we render thoughtful, heartfelt praise? Wouldn't an increased awareness of these wonders enhance the pointedness of the Christian prayer life? If a child at the dinner table offers a rather hurried prayer in which she says no more than, "Dear God, thanks for everything, Amen," there is good reason to wonder how thoughtful she is being or how well she has paid attention to how God has blessed her in the day gone by. But if a child were to pray, "Dear God, thank you that I did well on my spelling test and that Jimmy was my friend again on the playground, Amen," this would reveal a much greater and more moving attentiveness to the things of God. Believers who wish to praise God for the gift of creation would similarly do well to look for ways to make their prayers of thanksgiving and adoration more specific. Knowing at least some of what is "out there" in the physical creation as revealed by science could perhaps assist us in doing just that and would therefore be yet another area where faith and science naturally overlap.

Another wide subject that Christians often think about is the matter of hope. But what does it mean to have hope—cosmic hope for the future of the world and personal hope for a continuing life with God even after death—in a world that science frequently reveals to be entropic, subject to decay and diminishment, and pervaded by death? Many people today, scientists and nonscientists alike, proclaim some version of the "death as destiny" viewpoint, which says that death is built into the universe, death comes to all eventually, and the only thing more we can say about it from this side of death is that death is a cruel fact. Again, Christians have much to say on these subjects, but wouldn't the Christian voice be more credible and clear if hope were articulated from within a context that does not seek to escape the darker facts of our current existence?

Clearly, when it comes to such topics, it would be helpful if preachers knew not just that there *are* some debates and dialogues between science and theology but also some of the specific issues involved. Surely it would be helpful if preachers knew at least the broad contours of current scientific claims about the physical cosmos, just as preachers quite naturally tend to know the contours of the current political and cultural landscape, the history of literature, and some of the "hot" topics in wider theological and philosophical realms. When theology and science make pronouncements on the same phenomena, Christians may well find areas of agreement as well as of disagreement, things to appreciate about what science teaches as well as things about which to be a bit wary. But there can be no interaction between science and theology if people of faith have no clue what science is saying in the first place.

For this reason, the first part of this book will present some contemporary scientific theories about the universe in order to lay the groundwork for the specific preaching strategies I will suggest later in the book. Reviewing the claims of science is a necessary prelude to my suggestion that preachers should look for natural and positive ways to reflect on science in their sermons. Preachers may feel they are on shaky ground when it comes to science and may perceive science as an adversary to religious faith. I will therefore attempt to show that even in the face of scientific counterclaims, very strong cases have been made for the rationality and validity of religious knowledge, particularly the knowledge Christians receive from the Holy Spirit through the Bible. People of faith can, so to speak, "hold their heads high" instead of feeling they must duck their heads and retreat before the blows that science inflicts on the faith.

Reviewing the specifics of scientific claims may also help to stock the homiletical larder with facts and images that preachers can use illustratively in their preaching, or at least it might be helpful for preachers to be aware of such specifics when Scripture and theology intersect with the teachings and findings of science. Additionally, a sketch of what science is teaching today will provide the broad backdrop against which all preaching in the modern world takes place, whether or not science is specifically mentioned in a given sermon.

Most preachers would probably agree that preaching successfully in a given culture requires at least a broad understanding of what that culture is like. One would not, for instance, be able to preach successfully to Americans without a general knowledge of the structure of the American government, the nature of the entertainment industry in this country, and the key social and political issues of the day. Although a preacher need not know the minutiae of how the American government is structured, he would want to know enough to avoid saying "Parliament" in a sermon when he meant "Congress." One need not be a maven of the entertainment industry to know at least the differences between movie theaters and cable television. A preacher who routinely used the wrong political vocabulary or who demonstrated a repeated ignorance of the various outlets of the mass media would surely lose a little bit of credibility among the congregation, even as his or her sermons might be less effective in bringing God's Word (the gospel *content*) to bear on the real lives of the parishioners (the gospel *context*).[10]

Likewise, if a preacher were to completely bracket science (in the sense of never referring to it) or to speak of science in antiquated words and concepts (such that even eighth graders would notice the difference between what they learn in their science classes and what the preacher is now saying), there could, over time, be a loss of credibility and homiletical effectiveness. A friend once related the story of a preacher who, in a sermon early in his career, spoke of science so inaccurately that his wife, a physician, was horrified. She made him promise *never* to try to use science in a sermon again—a promise that he unfortunately kept. But in the face of homiletical mistakes—be they theological, factual, historical, scientific, or whatever—a preacher's response should be to attempt to gain more knowledge so that she can avoid such a faux pas in the future, not to practice a wholesale avoidance of the subject matter in question. A preacher who inadvertently misquoted a Shakespeare sonnet one week could respond to this gaffe by being more careful the next time, perhaps double-checking the exact quotation in his copy of the Riverside Shakespeare anthology. But a sensible reaction to such a homiletical mistake most certainly would not be a decision against all future poetry citations!

A sermon, of course, should never be a science lecture, any more than it should ever be a movie review, political speech, or history lesson. Sermons do, however, use contemporary cinema, current political issues, and historical events in illustrative and applicatory ways. Preachers who know something about the history of the ancient Near East will be better poised to preach from the Old Testament than those who have given history only a glance. Preachers who read thoughtful novels and biographies or who view well-crafted films will have more resources to draw on for sermon illustrations than those who read only biblical commentaries. Good novels or films, after all, frequently deal with some of the same topics dealt with in Scripture and therefore also in preaching. So, for instance, if a preacher has read a good novel by Russell Banks, the next time this pastor wants to deal with the despair and rage that so often grip working-class people (an aspect of modern life that Banks has sketched quite brilliantly in several novels), the force of what the pastor has learned by peering through this particular window on reality will be something the pastor can draw on naturally when presenting the nature of Christian hope and how it may interact with or bring healing to the despair in our country and our world.

Similarly, it is my contention that preachers who understand the larger picture of our cosmos (of *God's* cosmos) as science helps us better to understand it will be in a better position to talk about creation, providence, and even eschatological hope than those preachers who either chalk up science as a singularly godless enterprise or who simply ignore science as being of no use to believers, whose minds are better focused on "spiritual" matters only ("spiritual" in the Gnostic sense of all that is opposed to physical and earthly concerns).

The Preacher as Scout

But how might illustrations that utilize the findings of science actually work in sermons? A number of specific strategies and general ideas will be presented at the conclusion of this book, but in order to set the coming pages in a clear context, perhaps I can provide an overall strategy gleaned from the work of Roger Van Harn. In his book *Pew Rights*, Van Harn writes about preaching, not from the minister's viewpoint but rather from the viewpoint of those who sit in the pews each week. What do these faithful folks have a right to expect from sermons? Among Van Harn's many good suggestions is the notion of the preacher as a "pioneer listener" to the biblical text. "Preachers are pioneer listeners on behalf of the community of faith. Preachers who remain behind the travelers to take pictures and keep records of what happened along the way cannot help us with what is ahead. Preachers who remain in the company of the faithful without risking the look ahead and around may be able to help us with what's happening now but they will not be able to help us with what's around the bend. Preachers should be listeners before they are speakers."[11]

Van Harn applies this useful image principally to biblical text. Preachers should spend their week listening to the biblical text for the upcoming Sunday, taking the time to hear the text in ways that the average parishioner does not have the time to do. Come Sunday, the preacher then divulges the insights garnered during this pioneer voyage into Scripture. Like a scout who has gone ahead to investigate new territory, so the preacher goes in advance of the congregation to learn the contours of some new landscape. When the members of the congregation join the journey on Sunday morning, the pastor can assure them that he or she has already explored the region up ahead and has much to tell and much to show as a result of this exploratory foray into the textual landscape.

While working on this manuscript, I lived for four months in Princeton, New Jersey. My family and I had lived in Princeton for nearly two months before any of our friends or family from the Midwest were able to come for a visit. During those two months my wife and I did a lot of exploring throughout the university campus and the town as well as in the surrounding regions, parks, and wildlife refuges. We explored this new terrain for our own enjoyment and benefit, but we always had in mind our desire to discover new sites and to learn key information about those sites so that when our visitors arrived, we would be able to take them on a guided tour. Since our guests would have limited time in the area, we wanted to know enough to be able to select the highlights our guests simply should not miss while visiting Princeton.

So it is with sermon preparation: the preacher gets to spend longer stretches of time immersing himself in the biblical text in advance of the congregation's arrival for a visit. No preacher can share everything he has discovered in the process of writing the sermon, but at the very least the highlights of the text and the key points of interest and instruction can be summarized and passed on. Knowing which things to focus on and which things to leave to one side for the time being is one of the responsibilities and benefits of being a pioneer explorer on behalf of other people.

Expanding on Van Harn's image, I would say that the preacher needs to function in a similar role in relation to the wider culture and society in which the congregation finds itself week in and week out. As in the Bible, the preacher needs to be a pioneer explorer in society, investigating what's "out there" in the world so as to be better poised to bring the Bible's content into meaningful interaction with cultural context. But the preacher will not be in a very good position to do this if most members of the congregation are already much farther down the cultural road than the preacher is. If the preacher is the last one to find out about this or that new development in culture, science, or society and if this is routinely the case, how can this preacher's sermons help people to find their way in the world? If, culturally speaking, the preacher is always trotting along well behind the congregation, then clearly the members of the congregation are left to fend for themselves in society, with Sunday's sermons providing little guidance as they seek to find their way.

Obviously, in most congregations any number of people will know far more about specific subjects than the preacher ever could. It would be absurd to suggest that the only way a preacher could help, say, a doctor find her way in her profession as a Christian would be for the preacher to know more about new developments in medicine or genetic engineering than does the doctor who is a specialist in that field. The same could be said for most any professional or vocational field: any given person in the congregation will know more about certain narrowly defined subject areas than the pastor ever could (or should). The goal here is not that the pastor become a polymath expert in every conceivable field. Rather the goal is more modest, though not any less important, namely, preachers should have at least a general knowledge of what is going on in society as well as in the larger world. One need not be a geopolitical policy expert to know the broad contours of what is happening in the Middle East or on the African continent. One need not be a financial genius to understand what a dramatic drop in the stock market may mean for many people in the congregation. And one need not be a physicist or a well-read cosmologist to understand the basics of what science now reveals about the structure of the universe.

Preaching, of course, is always a delicate balancing act. On the one hand, the preacher does not and must not take his or her cues from science, economics, or the mass media in deciding the *content* of the Christian gospel that must be proclaimed each week. On the other hand, for the gospel content to relate meaningfully to the day-to-day lives of the parishioners, the preacher must acknowledge the reality of the larger world (including, therefore, science as well as the developing portrait of the world that science provides). In one sense, preaching provides an alternative view of the world to the view that bombards people all week through the mass media (which for the most part gets along just fine without any recourse to God's existence or God's work). At the same time, the reason the church needs preachers is because people need to know how to live out their faith in the world. Christian proclamation recognizes the myriad ways in which society "gets life wrong" and yet does not conclude each week's sermon by declaring, "Therefore, beloved, go home, bolt your door shut, and don't set foot outside again or read a newspaper until you are ready to return to church next Sunday morning!"

Instead, preachers hope that their presentation of the gospel's content in a given context will help people to keep in mind (and firmly believe) the things of God even *while* reading the newspaper, watching television, going to the movies, or jostling with other shoppers at the mall. Preaching needs to help people make sense of the world in which they live, but sermons accomplish this goal neither by thoroughly rejecting the world nor by making the Christian life look like a neat, simple, black-and-white alternative to the world.

Preachers are first and foremost students of God's Word. If preachers fail on that front, little else they could ever say about the wider culture or society will amount to much, spiritually speaking. But preachers should also attempt, as best as they are able, to be students of what goes on in the wider world. This, of course, is hardly a new thought. John Stott has written about the preacher as being "between two worlds" (the biblical world and the contemporary world), even as others have utilized the picture of preachers holding the Bible in one hand and the daily newspaper in the other. Obviously, it is my contention that science needs to be factored in to such imagery. Science now has significant influence on the contemporary world and makes up a significant portion of what gets printed in the newspaper every day. Preachers would do well to know at least a little about this subject.

It should be noted, however, that wondering how to bring science into religion is a different, albeit somewhat related, question from how to bring religion into science. Helping scientists understand and perhaps make use of faith in their work is an intriguing subject but not one that the average Christian congregation can do much about. Perhaps if the church were to do a better job from its pulpits of integrating faith and science, the scientists who are members of those congregations would be better equipped to return to their labs and observatories *as* Christians. But that would be a side benefit to the larger ideas I wish to propose; although it is possible that if, as I will suggest, the Christian community could have a more relaxed approach to the theology-and-science relationship, perhaps over time the relationship between these two fields would warm up sufficiently so that science would begin to be a greater respecter of religion and its beliefs concurrent to religion's ability to become a greater respecter of science and its methods and results.

But the primary goal of this book is not to get more religion into the lab but to get more of the lab into the sanctuary and, hence, into the warp and woof of the Christian life. In general terms, however, this is not something we commonly do. Preacher and writer Barbara Brown Taylor notes that at one point in her life she had a real interest in science. But she further notes, "As soon as I decided to go to seminary, science dropped off my radar screen altogether. As an ordained minister, I would not be required to deal in precise measurements or verifiable facts. I would deal in meaning, faith, morality, and love—all those invisible things that cannot be seen through a microscope or mounted on a pin."[12]

Perhaps because we have traditionally kept science and theology in separate categories, theology now finds itself marginalized in a scientifically informed world. When I became an ordained pastor in my first church, in Fremont, Michigan, I naturally had frequent cause to visit the nearby Gerber Memorial Hospital to call on parishioners who were ill. Perhaps partly because I have long been fascinated with the medical profession, but perhaps also because I longed for the kind of recognition and respect a doctor typically receives, I frequently wished I could drape a stethoscope around *my* neck and thereby feel as if I had a niche in the hospital setting. I never did so, of course, but when some months later the hospital arranged to give all clergy a clip-on photo I.D. similar to those worn by the doctors and nurses, I finally began to feel like somebody in a way I had never quite felt just by carrying around a Bible. Truth is, the photo I.D. still didn't garner the level of recognition that a shiny stethoscope attracts!

Perhaps this is because society is fascinated with science and particularly with medical practitioners of science. Consider the plethora of prime-time television dramas, not to mention afternoon soap operas, that revolve around doctors. Then consider the handful of (largely unsuccessful) shows in the history of TV that have had anything to do with clergy. Most shows that have regularly featured a pastor in a lead role either have been inane comedies that poked fun at the quirks of religion or have featured priests who do no religious work at all but are instead private detectives on the side (in which case the sleuth work, not any recognizable pastoral duties or religious practices, is what the show is about). People of science, as opposed to people of faith, carry great weight in our society. They are the stuff of good drama.

Barbara Brown Taylor tells her own hospital-related experience, noting that years ago when she served as a hospital chaplain, she was called in only when "all else had failed" and the doctor could do no more than depart from the dying or dead patient. Perhaps, Brown Taylor concludes, this marginalization of clergy and of matters related to faith is why the phrase "Scientific studies show . . ." carries far more weight in our day, even among some religious people, than "Thus says the Lord . . ."[13]

Similarly, a researcher recently conducted an informal experiment to test how credulous folks are today. He found that as long as you cloak some bit of information in the garb of a scientific study from some respected institution, people are willing to believe, or at least to consider believing, almost anything. "Say, did you hear about that new study from M.I.T. that showed a connection between jogging and lower intelligence?" Or, "Did you know that according to recent research at Berkeley, a diet that includes three chocolate eclairs a day can dramatically help you lose weight? Yeah, it seems there is an enzyme unique to eclairs called protoleptic amino oxide that actually stimulates the burning of fat!" This experiment showed that no matter how outrageous the claims were, as long as they sounded scientific, people typically responded in one of three ways. Some said, "Really? Can that be true? Interesting." Others would respond, "*Where* did you say that study was conducted?"

And many put themselves into the scientific know by proclaiming, "You know, I've *heard* that!"

There may be, of course, any number of reasons for the automatic credence given to apparently scientific matters (as opposed to the skepticism that typically attends faith claims), but maybe it is partly because those who speak for the Lord in pulpits have so long distanced themselves (passively, if not actively) from all things scientific. Maybe a lack of scientific interest or awareness on the part of preachers has served to give the impression that what scientific studies show and what the Lord says have very little to do with one another (and just maybe science works *against* what the Lord says). Thus, perhaps a tighter connection between science and faith, as fostered by realistic preaching that connects with the wider scientific world, would be a better way to proceed.

Hence, the principal aim of this book is to find a way to acknowledge science in the sanctuary more successfully and naturally. The idea is to do this not as a way to enhance the professional courtesies afforded to clergy but as a way to keep theology from seeming—even to Christians, much less to non-Christians—irrelevant over against all things scientific. A parallel aim, however, is to bring the lab into the sanctuary in a way that will honor both science and theology and each field's legitimate, albeit different, ways of knowing. Some Christian communities are already highly adept at "bringing the lab into the sanctuary," but this is done in such a way that the lab trumps Scripture rather easily. Needless to say, when other Christian communities who fear the encroachment of science see science having this kind of retrofitting effect on theology, they feel that their initial suspicions have been confirmed: when science comes into the church, the faith of our fathers and mothers goes to smash. So in our attempt to acknowledge science in a positive way, I believe we must first deal with questions on the authority of Scripture to affirm the Bible's traditional authority. I hope to demonstrate that a mediating way to bring the lab into the sanctuary is possible—one that maintains the integrity of both areas of inquiry and knowledge.

Overview

This book will therefore begin in chapter 1 with a defense of the authority of Scripture against those who assert that the only reliable authority on which to base one's life is the scientific authority that results from rigorous investigation, experimentation, and proof. Since this is a book about preaching and science, it makes sense to begin with a defense of that which, in traditional churches at least, is the bedrock of every sermon: the Bible. But as will become evident, the argument by which I think the Bible (and religious knowledge in general) can be affirmed and defended may also be useful in encounters with scientific naturalists who scorn faith-based claims to truth in favor of holding up science alone as the key to reliable knowledge.

In other words, chapter 1 will not only establish the gospel basis of the kind of preaching I want to recommend but will also present a good argument against those in the sciences today who believe that they alone have a corner on truth. This strikes me as a necessary starting point if readers are going to find it possible to acknowledge and learn more about science. After all, if science *necessarily* undercuts the Bible, from which Christian hope and joy is proclaimed, then science would definitely be something to be avoided in the pulpit and everywhere else in the Christian life. But if we can come to see that there are very good reasons to believe that the voice of God's Spirit that believers hear in Scripture is real (in ways science can neither prove nor disprove), then the nature of the discussion between theology and science may become a bit more relaxed and hence more fruitful right from the start.

Chapter 2 will focus on celebrating science. If believers do indeed believe that the Bible is the best lens through which to view life and the world, then elements in that same Bible lead us to a positive investigation into God's creation. The Bible itself suggests that as we find out more and more about God's work, we will find more and more reasons to praise God, from whom all blessings and wonders flow. It will be my contention that science can be a good partner in helping us to further explore the handiwork of our God.

But of course not everything in the realm of science is going to be acceptable to Christians (much less a cause to praise God!). So in chapter 3 we will take a critical look at some of the anti-religious sentiments that some contemporary scientists express. As I noted earlier, such statements typically have less to do with science's physical findings and more to do with the religious bent (or lack thereof) of the scientist doing the work. This chapter will try, therefore, to distinguish the proper work of science (investigating, say, the nature of an electron) from the nonscientific imposition of the scientist's own religious and philosophical positions on his or her work (claiming, for instance, that there is no God because the electron whirs around just fine without the help of any outside force, divine or otherwise). Building on chapter 1, we will note that science's more religious pronouncements are out of place and do not destroy or even diminish the existence of religious experience of God. But if science as investigation into the world is, even from a biblical perspective, a proper enterprise to pursue (as highlighted in chapter 2), and if theology is also a wholly legitimate way to find out still more about the universe—in short, if *both* theology and science have good and valid things to say—then clearly the next task will be to suggest ways to relate these two subjects. Hence, chapter 3 will conclude with some suggestions on how to do precisely that. I will outline my own model for how I think theology can fruitfully acknowledge what is legitimately good about science, even if at the same time people of faith critique what is illegitimately said by at least some scientists today.

Chapter 4 will build on my belief that there is no *necessary* clash between theology and science and will then attempt to summarize some more recent discoveries, particularly discoveries in the fields of physics and cosmology, though we will also ponder some of the ideas currently being advanced by those sciences that deal with the biological and mental nature of the human person. Chapter 4 will attempt to accomplish in a limited way what I am suggesting should become a goal of all preachers; namely, to find out a little bit more of what science is now saying about this universe and our place in it.

The dazzling scientific facts presented in chapter 4 will be followed in chapter 5 by my attempt to provide a theological interpretation of the emerging scientific picture of the universe. If, as Christians believe with a passion, God continues to uphold this universe by divine providence, and if this God is also active in revealing himself to his creatures, how does that enrich our Christian appreciation for the scientific picture of the universe? How does our belief in God's abiding presence and providential guidance cause Christians to nuance or at least to add to our understanding of the quantum universe and humanity's place within it?

Finally, the last chapters of the book will turn to the preaching task of pastors in the church. Some very specific suggestions and strategies will be presented to flesh out ways preachers can acknowledge the scientific picture in those areas where theology and science naturally overlap. When such occasions of overlap and interaction arise in the course of presenting God's Word in sermons, how can theology and science most fruitfully interact in the pulpit? Are there some overarching ideas preachers would do well to bear in mind week in and week out that will serve to enhance the congregation's ability to appreciate God's creation and science's ability to help us celebrate that creation? In partial answer to such questions, the book will conclude with a few sample sermons from my own preaching—occasions when I tried to take my own advice in bringing preaching and science together.

But long before we get to that nitty-gritty level of homiletical strategies and practices, significant groundwork needs to be laid so that Christians can begin to relax when theology meets science. To this task we now turn, beginning with some reflections on the properly central place that the Bible occupies in the life of the church as well as in the life of the Christian in the wider world.

Part 1

1

Biblical Authority
in an Age of Science

The Church's Script

With each technological advance in history, the text of the Bible and perhaps also people's perceptions and use of the Bible have in some way changed *with* the new technology and often as a direct result *of* the technology. In our day, when many homes have ten or more Bibles lying around and almost every hotel room contains a Gideon Bible, we do not often recall that for nearly three-quarters of the two millennia Christianity has existed as a religion, precious few Bibles were available. Prior to Gutenberg's invention of printing via movable type, copies of sacred Scripture were for the most part possessed only by monasteries, the very wealthy, and the clergy—which was just as well, since many Christians prior to that time couldn't read anyway. The prospect of a person carrying his or her own personal copy of the Bible to church or even the prospect of a church sanctuary containing scores of Bibles in the pew racks would have seemed a near impossibility to the many Christians who lived prior to the 1400s.

But all of that changed when printing was invented. After all, the Bible was the first book to be published. Not long after printed Bibles became available, Martin Luther took pains to do something that had seldom been done before: he translated the Bible into the vernacular language of ordinary people. Suddenly the Bible was no longer the book of the clergy alone but was for all believers. What's more, Luther and other Reformers of the sixteenth century, though still recognizing the communal nature of biblical interpretation within the context of the wider church, encouraged each person not only to read God's written Word but to be his or her own biblical interpreter. So the invention of printing gave people a reason to learn to read in that they could now actually lay their hands on reading material. After all, when there had been nothing to read in the first place, illiteracy was not perceived as a grave deficit.

By making the Bible available to all people, which led to the idea of publishing vernacular translations of the Bible, printing may also have contributed in some measure to the splintering of the Protestant wing of the church into ever-increasing subgroups, sects, and denominations. After all, once people could read the Bible for themselves, the possibility arose that they might disagree about what they read. Gone were the days when the only way people could learn what the Bible said was to listen to the priest, who would *tell* them what it said. Now they could look it up for themselves. Although this is an admittedly brief summary of printing's impact, the point is that the technological innovation of printing had significant effects on how people perceived and used the Bible.

At the close of the second millennium, technology surged ahead once again, this time via the electronic medium of the Internet and the World Wide Web. Suddenly we had not only printed text but *hypertext*. Hypertext is a computer format in which certain "hot" words or links are highlighted (usually in bright blue). By clicking the computer's mouse on a hot text, one can instantly be linked to other web sites that provide further and more specific information. So, for instance, if you were reading a forecast on a weather web site, you might see the word "hurricane" lit up in bright blue. Were you to click on "hurricane," your computer might then display a dictionary definition of what constitutes a hurricane, a list of the century's worst hurricanes, or maybe even videotape footage of what a hurricane looks like as it comes onshore.

One might not have guessed this technological advance would have much of an effect on the Bible as God's authoritative Word, but evidence of the Internet's impact on people's perceptions and use of Scripture can already be seen. In his 1998 book *Virtual Faith*, Tom Beaudoin traces some of the main lines of Generation X spirituality. Generation X is somewhat loosely defined as those born between 1964 and 1979. Members of this generation were in their twenties and thirties when the year 2000 arrived and cannot remember a time when computers and cable television were not common. Gen Xers are cyber-suckled and cyber-savvy.

For our purposes, it is instructive to examine one of the effects Beaudoin claims the Internet culture has had on Scripture. Beaudoin says his attitudes toward the Bible changed radically the first time he saw Scripture laid out as hypertext on a web site. Suddenly he could click on various portions of Bible verses and get whisked to other web sites that provided commentary on the verses and sometimes even to sites that questioned the credibility of the verses. For Beaudoin and many other Gen Xers, this opened up a new way of reading the Bible. "I realized that hypertext makes us read Scripture in a new way, as a cyberBible. . . . When Scripture is hypertext, readers take control of the text, in effect rewriting it and becoming biblical coauthors. This makes a whole new claim on Xers of faith. I could not navigate through the cyberBible without continually selecting where I should go from among seemingly endless hypertext links. The responsibility of coauthoring sacred texts . . . becomes more explicit in cyberspace. This possibility of Xers as biblical coauthors is perhaps the most shocking threat to old orthodoxies."[1]

Indeed it is. Whether or not other people of his generation would agree with him on this particular point, Beaudoin nevertheless serves as just one illustration of how science, the technological tools it makes available, and the larger worldview it fosters may have an impact on the Christian faith and on Scripture, which has traditionally been seen as the bedrock on whose unchanging authority the faith depends. Beaudoin says he grew up believing that the Bible provides believers with "a firm theological foundation." Although his new ideas about the cyberBible are clearly presented as a positive advance, Beaudoin admits that these ideas shook his "firm foundation," making even the Bible seem "as slippery as the old orthodoxies that my culture's music videos skewered."[2] Apparently, for the Bible to mean anything to members of Generation X, it needs to undergo a technological makeover, the first effect of which is the replacement of the overarching authority (which has traditionally stemmed from the Bible's divine *Author*) with the ad hoc, experiential authority that each reader creates for him- or herself through cobbling together information made available by surfing hyperlinks in the ever-restless, fast-paced world of cyberspace.

While the goal of this book is to foster a positive attitude toward science and to encourage positive acknowledgments in sermons of what is good about science, it may be useful to first deal with a few of the genuine drawbacks of the scientific mentality. As we have just seen, the rise of science and technological innovations (like the Internet) has clearly done damage to people's perceptions and use of the Bible. More dire yet, however, is that in some circles the scientific mentality has led to a dismissal of the Bible because the Bible's various claims, including its overall claim to inspired authority, cannot pass scientific muster. So why would a modern person want to base much (or all) of his or her life on something whose validity, truth, and authority seems vastly *less* certain than the many things science can teach us?

As I noted in the introduction, some scientists regard the rejection of theological claims as easy. Although proving a new scientific postulate on relativity or cosmic string theory may be difficult, many scientists are certain that the *dis*proof of anything scientific most assuredly will not come from a document several thousands of years old (or from those who adhere to that outdated document). Ironically, it seems that secular thinkers may not be the only ones skeptical about Scripture's ability to speak to the modern world. The crisis of biblical authority bears witness to the faith community's struggle with this issue, a struggle in which the Gen Xers' attempt to be "coauthors" of Scripture is but one small example of the larger crisis.

This is a book about preaching, science, and the possible intersections of these two enterprises. I will contend that preaching and science can be brought together very naturally, with neither field necessarily impugning the validity of the other. But it is patently obvious to almost any observer of the contemporary scene that certain elements of our postmodern setting tend to corrode the authority of the very book on which, I believe, all preaching must be based: the Bible. So how can a Christian preacher committed to a faithful proclamation of Scripture find occasions to speak of science in a positive, affirming way if a scientific frame of mind tends to undercut the very book on which the sermon is based in the first place? Some Christians today see science as the enemy of faith, the foe of what the Bible says, and the countervoice of the divine voice believers claim speaks to them in Scripture. If science truly is the enemy of the Christian faith, it simply cannot be given much, if any, voice in a sermon.

Perhaps an analogy would be helpful at this point. Some time ago I saw an outstanding play on Broadway in New York City. For nearly two and a half hours the actors in this play were completely absorbed in their respective roles. During this time the script of the play dictated each actor's every word, gesture, facial expression, and movement. The art of acting and staging a play, however, is to create the illusion that the characters being portrayed are real, that they truly are a part of the story being told, and that the events and dialogue are developing naturally and spontaneously. But suppose that midway through a performance some person off the street wandered onto the stage. Suppose further that this intruder began relating to the actors not as the characters they were portraying but indeed as *actors* and started saying to the audience things like, "They're just mouthing words from a script! It's not real!" Clearly, this would shatter the illusion of the play. By directly calling attention to the script, the intruder would ruin the script's purpose, which is to dramatically tell a story in a way gripping enough to make a deep impression on the members of the audience.

Christians, of course, also have a "script," but the purpose of their script is not to create a temporary sense of reality but to convey the true, abiding nature of the reality of life in this world. As we will see, however, the way Scripture conveys information is quite different from the way science conveys information. What's more, a scientific approach to truth and knowledge has led some (professional scientists and laypeople alike) to dispute and sometimes to *dismiss* the Bible's authority to reveal the truth about anything. Thus, one might fear that bringing science into the pulpit might be like letting an intruder onto the stage during a play. Would the voice of science in a pulpit point to the "script" of Scripture and say, "It's not real, you know! None of it can be proven, so it's just not rational to believe a word of it!" If this is the effect science has on faith, the voice of science would ruin a convincing presentation of the script of Scripture, which is what the sermon aims to accomplish in the first place.

Some in the scientific community quite obviously think that this is precisely the shattering effect science has on religion and particularly on religious texts. It is equally obvious that some in the church *fear* that this effect may be the inevitable outcome of mixing religion and science and therefore believe that the only things to be said about science from the pulpit are negative, critical things. Just as the director of a play would want to immediately toss an intruder off the stage, so some in the church want to grab science by its lapels and toss it back out into the streets.

But I believe we do not need to take such a hostile approach. Shortly I will attempt to summarize recent efforts to demonstrate that the claims Christians make for theological and spiritual knowledge are similar to, and as rational as, many other things people claim to know about in the normal course of life in this world. Theology's way of knowing, therefore, neither supplants nor impeaches science's various ways of gaining knowledge. Instead, theology stands alongside science as yet another, albeit very different, way to learn about the universe in which we find ourselves.

The crux of this important issue is whether Christians can reliably discover and reliably know true and valid information despite their not using scientific methods. To answer this question, we need to first consider the nature of the Bible's authority as the church has tradition-ally thought about it and then examine why those who claim to have destroyed that authority by scientific means are wrong. Only then can we pursue the suggestion that preaching and science can be fruitfully combined.

Those familiar with church history know that once upon a time theology itself was regarded as a form of science. Around the time of Thomas Aquinas in the thirteenth century, theology was even regarded as "the queen of the sciences" in that theology was thought to be based on a more certain foundation (the light of divine revelation) than other fields of inquiry that rely on human rationality. At that time *scientia* was the generic term for all forms of knowledge. With the rise of the empirical or "natural" sciences in and following the sixteenth century, the meaning of "science" narrowed and was increasingly restricted to those pursuits that examine the observable physical universe, and today very few people would associate the word "science" with disciplines such as theology or philosophy. Indeed, the fact that many people today would be *startled* to discover that anyone ever regarded theology as a science, much less a superior, more reliable form of science than even geology or physics, is a good indication of how much our world has changed. With the rise of the scientific mentality and its widely accepted methodology of empirical research and discovery, many people have become suspi-cious of any theories that do not in some way result from experimental science and the technological tools through which scientists learn about this universe.

But even when theology was regarded not just as a science but indeed as the queen of the sciences, people recognized that theology's way of knowing was very different from, say, astronomy's way of knowing. Obviously, theology deals with a peculiar (even unique) type of data and operates in realms quite different from the other sciences. What allowed thinkers like Aquinas to nevertheless regard theology as a superior form of science was that in that day a good many people were inclined to grant both the reality and the validity of divinely revealed knowledge *(scientia)*. That inclination, however, is for the most part no longer present in the modern academy.

Today not only does our more narrow definition of "science" prevent most people from identifying theology as a science in any sense, but many even question, if not debunk, what was once the very foundation of theology as science: the reality of divine knowledge coming through a Spirit-led process of revelation. If information is not gleaned through rigorous physical observation via methods that are empirically repeatable, verifiable, and controlled, that information is labeled suspect at best or is dismissed as the product of sheer fantasy or personal preference or opinion. Recent attempts have even been made in the neurosciences to suggest that religion and spirituality may be the result of nothing more than abnormalities in the brain or a certain kind of neural stimulation that, if absent, renders a person religiously tone deaf after all. Whether intended or not, such theories are clearly attempts to undercut the basis of theology, which is divine knowledge reliably revealed to us by God through the Spirit.

As recently as the time of Karl Barth (1886–1968), the question of whether theology could in any sense be labeled a form of science *(Wissenschaft)* was still being bandied about in some academic circles. The ins and outs of such debates on nomenclature and classification need not detain us in this book. The vital question to address in this chapter, and to apply to scientific naturalism in a later chapter, is whether Christians are being rational in claiming to derive genuine and reliable knowledge from God's Word as it comes to us through the Holy Spirit.

Examining the validity of theology's way of knowing is a necessary beginning for a project like this one. Both theology and science offer legitimate access to truths about reality. But the attempt to live meaningfully with both religion and science breaks down if either attempts to cancel out the other, which is exactly what happens all too often. As we will see in detail in later chapters, some vocal figures in science today claim that religion and theology do not have *any* true way to know anything; only that which passes scientific proof tests is allowed to count as knowledge. Conversely (though with equally bad results), some Christians today routinely question whether science can really be trusted to uncover facts that we ought to embrace as reliable descriptions of the world.

Some Christians may not directly challenge science's ability to work toward true and reliable descriptions of the universe but nevertheless bracket that ability by juxtaposing divine revelation (principally from the Bible) and science in ways that make it appear we always face a choice: either accept the valid way by which Christians know about God and creation *or* accept the falsehoods of science. When one is frequently or routinely presented with this choice, slowly but surely the impression is made that either science or theology is right, but not both; if the one is true, the other cannot be.

My goal is to grant each field its due. Christians do not need to accept the either-or scenario laid down by some scientists and even by some well-meaning religious writers. Again, however, my aim here is not to convince the scientific community that Christians really do have access to truth but rather to remind believers that our faith *does* have a solid, rational foundation—we do not blindly embrace sheer fantasy. Once Christians feel more secure in their own position, this may in turn help foster a willingness on their part to grant science its own reliable way of getting in touch with truth (even if science does not return the favor!).

If either faith or science is necessarily and totally wrong, there is nothing to ponder in terms of a relationship between the two; it would be like trying to relate the World War II military strategies of General Dwight D. Eisenhower to *Star Trek's* Captain James T. Kirk and his battle strategies against the Klingons. Since one character is historically real and the other is a fictitious character who never existed, no real relationship between the two strategists can be pursued. So also, if either science or theology is granted only a tiny sliver of truth, virtually no relationship can be pursued; overlaps between the two would almost never occur.

Perhaps another analogy would best explain this point. Consider the two fields of gourmet cooking and agriculture. Ordinarily, of course, you wouldn't find a chef in a white cooking jacket sitting on a tractor harvesting corn, any more than you would find an overall-clad farmer in a Dekalb's cap whipping up smoked chicken and corn chowder in one of New York City's finer restaurant kitchens. Nevertheless, only a fool would deny the important links between agriculture and cooking. Not only would chefs have nothing to cook were it not for farmers, but the chef's ability to produce truly excellent cuisine actually *depends* on the farmer's skill in cultivating high-quality produce. Thus, it is no surprise that some of the finest chefs in the world have taken the time to learn from farmers about agriculture. Smart farmers who want to sell their products likewise take the time to learn from chefs about what kinds of food taste best and hold up best under various forms of cooking preparation. The farmer can then try to produce just such foods, knowing that good chefs will pay top dollar to acquire these agricultural products.

World-class chef Jean Georges Vongerichten even owns some farmland in upstate New York where he helps growers cultivate the herbs and other fresh foods that ultimately go into his culinary creations at his four-star restaurant in New York City. Farmers and chefs who understand how important each is to the other nurture good relationships, thereby acknowledging that their respective fields of endeavor overlap and affect each other at many significant junctures. Lesser cooks think less about agriculture, perhaps believing that it really doesn't matter what foods they use: corn is corn is corn, and one source of fresh herbs is as good as the next. That is not true, but a cook who believes it anyway won't work on a relationship with those involved in agriculture; he figures he can get along without it.

So also with religion and science: if you think the two have very little to do with one another or that either field is just too remote, uncertain, or strange to bother thinking about, then you can live happily without trying to nurture some crossover ties and relationships. But it is my contention that such an approach is a little like the chef who thinks he can get along just fine without farmers. If we as Christians can come to understand that theology and science both have good and legitimate ways of knowing about the larger reality in which we live, then we can respect and honor both. And if, like a smart chef who understands the important links between cooking and agriculture, believers can recognize that theology and science have many areas of appropriate overlap and mutual interest, then we will move from a mere acknowledgment of science to a desire to learn from it and thereby bring science into preaching and into the life of faith.

But first things first. Clearly, in an environment where there is enough mutual suspicion and hostility to go around, our first order of business is to examine why Christians are right to believe in the reality not just of God but also of God's ability to speak to us in Scripture. Once this matter is secured, especially in the face of those who claim the opposite, we can move on in subsequent chapters to more fruitful engagements with the scientific enterprise and some of the specific things it now teaches.

Scripture: Authority or Dialogue Partner?

When examining the validity of scriptural authority, the key question with which we must grapple is whether Christians, via their faith, can legitimately claim to know anything true and real about life in this cosmos. This question comes at us with peculiar force these days. According to Walter Brueggemann, the key challenges that modern preachers face are mainly consistent with, and actually stem from, the modern world's problem with any text that claims an authority weighty enough to make demands on its readers or hearers. "Listening is difficult . . .

because the modern world is organized against serious speech, against authoritative speech, against listening, against passionate discourse that binds one to another and causes one to yield to another. The notions of self-sufficiency and autonomy that govern our consciousness make listening difficult and obedience nearly impossible. . . . The preacher, with the congregation, is set in an epistemological crisis: she must make an appeal that violates the way we think and know and believe in our culture."[3] In other words, even some Christians are struggling with questions about what believers can reliably know and whether the traditional claim of Scripture's authority (on which the reliability of Christian knowledge has long been based) is sufficient to ground our faith-based beliefs in reality.

Brueggemann has highlighted what some have called "the crisis of biblical authority in the church today,"[4] in which a key question is whether we are willing and able to be confronted by any biblical text that makes claims on us, that seeks not for our consent but rather to reshape and remold our perspectives. Are we willing not just to learn *about* texts but above all also to learn *from* them? C. S. Lewis used to write lovingly about the family dog, Tim. According to Lewis, Tim was a good, albeit somewhat headstrong, dog. Lewis summed up Tim's attitude toward life this way: "Tim never obeyed you exactly, but sometimes he agreed with you." Does something similar characterize a contemporary approach to Scripture? Is Scripture something not so much to obey as to now and again agree with? Even more central to the issue of biblical authority is, *Why do we read and study the Bible at all?* There may be a bevy of answers to that question among the many people who study the Bible, including (but by no means limited to) those who study it as great literature, those who study it as a historical curiosity, those who study it for personal edification in the nurturing of piety, and those who study it for use in the upbuilding and education of the church.

As my congregation's minister of preaching, I am expected to be a student of Scripture, and as such, it is also expected that I will be in touch with the many areas of scholarly inquiry into the Bible, with the goal of sharing the fruits of my studies in sermons that will bring God's Word into contact with the real lives of the members of my congregation. These sermons will then perhaps provide guidance, wisdom, truth, correction, and purpose and thereby enable faithful attempts to follow God in Christ.

But why am I charged to explicate the Bible specifically, as opposed to some other document or my own freewheeling ideas? What is it about the nature of this book, with all its wild and rich diversity, that makes it the basic source for the sermon? Most of the people to whom I preach would say (and would hope I would say) that the reason the Bible occupies this place of prominence is because somehow, some way, *God* is revealed in the Bible in a way true of no other book. Thus, the most basic assumption with which I approach, study, and finally proclaim Scripture is that it is a holy revelation that teaches us about God, creation, and their relation. In the mystery of inspiration and through the myriad of human hands that had something to do with the composition, redaction, transmission, and preservation of these texts (and scholarly inquiry in recent centuries has increased our awareness of the process by which the Bible was composed and preserved), somehow it has ultimately been God through the Holy Spirit who has woven the rich tapestry on which is embroidered the nature of God, creation, and their relation.

This position was articulated by John Calvin at the very outset of his *Institutes of the Christian Religion:* "The Scriptures obtain full authority among believers only when men regard them as having sprung from heaven, as if there the living words of God were heard."[5] Contrary to those who believed that the chief authority of Scripture was granted by the church, Calvin advanced the thesis that true authority could be grounded only on God's being the ultimate author. Any other reckoning of biblical authority would, in his opinion, render faith a "precarious" enterprise. Although he admitted that this claim could not be proven to the satisfaction of nonbelievers, Calvin wrote that for the believer there is neither doubt nor need of further proof: the internal testimony of the Holy Spirit convinces the heart that God is both the original author of the text and the one who even now speaks in and through it. "The testimony of the Spirit is more excellent than all reason. For as God alone is a fit witness of himself in his Word, so also the Word will not find acceptance in men's hearts before it is sealed by the inward testimony of the Spirit."[6]

In short, Calvin's claim of the divine inspiration of the Bible rests on faith. Building on this claim, Calvin went on to say that we can have confidence that the same Spirit who inspired the truth of the text in the first place will not now abandon that text but will instead continue to bring it into people's hearts, applying God's Word in the church throughout history and its ever-changing challenges, including the present challenge of a scientific naturalist worldview that insists on ruling out, a priori, any claims to valid knowledge about reality that do not open themselves up to empirical scrutiny. As Calvin stated, "God did not bring forth his Word among men for the sake of a momentary display, intending at the coming of his Spirit to abolish it. Rather, he sent down the same Spirit by whose power he had dispensed the Word, to complete his work by the efficacious confirmation of the Word."[7]

This fundamental assumption on the divine authorship of Scripture is now, of course, routinely questioned. As Wolfhart Pannenberg notes, by the beginning of the nineteenth century one could witness "the decay of the older Protestant doctrine of the authority of scripture that viewed revelation as divine inspiration. . . . The historico-critical dissolution of the doctrine of inspiration had cut the ground out from under the authority of scripture as a direct expression of divine revelation."[8] In addition to the historical-critical methodology that has revealed the Bible's compositional history to be more complex than once thought, the entire modern ethos has rendered Calvin's approach incomprehensible for many.

Langdon Gilkey claims that the modern ethos is characterized by four salient traits, each of which corrodes the acknowledgment of and submission to claims of external authority. These four traits are: a sense of contingency that doubts overarching purposiveness, a relativism that renders everything transient and prevents the past from making claims on the present, a temporality that claims human knowledge and understanding have been evolving and building over time so that we're farther along the road to human maturity than people in the past, and an autonomy that claims nothing can or will come from the outside to help us. Gilkey says these traits lead to the following conclusion: "The modern spirit is dedicated to the proposition that any external social authority will in the end only crush man's humanity if his own personal being does not participate fully and voluntarily . . . in whatever creative turns his life may take."[9] By quoting Gilkey's conclusion, J. Christiaan Beker confirms how greatly even the church and the academy have been affected by the modern ethos. Beker goes on to say, "A visit to any recent conference of the guild of biblical scholars will demonstrate the extent to which we have cast aside the issue of biblical authority. Instead, we have substituted the idea of the Bible as an archaeological deposit for the Bible as an authority. . . . It seems that Scripture is no longer normative but is at best incidental, becoming authoritative when and if it conforms in some of its expressions to what we consider to be helpful guidelines for our present situation."[10]

Indeed, there is now a vastly increased variety of approaches to Scripture, many of which assume that our contemporary experience, historical awareness, and scientifically informed worldview must be the lens through which Scripture is read (thus undercutting the possibility of Scripture's being the lens through which we make sense of contemporary views). In a February 1997 article in the *Christian Century*, Richard B. Hays illustrated the modern hermeneutic of suspicion, and where it can lead, by quoting from Elizabeth Schüssler Fiorenza, whose approach to life and theology "does not appeal to the Bible as its primary source but begins with women's own experience." Thus, as Hays notes, our contemporary experience (be it women's experience or some other form of experience and modern thought) is often treated "as unambiguously revelatory, and the Bible is critically scrutinized in its light. . . . As a result, [such people] endlessly critique the biblical texts but rarely get around to hearing scripture's critique of us or hearing its message of grace."[11]

As though to confirm and illustrate this contention, two months later the *Christian Century* published a letter to the editor in which Episcopal priest Harry T. Cook scathingly critiqued Hays's essay. How sad it is, Cook declared, that someone like Hays, who instructs the next generation of preachers, can neither recognize nor tell his students to recognize that the Bible is a fragmentary collection of documents whose content is suspect where history is concerned. "The Gospels do not reveal Jesus. They reveal what various first-century communities wanted themselves and others to believe about Jesus."[12] The solution, according to Cook, is to vet the Scriptures of all antiquated and false views of Jesus, to "filter out Paul's theological and social biases and to dismiss of him what needs to be dismissed" so that tomorrow's seminarians (and presumably all of us) can "put away the childish things of credalism."[13]

In reply, Hays pointed out that Cook's letter and the views it espouses highlight precisely the mess we're in as far as biblical authority is concerned. This thinking says that what the New Testament (in both the Gospels and the Pauline and other Epistles) claims about Jesus need have no weight for us whatsoever. The content of Scripture is not so much something to form us as it is something to be formed *by* us. Our ideas and knowledge are so far superior to that of the biblical writers that their words should be regarded as little more than historical examples of what people *used* to be able to believe prior to what we have only lately come to learn. Scripture is not an authority from which we learn how we are supposed to think; it is, as one writer put it, more like a friend with whom we can have discussions but with whom we can also respectfully disagree. Cast into a world increasingly informed by science, the points of disagreement with our "friend" the Bible would be any claim it makes that could not be proven with scientific precision according to scientific methodology.

Clearly, many people, particularly those in the scientific community, believe just this. If a belief cannot be subjected to experimental investigation, and perhaps thereby also proven to some measure of scientific precision, such a belief should be seen as irrational and therefore quite probably false. In short, religious knowledge does not count. The claim that the Holy Spirit relays information to us is chalked up by people of science as being no more valid or reputable a claim than saying you learned something because a little green man from Mars radioed it to you. For something to count as reliable knowledge, it must be provable and testable on a par with everything else that typically emerges from the scientific way of investigating physical reality.

But does everything the average, well-functioning human being believes on a day-to-day basis meet the requirements of such rigorous scientific investigation? In recent years philosophers like Alvin Plantinga and Nicholas Wolterstorff have addressed such questions and have concluded that a large number of the beliefs to which people firmly adhere are not open to experimental confirmation or disproof, yet these beliefs are not regarded as irrational, much less false, just because they have a different nature than, say, their belief that water consists of two hydrogen atoms bonded to one oxygen atom. Beliefs don't need to be scientific to count as being rational or true.

This line of thought is worthy of further elaboration here for two reasons: First, it nicely demonstrates that Christians have good reason to regard the Bible as God's inspired Word, which therefore stands as a legitimate conversation partner with other valid sources of knowledge about life, including science. Second, as we will see a bit later in this book, this line of thought can quite readily be employed against those who claim that everything true and knowable in reality can be, and one day will be, discovered by the natural sciences alone. There is good reason to resist and refute that kind of reductionism; science is not the only avenue by which to discover truths about reality. Thus, faith insists it also has reliable access to truth, as revealed by God and as found in Scripture. So as we proceed in this chapter to defend the rationality and coherence of the belief that a Christian can hear the voice of God speaking through Scripture, we are simultaneously building a case against the claims of scientific naturalists who want to privilege the scientific way of finding out about life as the *only* access to truth.

Knowing

Whether they know it or not, those who today claim that the only rational beliefs are ones open to scientific scrutiny are in some ways coming very close to an old traditional approach to human knowledge called classical foundationalism. Picture a skyscraper like the Empire State Building in New York City. When you stand next to this edifice and look up, it boggles the mind how a building can rise so high without toppling. One of my son's favorite activities is to build skyscrapers with his interlocking Lego blocks. If you've ever tried this, you have experienced the moment at which the laws of physics catch up with your little Lego edifice: it becomes too top-heavy, begins to bow out in the middle, and eventually topples. I've discovered, however, that your Lego tower will stand much higher if you first take care to build a foundation around the four edges of the tower. A good foundation is the key, and for actual skyscrapers like the Empire State Building, much of what keeps the building upright is below ground, in the pilings and foundations sunk deep into the earth.

The edifice of human knowledge is similar. If we want to mount ever higher in our understanding of life's truths, we had better be certain in the very beginning to lay a good foundation of basic truths on which to build. Because if we start off on the wrong foot (or the wrong *footing* in this case!), the structure of our knowledge will eventually collapse. I once saw on the office door of a village building inspector a cartoon depicting the construction site of the tower in Pisa, Italy—now the *Leaning* Tower of Pisa, of course. But in the cartoon the nearly completed tower is still upright and straight. In the foreground the construction foreman whispers to the architect, "I saved a little money on the foundations; but don't worry, no one will ever know." Foundations are important.

When it comes to human knowledge, what constitutes a good foundation? What can legitimately be considered as undeniably reliable beliefs? The theory of classical foundationalism sought to answer such questions. We should note up front, however, that many contemporary philosophers, such as Plantinga and Wolterstorff, have cogently argued that classical foundationalism is self-referentially false and incoherent.[14] Classical foundationalism claims that a person is justified in believing something if and only if she can demonstrate that this belief is reliably evident to one's senses, self-evident, or incorrigible.[15] On the basis of this approach many philosophers and theologians in history have claimed that belief in God (and by extension the belief that God reliably spoke and inspired a record of his nature and actions in the Holy Bible) is irrational in that it can rest on no other foundation than faith (and the leap into the unknown that faith enables). And faith, they assert, does not qualify as suitable material for the foundation of knowledge. Faith seems to them squishy and not nearly solid enough; for them, using faith in the foundation of human knowledge would be like building a skyscraper with Silly Putty in the footings instead of steel and cement. God's existence and revelation in Scripture is not available to our senses, self-evident, or incorrigible. God is not available to our senses; we cannot see, taste, touch, or hear God. God's existence is not as obvious as just seeing that 2 + 2 = 4. Nor is belief in God incorrigible; one could be wrong about it. Hence, some thinkers have concluded that a person cannot justifiably claim that belief in God or his Word is properly rational or intelligently foundational enough to build a life upon. A person may hold to such a belief if she wishes, but she may not claim that it is a rational or sensible thing to do.

The empirical approach that Richard Dawkins, Daniel Dennett, and other contemporary scientists now espouse uses essentially the same reasoning as classical foundationalism, as will be shown when we consider the areas where science and theology clash. More accurately, we will explore *not* those places where science and theology clash but rather the skirmish points where scientific *naturalism* and theology clash. As we will see, the reason used by some scientists to dismiss theology and the claims of faith blithely and totally cannot itself be tested or corroborated based on the model of classical foundationalism. Further, the antireligious claims of some scientists also fail to pass muster in the realm of empirically verifiable science—even scientists can only *assert* their disbelief in God's existence and God's ability to reveal information. They cannot prove it. Of course, some may say that lack of proof on the part of Christians constitutes a disproof, but as we are already beginning to see, that is simply false. There are any number of true and valid things that perfectly rational people accept and believe every day that are not disputed simply because they cannot be logically or empirically proven.

Plantinga in particular has argued that as a theory, classical foundationalism itself is not evident to the senses, self-evident, or incorrigible; it is thus self-referentially false. Classical foundationalism cannot meet its own standards. Suppose you met someone who stated the following theorem about human life: "We should *always* doubt the truth of what people say because people always tend to embrace beliefs that serve their own best interests." Well, by that same token, we would have to doubt *this* person also and thus his belief that people are always self-serving. If what he says is true, his own claim would likewise have to be doubted. Similarly, as a theory, classical foundationalism explodes, or implodes, upon itself.

In addition to pointing out this self-referential difficulty, Plantinga also demonstrated that following a classical foundationalist approach to what constitutes a rational and sane belief, one cannot reliably prove the existence of other minds or the truth of one's own memories—at least one could not verify such beliefs as being properly rational components at the bedrock level of your mind. On a strictly evidentialist, foundationalist approach, one could not rationally refute someone who claimed that the entire universe, including all memories of the past, was created in a flash five minutes ago. Neither could one refute someone who claimed that she alone was the only truly existing person and that everyone else was merely a dream within the confines of her own mind.

Similarly, my belief that my wife really exists is not incorrigible; I could be wrong were I insane or brain damaged. (Think of the figments of John Nash's schizophrenic imagination, as depicted in the film *A Beautiful Mind*. They seemed real enough to *him!*) My belief in my wife's existence is not self-evident in terms of being able to see it in the same sense I can see that 2 + 2 = 4. Nor is my wife's existence necessarily evident to my senses, at least not if I am attending a seminar and my wife is three hundred miles away. (And if the entire universe and I myself popped into existence five minutes ago, replete with memories already in my mind, the memory that my wife has *at times past* been evident to my senses would not cut it as rational and irrefutable evidence, either.) So if I am away from home and someone were to ask me if I have a wife, a classical foundationalist approach would conclude that my definitively answering "Yes" is not a properly basic or rational thing to say. I would have to prove my answer by basing it on some other beliefs that *are* properly foundational, but how could I do that? To what could I appeal?

Of course, as my wife herself once pointed out (seeing as she has a stake in this, after all), if I were to meet up with someone who doubted the existence of my wife, I could refute such a doubter by going home, fetching my wife, and presenting her to the skeptic. Or I could call her on the phone and then give the receiver to my interlocuter and say, "Here she is. You can talk with her, and that ought to convince you she's real!" In this sense, belief in God may seem different from belief in the reality of my wife when she's not present: I can go and fetch my wife, but I cannot go and fetch God; I can present physical evidence of my wife through photographs or by letting you hear her voice on the phone, but I cannot similarly produce any such evidence of God.

The point of this analogy, however, is that my belief in my wife's existence when she is not present does not *hinge* on my ability to fetch her, call her, or produce some other tangible, physical evidence of her.

Instead, even in the absence of physical evidence, my belief in her existence is basic for me in the same way as is my belief in the previous
existence of people who are now dead. For most of human history there
were no such things as photographs or videotapes. When a loved one
drowned at sea, the man's survivors would have only their memories by
which to recall and recount the fact that he really did once live. They
would have no pictographic evidence of him, and since he drowned at
sea, they would not have even a corpse or a grave to prove that he once
lived. They could not, in any sense, go and "get" him to demonstrate
his previous existence. Yet they would continue to believe he had lived,
for the same reason and based on the same set of mental and rational
assumptions by which I believe in the reality of people whom I likewise
cannot see or touch at a given moment.

So despite the inability to logically prove history's reality or the existence of other people, few would want to claim that my rock-solid belief
in the ontological reality of other persons is absurd. Few people would
challenge that my memory of what I ate for breakfast this morning or of
the last time I saw and hugged my wife is an irrational fiction that may
have popped into my mind five minutes ago along with the sum total
awareness of a personal history that never actually occurred outside
the confines of my own brain. Instead, we are correct to regard such
beliefs as "properly basic" and as properly sane and rational extensions of
what it means to be alive and to be human, particularly insofar as these
beliefs are held with deep conviction, are consistent with experience,
and are shared by other people.[16] So also, Plantinga has said, the belief
that there is a God can be numbered among the same set of intuitive
beliefs, such that even if this belief has a strong component of faith,
that hardly renders the belief and its attending corollaries irrational
or baseless. (And as Plantinga once wryly noted, even as a wife would
not be much moved or flattered were her husband to defend his belief
in her existence through rigorous and dry philosophical permutations,
perhaps God feels the same way!)

Obviously, so quick a summary of such deep philosophical arguments
glosses over more than it captures. But I mention this line of reasoning to provide background for my contention that even as a belief in
God is properly basic, so also is the corollary belief that this same God
has inspired a reliable account of what he has done in and intends for
creation and redemption. As Plantinga claims, whether the belief that
God speaks through Scripture stems from the basic belief that God
exists or whether this contention about Scripture leads to or at least
helps to corroborate a belief in God, either way such a contention can

be seen as properly basic.[17] From a rational point of view, we are entitled to such basic beliefs until they are decisively defeated or shown to be incoherent.

This excursus into philosophy may seem strange in a book such as this. But as I have stated, my purpose in reviewing this line of thought is to counter those who claim that in this day and age, to deal with the question of Scripture's authority (if not the overall content of faith over against the findings of pure science) by merely positing faith as a valid and warranted source of genuine knowledge about reality is facile if not flat-out false. Despite believing in God's necessary ability to reveal himself if we are to know God at all, Pannenberg seems to doubt that an appeal to faith can accomplish much today. "Today all such claims to authority [that is, to Scripture as God's Word] inevitably involve faith subjectivism. There is thus something forced when theology must begin with the expectation that is implicit in the concept of the Word of God. . . . To assert [this] directly, arguing that what is communicated has an inescapable claim to supreme authority, is to make an authoritarian demand outside the agreed consensus of the church's discourse, and the people who make use of this language are those who actually make the demand. In modern circumstances demands of this kind fortunately carry no weight by their very nature."[18] Pannenberg also comments on the work of Eberhard Jüngel, who addresses the role of faith in coming to believe that God speaks to us. Pannenberg questions this move: "But if faith is the presupposition of the validity of expectation of the speaking God, how can Jüngel ask us to begin with the expectation and not its presupposition; i.e., faith? Or is the beginning with this expectation simply an expression of faith? But how is the presupposition of faith itself grounded?"[19]

Others today make similar observations and ask similar questions. As Beker notes, the eclipse of biblical authority in the face of the new historical-critical consciousness "is all the more apparent when we notice the desperate attempt of fundamentalistic and evangelical theologians and preachers to reestablish biblical authority by hardening their views on the inerrancy, infallibility, and inspiration of Scripture."[20] As one such evangelical preacher, I do not wish to be accused of or characterized by a simple retreat into "faith subjectivism" or a stubborn (and so perhaps mindless) "hardening" of a traditional theological tenet that is manifestly no longer tenable in any rational, commonsense way. It is precisely because a position on biblical inspiration is so often attacked with these accusations that I have outlined Plantinga's work.[21]

I contend that the God who took care first to create and then, through
the long process of salvation history, to redeem this cosmos is a God
who also took equal care to reveal and to preserve the truth of this history for us. Maintaining this faith today requires neither that we reject
modern consciousness nor that we ignore historical-critical studies and
all their fruits. Rather, we reject the underlying premise (or perhaps the
unnecessary conclusion) of some of those studies. I reject the claim that
because the text came to us via a complex set of historical contingen-
cies, it *cannot* also be of God's Spirit; and that *because* we now have
such a detailed understanding of the human element of Scripture's
composition, we *must not* maintain that God was somehow intimately
involved in every part of that process. Faith in the God of the universe
would declare that no matter how prolix, prolonged, or protracted the
process of textual composition and transmission may have been, God
is powerful enough to have been in it all. Similarly, faith can proffer a
proper challenge to the notion that our position in history and our high
level of scholarship automatically bestow on us the right to declare which
parts of, say, Matthew's teaching about Jesus are correct (because they
accord with contemporary consciousness) and which parts are wrong
(because they smack too much of ancient ways of thinking).

As Richard Hays writes, "In order to read scripture rightly, we must
trust the God who speaks through scripture. . . . The German New
Testament scholar Peter Stuhlmacher says something similar when he
speaks of a 'hermeneutics of consent'—a readiness to receive trustingly
what a loving God desires to give us through the testimony of those
who have preceded us in the faith."[22] Such an approach of trust (born
of faith) need not reduce hermeneutics and biblical interpretation to
simpleminded literalism, need not override the importance of discerning what is central to a given pericope and what is peripheral, and need
not replace trust in God with a naive trust in the Bible. But what an
approach of trust *does* claim is that Scripture is received by faith, for
faith, within the community of faith. Far from being an unwarranted or
irrational leap into the unknown, approaching Scripture in this way is
an appropriate corollary to the belief that God in Christ is reconciling
the world to himself.

Furthermore, as Plantinga points out in his recent volume *Warranted
Christian Belief* (which is Plantinga's most exhaustive treatment of specifically Christian beliefs), most believers testify that their belief in God's
reality and in God's speaking to them through the Bible is basic, in the
sense that they simply believe it and feel it outright and that it is not
based on a series of other factors or beliefs. Plantinga presents a good

analogy to illustrate the kind of belief that simply wells up in a person's mind: "I look out into the backyard; I see that coral tiger lilies are in bloom. I don't note that I am being appeared to a certain complicated way . . . and then make an argument from my being appeared to in that way to the conclusion that in fact there are coral tiger lilies in bloom there. . . . It is rather that upon being appeared to in that way (and given my previous training), the belief that the coral tiger lilies are in bloom spontaneously arises in me. This belief will ordinarily be *basic,* in the sense that it is not accepted on the evidential basis of other propositions. The same goes for memory. You ask me what I had for breakfast; I think for a moment and then remember: pancakes with blueberries. I don't argue from the fact that it *seems* to me that I remember having pancakes for breakfast to the conclusion that I did; rather, you ask me what I had for breakfast and the answer simply comes to mind."[23]

Plantinga then goes on to say that belief in a real God who left a record of his nature and actions in history simply arises in the believer's heart, and so, similar to tiger lilies and pancakes, this belief can count as being properly basic, natural, and rational for a person to believe. According to a person of faith, a sense of God's presence and "voice" simply wells up in a person because God, through the Spirit, is real and so causes this belief in us in the same way that seeing tiger lilies in a garden is enough to make us believe they really are in bloom.

An atheist, of course, would not buy that. If you deny God's existence, then you must of course deny the possibility that God could in any sense "appear" to a believer in ways on a par with the presence of a real tiger lily or the remembrance of a real pancake. Therefore, an atheist would conclude that a belief in God *must* be irrational and false since there is no God (and so no Holy Spirit) who could appear to a person and thus cause a belief. Without a God to cause a belief to arise in a believer, what other conclusion could there be, therefore, than that the belief is not just false but is silly, irrational, and perhaps the result of some malfunction in the believer's brain? A belief in God would be compared not to spying coral tiger lilies in the backyard but rather to someone who claims to see the coral tiger lilies doing a waltz together in the backyard. Since lilies do not dance, the belief that you saw them performing a waltz can never be true and is almost certainly the result of a delusion or hallucination. So also, if there is no God, then a belief in God (much less a belief that God speaks to you through Scripture) must be not just wrong but sick.

The point is that when a scientific naturalist or an atheist tries to impeach a person's belief in God's existence (and in God's speaking through Scripture) as not just wrong but irrational, at bottom it is not the nature of the belief itself that causes the atheist's scorn but rather the larger issue of this person's having previously rejected the existence of God altogether. An atheist might present many reasons why he or she does not believe in God, but this unbelief is not itself subject to empirical proof. So although such unbelief may say much about the atheist, it says nothing about the rationality of those who do believe in God (and who have their own good reasons for so believing) or in God's ability to communicate with God's creatures. Plantinga's point is that the nature of spiritual beliefs that arise spontaneously in a believer's mind is similar to a great many other beliefs that arise spontaneously in a person's mind, so if the basic nature of a belief in tiger lilies is rational so is a belief in God—especially if, as a matter of fact, God does indeed exist! If God does exist, there is nothing irrational about believing in God.

Conclusion

As I have stated, this is a book about preaching in the scientifically shaped world of the twenty-first century. I will eventually claim that by not acknowledging science as a legitimate way to learn about this world, preachers impoverish their listeners' ability to connect a living faith with the wider world. Although it can be very difficult to separate the wheat of genuine scientific discovery from the chaff of the scientific and philosophical naturalism in which some scientists cloak their work, when proper distinctions are made, the life of the church and its celebratory awareness of the universe God crafted will be enhanced. But we cannot naturally acknowledge and mention science in sermons in a way that will enliven the active faith of Christians unless we first make certain that the source of that faith, the Word of God, is in a strong enough position to still speak to us, shape us, mold us, and confront us authoritatively.

Curiously, as we have seen in this chapter, the way that Scripture's authority can be defended is the same line of reasoning that can help us to combat the philosophical and scientific naturalism of someone like Richard Dawkins. Dawkins and many other scientists today seek to privilege the scientific way of knowing even as they dismiss as invalid and untrue all other possible ways of knowing about life, starting with the Bible. This chapter has laid the groundwork for the balance of the book by enabling us to warrant the claims of faith over against the claims of its epistemic critics and by establishing that though the preaching I am advocating makes full use of all that is right and true in science, it is nevertheless firmly rooted in the faith handed down by the apostles, inscripturated in the Bible, and now known by Christian believers in fully rational ways.

With this basis established, we turn to the question of how preachers can bring science into the sanctuary in some way *other* than introducing a straw scientist or a watered-down scientific theory, which is no more than a pretext for knocking science down in a kind of faux triumph of the Bible over science. Too often and in too many pulpits, science is mentioned mostly in regard to what Christians must *not* believe. Of course, scientists do sometimes make claims with which faith properly takes issue. Still, I suggest we can embrace science and its findings (and the entire enterprise of science, for that matter) in ways that will, over time, have a positive impact on the church community and hence on its ability to articulate and apply its faith in the modern world.

Holy Curiosity and Science

The Church's Brainchild

People who love words often love etymology also, the study of the origin and history of words and phrases. Sometimes discovering how a certain word was first coined can be amusing or interesting, and sometimes this verbal history provides a kind of key as to what the word really means even yet today. But that is not always the case, as words and phrases have a way of taking on a life of their own. A word often develops and evolves in common parlance to the point that it no longer has much to do with how the word first got coined, which is why most people can use words very accurately even if they have no clue about etymology.

So, for instance, the common phrase "hocus pocus" has come to mean "magic," maybe even with a hint of witchcraft. For most people, this phrase does not have a religious connotation; if anything, it conjures up mental images that most definitely have *nothing* to do with church. Yet it was in the church, and in the church's most sacred sacrament, that "hocus pocus" was born. In medieval times church services were conducted mostly if not exclusively in Latin, though the common folk who attended church largely did not understand Latin. The priests of the church often breezed through the routine elements of the liturgy, muttering rote phrases in ways scarcely intelligible to the hearers. The phrase from Jesus "This is my body," recorded in the New Testament and always spoken at the Lord's Supper, was one such rote phrase. In Latin this phrase is "Hoc est corpus meum." Something mystical was clearly taking place when the priest spoke these words over the bread of communion, but because the common folk did not understand Latin and because the priests muttered these words rather briskly, "Hoc est corpus meum" started to sound like "hocus pocus." Thus was this phrase coined and thus began its association with something mystical and rather difficult to understand.

While the background of this phrase may be interesting, a person does not need to know the etymology of "hocus pocus" to use it correctly today. The phrase has taken on a life of its own that is only remotely connected to its origin. A similar example is the common yet strange word "scuttlebutt." Most people know that "scuttlebutt" refers to gossip and rumors, to a story that is being whispered about so-and-so. What most people do not know, however, is that "scuttlebutt" is one of a bevy of English words and phrases that began aboard sailing vessels and oceangoing ships. In his wonderful book *Wordstruck*, Robert MacNeil filled nearly an entire page with a list of common phrases like "three sheets to the wind," "pooped," "all in the same boat," "give him a wide berth," "lower the boom," and "keeled over," all of which are nautical images.[1] In the case of "scuttlebutt," the "butt" refers to large barrels that were used to transport wine or other goods. A "scuttled butt" was a barrel that had a large hole cut in the top. (Similarly, if you scuttle a ship, it means you intentionally sink it by cutting a hole into the hull.) The reason some barrels were scuttled was so that they could then be filled with fresh drinking water for thirsty sailors, who would dip their cups into the barrel for a drink. Thus, the scuttled butt was an early form of the latter-day office watercooler; it was the place sailors gathered for a sip of fresh water and hence was also the place where the latest shipboard gossip could be exchanged.

Again, however, knowledge of the historical origins of words will not necessarily make a person's use of words or phrases more accurate. History does not tell you everything, nor is it necessarily descriptive of the current state of affairs. Similar observations could be made about the origins of modern science as we now know and understand it: the historical origins of science in the Western world are interesting and perhaps important to know, but that background alone won't tell you about everything that science eventually became (and is still becoming). Nevertheless, a brief review of the history behind science may be a good place to begin in my attempt to help Christians appreciate and even celebrate those aspects of science that have faith-based underpinnings.

Although many people no longer realize it, the modern scientific tradition of the Western world began, in no small measure, in theological and ecclesiastical circles. Yet because the relationship between science and theology has been one more of controversy than of concord for at least the last several centuries, many people, including many who are in a position intellectually to know better, tacitly assume that it has *always* been so. As Diogenes Allen once noted, in the popular imagination science stands for all that is rational and evident, the investigation of which brings enlightenment and progress through science's scrupulous and open methods. Religion, on the other hand, stands for all that is irrational and invisible, the proclamation of which squelches scientific investigation and hinders progress in its backward adherence to beliefs that the human race ought properly, and at long last, to outgrow.

In a 1999 public forum in London, evolutionary biologist Richard Dawkins went even further when he claimed that science, over against religion, not only stands for all that is rational and evident but even exhibits in a better way the merits people once believed were the provenance of religion. "Well, it's common enough for people to agree that religions have got the facts all wrong, but 'Nevertheless,' they go on to say, 'you have to admit that religions do provide something that people need. We crave a deeper meaning to life, a deeper, more imaginative understanding of the mystery of existence. . . .' [But] religions are *not* imaginative, not poetic, not soulful. On the contrary, they are parochial, small-minded, niggardly with the human imagination, precisely where science is generous."[2] In short, Dawkins claims science is vastly superior to religion (and that science could do very well without religion, to which science is almost diametrically opposed). In truth, however, as Diogenes Allen notes, "We have begun to realize that for its very birth science owed a great deal to Christianity."[3]

Indeed, classical science as the world now knows it is of fairly recent origin, having arisen in Europe in the late sixteenth century.[4] The entire enterprise of investigating the physical world was, at its inception at least, aided by certain underpinning Christian beliefs about the physical cosmos. Christianity, Allen notes, is not an ascetic, world-shunning faith but a faith that proclaims the holy goodness of the Creator. The handiwork of the Creator is therefore also good and worthy of investigation. We human beings have even been created in God's image, precisely to endow us (unlike all other creatures of which we are aware) with the abilities to understand how God's various creations function and interact. The doctrine of creation affirms the goodness and beauty of this world. The doctrine of providence affirms that this world, fallen though it may be, is still held in the hands of this good Creator and so may yield itself to our orderly investigations of it.[5] The Christian faith was by no means the sole source of science's genesis. It was, however, a kind of incubator that helped to create the conditions under which it occurred to some geniuses of the sixteenth century that this world could open up its wonders, beauties, and mysteries to us precisely because the God who superintends it all is the same God who fashioned our minds to be capable of the Godlike thing of seeing creation and understanding how it is "very good."

As I have written elsewhere, humanity does indeed appear to be unique in its ability to soak up, appreciate, enjoy, and also rigorously investigate the physical world.[6] A white-tailed deer in the deep forests of Michigan may live side by side with the wood thrush, but there is no evidence that this deer ever pauses to listen to or enjoy the thrush's clear, liquid melodies.

Only humanity, created to be intensely reminiscent of God, has the ability to appreciate otherness. Simone Weil once said that one of the most striking features of the biblical book of Genesis and its account of the origin of the universe is God's ability to appreciate others. God is not God-centered. Despite the riches of glory and power that God most assuredly possesses within Godself, the true joy and playful delight that emerges in Genesis 1 comes when God adores and studies *others*. Similarly, our ability to get out of ourselves and into others is a hallmark of what distinguishes humanity.

If you walk into the science section of any library, you will be amazed at the great number of shelves sagging under the weight of animal, bird, reptile, insect, arachnid, fish, coral, plant, tree, and even grass identification books. Humanity has both the ability and the yen to observe this world and to catalog what it sees (and to be as exhaustive as possible in doing so). The biblical account of Eden claims that God gave Adam the task of naming the animals. In truth, the task of assigning nomenclature has never stopped. If this were a dry and tiresome exercise, human beings would surely have given up on it long ago and simply joined the rest of this planet's creatures in being content with the rudimentary knowledge of one's immediate surroundings necessary for mere survival. We do not *need* to know the names or habits of earthworms, nor did we ever need to develop equipment to plunge under the sea in order to discover, among many other things, those tiny cleaning shrimp that we now know cleanse other fish of external parasites in so-called fish "cleaning stations" on the reef. We don't need any of this knowledge to survive.

Knowledge of such things has nothing to do with our species or its continuation. But pursuing this knowledge is at once something we *can* do and something that brings us joy. The spectacles visible in nature move and inspire us in a way that appears not to affect other creatures. A male peacock who fans out his spectacular tail feathers is a gorgeous spectacle (actually, a single peacock feather is a wonder all its own). We know that what motivates the peacock is likely no more than the desire to survive and to propagate himself by attracting a mate. Beyond that, however, it is obvious the peacock is unaware that in the process of attracting a mate, he is simultaneously providing a sight we humans regard as arrestingly beautiful. The peacock knows neither that it is beautiful nor that anyone other than a peahen would find his tail feathers worth looking at. Only humanity seems able to both know and appreciate beauty—both the beauty we ourselves may possess or produce (in, say, a lilting piece of music we may compose) and the beauty displayed by nonhuman creatures.

In his book *When Science Meets Religion*, Ian Barbour makes a similar observation in connection with sociobiologist Edward O. Wilson, who claims—as do many others today—that the purpose of evolution is simple survival and that almost anything in the animal or human sphere can be explained through the Dawkins model of the "selfish gene," which seeks only to propagate itself and/or survive. Everything from predation to altruism can be chalked up to the deep-seated evolutionary need and desire to survive and reproduce (or perhaps at least to help ensure the survival of one's close kin, who bear nearly the same genetic code). But in some key aspects of his life, Wilson himself may be a counterexample of this simplistic reduction. Wilson is an ardent supporter of endangered species, yet it is very difficult to see how such an interest in others (and in otherness) has anything to do with his own genetic fitness or survival.[7] Ironically, even those who claim that life is only all about oneself and one's own survival find it difficult to resist the human yen to be curious about *others*. Richard Dawkins himself developed his theory of the selfish gene in large part through his ability to study other species like ants and bees, whose behavior in the colony or hive contributed to Dawkins's now widely quoted notion that what drives the world is self-propagation and/or the survival of close genetic kin. But might it not be considered contradictory to have a career devoted to a study that has little if anything to do with human survival yet all the while proclaim that self-interest is the most basic truth of the universe? Even if this proclamation is true of nonhuman species, history shows that it is not what humanity is all about. We are curious. What's more, we have the wherewithal to channel that curiosity in ways that yield significant fruits of knowledge and understanding about others.

In a real way, the entire scientific enterprise springs from childlike, zestful curiosity. Whether or not we need to know, we want to. This is where science begins. Couched in a belief in the basic orderliness of the universe and recognizing the mental hardware we alone possess to investigate that orderliness, we pursue experiments and catalog what we have seen and learned. In the twentieth century the advent of photography and motion pictures vastly magnified science's ability to take what is observed in the field and bring it home to even nonscientists. Not so very long ago the mere possibility of a Jacques Cousteau did not exist. But the invention of scuba gear, along with the innovation of undersea photography, allowed Cousteau to show the world what lies beneath the waves (and Cousteau did so in the hope that people would be so overwhelmed by what they saw that they would be the more motivated to preserve earth's oceans).

In an admittedly simple sense, science is little more than an adult extension of a three-year-old's reaction to the first anthill he encounters: "What's that? Let's look!" When in the late sixteenth century this basic human curiosity got cast into a Christian environment, replete with beliefs in providence and the image of God, the scientific enterprise became endowed with a kind of holy authorization.[8]

"Fear of the Lord"

In a recent lecture, theologian Jürgen Moltmann suggested that a sense of astonishment is a natural (God-given) avenue through which to learn. Our childlike sense of wonder leads to astonishment when we seek out and discover the unprecedented. Such wonder can continue throughout our lifetime and arises when we encounter not only the unprecedented but also the familiar—sunsets, the cry of a loon, the gravity-defying hovering of a hummingbird. Such sights or sounds may be familiar to us, but a part of the godly way of life is nurturing the ability to experience such things again and again as though for the first time and being able to marvel at and celebrate the unique beauty inherent in each of these experiences. This ability is what Moltmann called *Geistesgegenwart*, the ability to remain ever attentive to the present moment and the experiences it may hold for us. Similarly, theologian Sallie McFague has encouraged the cultivation of "attention epistemology," the art of knowing that develops by simply taking the time to look and observe the wonders in even one's own backyard.[9]

Moltmann goes on to connect this approach to life with the biblical wisdom tradition, claiming that if the "fear of the Lord is the beginning of wisdom," then a major part of developing such wisdom is paying attention to what the Lord has made and is still doing in creation. Indeed, Scripture differentiates between wisdom and knowledge. Knowledge could be described as "book learning": multiplication tables, the dates of history, and the recipe for coconut macaroons all qualify as the kind of knowledge acquired through studying books and assimilating the instruction of others. Wisdom, on the other hand, could be described as a kind of street smarts, the knack for getting along in life by paying close enough attention to figure out how things "go" in this world. Wisdom watches life and learns by the school of hard knocks why it is unwise to spit into the wind or saw off the branch you're sitting on, why anger is sometimes no more than an irrational outburst that damages all concerned and at other times the only appropriate and constructive response to have. But figuring all of this out and becoming a truly wise person takes time and requires a lifetime of very careful observation.

Wisdom is also required to apply one's wisdom correctly. Observant readers of the Book of Proverbs have long noted the "inconsistencies" of the proverbs, at least when taken and applied in a wooden, literalistic fashion. For instance, one proverb says to rebuke a fool sternly in his folly, while another proverb claims the soft response turns away wrath. One proverb preaches against the hollowness of life caused by too much food and drink, while another celebrates both as excellent gifts that gladden the heart and make life sweeter. The key to wisdom literature, it seems, is to pay sufficient attention to life—and to the many different kinds of people and situations we encounter in life—so as to know which proverb fits the occasion. Even if two different people act in very similar ways, a sharp answer may be called for with one and a smiling, gentle answer for the other. The difference is in your wise apprehension of who each person is, what makes him or her act that way, and whether a sharp answer will be productive in fomenting a change in behavior or whether it will be a wasted word that will only enflame the person and make matters worse. In short, it takes wisdom to apply wisdom. The one who treats any given proverb as a one-size-fits-all solution is not a wise person but a fool.

Wisdom is the art of steering one's way through life, but a person acquires this knack for going with the creation's proper flow only through long and patient observation. At least part of the reason that fearing and honoring the Lord is the beginning of wisdom is that if God truly is the creator and sustainer of all—the origin and destiny of all life—to oppose this God (or to live as though God were not real and so *de facto* oppose God) would be the spiritual equivalent of spitting into the wind (or worse, like sawing off the branch you're sitting on). It simply doesn't work out very well. But a secondary reason that fearing God leads to wisdom is that God has created a universe stable enough to yield itself to orderly investigation and has given us, his divine image-bearers, the mental capabilities needed to make such inquiries into the ways and workings of God's creation.

The wise person, therefore, astutely observes life as it goes on around him, in the belief that the perceivable world is knowable and that it will reveal something about its Maker. The wise person knows that the world is worth paying attention to, not only in terms of human interactions but also in terms of the whole sweep of the created order. We learn how best to get along in life if we nurture the ability to make careful observations.

After all, the first and greatest commandment in Scripture is to love the Lord our God with all our heart, soul, and strength but also with our *mind*. As Neal Plantinga has pointed out, to be such a lover of God is to love what God loves. That is the way of all lovers. A lover is interested in and ultimately loves the things that bring his lover joy and a sense of accomplishment. A man whose wife is an artist is a poor lover if he fails to ask his wife about her current projects in the studio, fails to attend her exhibits, and fails to listen when she discusses the works they encounter at an art museum—and this is true whether he himself possesses an artistic sense or not.

In the same way, loving God with our minds means we are attentive to what brings God joy. According to Scripture, the creation is a source of great joy to God. The wise lover of God who fears and honors God will incessantly desire to discover deeper layers of God's creative work. The wise Christian is one who *expects* to be astonished by the work of God and so investigates that work with the eagerness of a child exploring a new place. In the second part of this book, when we turn more directly to the task of preaching God's Word in the church, we will examine in greater detail the parts of the Bible that demonstrate God indeed loves his creation, pays attention to it, takes joy in it, and cares so much for the well-being of this physical cosmos that he sent his only begotten Son to die in order to salvage it. As we will see, Scripture consistently shows God taking an ardent interest in the whole sweep of creation.

Lovers of God, who bear the very image of God, should demonstrate a similar interest.

This brief excursion into the biblical wisdom tradition is appropriate to our topic, because in the modern world it is science—or at least a proper Christian apprehension of what science can show us—that blazes the trail into just such curious explorations of the what, the how, and the why of God's wonderful creation. It may be that short of the inner working of God's Holy Spirit, scientists will never fully be able to pursue wisdom in the sense of attaining a proper "fear of the Lord" or of fully understanding the spiritual, theological significance of the very phenomena they study. Indeed, it is patently obvious that science can be a kind of contemporary idolatry all its own. It isn't just that some scientists resist making any spiritual or theological connections, they go so far as to claim that it is flat-out wrong for *anyone* to put a spiritual or theological spin on scientific data. In the next chapter I will present a model for how I think Christians can appropriate and reflect on science in theological settings. Many in the scientific community today, however, scorn any attempt to bring theology and science together. Some scientists begin and end their scientific inquiries in order to achieve mastery over nature even as others seek, through these same inquiries, to demote humanity's perceived place in the universe by suggesting that in the larger scheme of things we human beings are a mere blip, a trifle, a happenstance that only deluded arrogance could presume amounts to anything.

The point of this chapter is not to deny any such antireligious tendencies within the scientific community. It could perhaps even be alleged that "pure science," in the sense of an unalloyed joy of discovery or unbiased presentation of data, does not exist; everything gets filtered through some world-and-life view or another. Still, on a strictly physical level, when science shows us what truly exists in the cosmos, Christians can properly take joy in scientific discoveries. The religious or philosophical bias of an individual scientist and the driving forces of his or her work are not necessarily a decisive factor in the reliability of the discoveries that result from that work (except, as we will see in the next chapter, when a scientist insists that his or her findings *must* wear a naturalistic cloak that defeats Christian belief). If an astronomer snaps a picture of a gorgeous nebula out in deep space or discovers a previously unknown but wonderfully interesting species here on earth, then Christians, of all people, can take proper, holy joy in such things, giving glory to God for a universe so wondrous and endlessly surprising. Further, we can experience this kind of joy even if the astronomer who took the photo is an atheist who grinds his teeth over religious appropriation of his work.

In short, seen through a proper, well-ground theological lens, science can be viewed as the creative exercise of a God-given curiosity that seeks to open up, to our mutual astonishment, a cosmos designed to be explored and a universe created to yield its orderliness and splendor to our investigation of it. It should be, therefore, no surprise that the Christian faith helped to birth the scientific enterprise. The fear of the Lord could demand nothing less.

3

Where Faith and Science Disagree

The Widened Gap

The previous chapter suggested that in a sense science is Christianity's brainchild. It is, however, a child who rather quickly grew up and struck out on its own. Science swiftly emancipated itself from its home of origin and sometimes even talked back to its parents in an unsettling way. At one time or another most parents look at their child and ask, "Where did he *come* from?" Children can be so different from mom and dad, coming into the world as little individuals replete with wills, personalities, and their own way of looking at things. Christianity's offspring of science was no different. By the time of Galileo, the church found itself openly at odds with at least a few of science's new discoveries. As many writers point out, the church's battle with Galileo, though not pleasant or noble, was perhaps not as horrid as it was later made out to be in the eighteenth century, when thinkers like Voltaire used this flap to caricature the church establishment as anti-intellectual and as no longer necessary for a now mature human race.

Yet there is no denying that in the centuries after science's debut on the European stage, the church's fear and suspicion of science grew. But did science per se ever threaten the core foundations of the Christian faith during this time? Granted, science overturned a great many things people once thought to be true about the universe. Granted, too, a great many people *thought* that those traditional truisms were affirmed by, or at least reflected in, Scripture. The notion that the earth is the center of the cosmos around which everything else revolves was one of the first traditional worldviews to be challenged and demolished, in this case by Copernicus, then Galileo, and still later Kepler and Newton. But was such a geocentric view of the universe really a biblical teaching? Many scholars over the centuries (and almost everyone today) have agreed that it most assuredly is not. At the most, the Bible's references to the sun's "rising" and "setting" as it "goes around" the earth reflects the view of the solar system held by biblical writers. *Reflecting* a certain view, however, is quite different from *teaching* it authoritatively.[1]

As Diogenes Allen points out, Galileo was not so much challenging any specific Bible verses as he was the Aristotelian philosophical system that had crept into Christian theology, the ultimate debunking of which turned out to be, even from a purely biblical and theological point of view, a helpful phenomenon in the history of the church in terms of recovering the true roots of Scripture and what it intends to teach.[2] Dava Sobel's recent historical memoir, *Galileo's Daughter,* presents a bevy of directives from the Catholic Church leadership of Galileo's day that make it clear that what many of those leaders were trying to defend against Galileo's teachings had less to do with specific Bible verses (though a few Scripture citations were marshaled) and more to do with the philosophical beliefs of Aristotle and his beliefs about motion, the immutability of the heavens, and the "fact" that the earth is the center of the universe. So ardent and deeply entrenched was the belief in the unchanging, stationary nature of the celestial sphere that the seventeenth-century followers of Aristotle's thought system refused to allow *any* hint of change or movement in the heavens. Hence, when a supernova star blazed in the night skies for weeks in late 1604, even this was explained away by the followers of Aristotle as some rogue element that existed between the earth and the moon (where change was permissible), *not* in the farther reaches of space where, according to Aristotle, no change could be permitted. Similarly, when Galileo discovered new sunspots on the surface of the sun, his Aristotelian opponents "sputtered that the sunspots must be a new fleet of 'stars' circling the Sun, the way the Medicean stars orbited Jupiter. Even professors who had vociferously rejected the moons of Jupiter, damning them as demonic visions spawned by the distorting lenses of Galileo's telescope, now turned to embrace them as the Sun's last hope for maintaining its steady stateliness."[3]

So was there an *inherent* clash between theology and science in the early days of scientific development? No. Not only did the Christian worldview contribute to the rise of science; science provided an opportunity for God's image-bearers to exercise a portion of their Godlikeness by rationally investigating the universe and, as some have traditionally put it, tracing the very footsteps and fingerprints of God himself.

But the tensions that nevertheless existed between church and academy—even though most scientists at this time were, like Galileo, Christians—grew more taut over the next centuries as an increasing number of scientists moved away from the Christian faith and began to substitute science's findings for theological claims. Near the turn of the nineteenth century, Emperor Napoleon is said to have complained to scientist Pierre Laplace that although his new book on cosmology was a fine book, he had neglected to deal with God. Laplace's now well-known rejoinder to Napoleon is said to have been, "Sire, I have no need of that hypothesis."[4]

Laplace was a harbinger of scientists to come. In the twentieth century many scientists, including prominent scientific popularizers like Carl Sagan, quietly bracketed theology as being of no use in the scientific enterprise. After many years of scientific research without even minimal recourse to God (and having not bumped into God along the way as they shuffled microscope slides, dug up fossils, or peered into distant quasars), scientists confidently proclaimed that life as we know it chugs along just fine without any god. As Sagan wrote in the introduction to Stephen Hawking's best-seller *A Brief History of Time*, Hawking ends up showing us "a universe with no edge in space, no beginning or end in time, and nothing for a Creator to do."[5]

Sagan's dismissal of God is mild compared to the outright hostility sometimes displayed by scientists today toward all matters religious. At times scientists have even made virulent attacks on religion. Peter Atkins backhands religion as "sentimental, wishful thinking. . . . The whole history of the church was based on a clever but understandable self-delusion (and in some cases, I think, on a straightforward, self-conscious lie). . . . Religion has failed, and its failures should be exposed. Science, with its currently successful pursuit of universal competence through its identification of the minimal, the supreme delight of the intellect, should be acknowledged king."[6] Similarly Edward O. Wilson claims that because "sacred narrative" has singularly failed to explain the cosmos in any comprehensive or accurate way, the right to tell the story of the cosmos should be seized from the religious community and turned over to science, whose evolutionary epic of blind galactic development over a span of billions of years possesses poetry and grandeur.[7]

But perhaps no one has done more in recent years to further the common notion that religion is not only science's enemy but is necessarily *defeated* by science than has Richard Dawkins. An eloquent writer and a brilliant evolutionary biologist, Dawkins at times displays what Keith Ward has called an almost willful distortion of the role of religion and of what faithful adherents, especially Christians, actually believe and claim.[8] Dawkins and other similar writers use the term "theologian" as an insult, perhaps on a par with calling someone a Neanderthal or a troglodyte. In a blatant attempt to privilege the scientific way of knowing as being superior to all other ways of knowing, Dawkins asserts that believers must "either admit that God is a scientific hypothesis and let him submit to the same judgment as any other scientific hypothesis or admit that his status is no higher than that of fairies and river sprites."[9] As a raging bull in an epistemological china shop, none is better than Dawkins at wreaking havoc. Daniel Dennett, however, gallops not far behind when he alleges, "There are no *factual* assertions that religion can reasonably claim as its own, off limits to science."[10] Religion, in short, has no real or reliable access to reality. Religious insights do not count as knowledge or fact; hence, theology is perforce fiction.

At times Dawkins displays an all-encompassing, fundamentalist-like arrogance about science's ability to explain absolutely everything. Admitting that at this point we are still ignorant about much in the realms of human consciousness, Dawkins concludes that the only honest thing to say about such gaps in our current level of knowledge is that we just don't know.

> We don't understand it. There's a cheap debating trick that implies that if, say, science can't explain something, this must mean that some other discipline can. If scientists suspect that all aspects of the mind have a scientific explanation but they can't actually say what that explanation is yet, then of course it's open to you to doubt whether the explanation will ever be forthcoming. That's a perfectly reasonable doubt. But it's *not* legitimately open to you to substitute a word like soul, or spirit, as if that constituted an explanation. It is not an explanation, it's an evasion. It's just a name for what we don't understand. The scientist may agree to use the word soul for that which we don't understand, but the scientist adds, "But we're working on it, and one day we shall explain it." The dishonest trick is to use a word like soul or spirit as if it constituted an explanation.[11]

Such pronouncements represent a sweeping, almost breathtaking, indictment against any way of knowing about or inquiring into reality that does not pass strict scientific muster. If the scientist can't know it, neither can or may anyone else—not now, not ever. Science, in Dennett's words, is king, and this monarch will not share the throne with anyone else. King Science is vaguely despotic with its power, disallowing anyone else in the kingdom to make any observations about reality unless the king can ultimately impress the royal signet ring's seal of approval on it. But such a view of science, in addition to being epistemically sloppy and false, caricatures religious believers as having a "God of the gaps" mentality and as having no reliable knowledge and no legitimate source of information about reality (say, the revelation of God's Spirit); they simply slap spiritual labels on whatever science, for the time being, cannot explain.

Of course, in the history of the relationship between science and religion there *have been* believers who were little more than gap fillers, touting the triumph of faith over science by making God the answer to any and all questions that science could not at the time answer. This is a dangerous way for believers to proceed, of course, in that the very nature of science is to fill its own gaps and plug its own holes. A God who comes into the picture only when science bumps up against an epistemological limit is a God on the run who will slowly but surely be marginalized. On a purely physical level, Dawkins is almost certainly correct in saying a day will come when science will be able to explain a great deal more than the already substantial amount it can now explain about a vast portion of the physical universe.

There may well be historical examples of such faux triumphs of religion over science that really amounted to no more than positing God wherever science hit a bump. What is deeply disingenuous on Dawkins's part, however, is his reducing all talk about religion and the tenets of faith to no more than a "cheap debating trick." As we saw earlier, people of faith have a fully valid way of knowing the reality of the existence of God and of the Holy Spirit revealing God to them through Scripture. True believers do not conjure up the idea of God and then use the vocabulary of faith as merely a convenient way to do an end run on scientists who now and again get stuck in their work. People of faith believe in God and in the existence of spiritual realities because of their encounter with the very personal presence of God in their lives. God is not merely a part of the cosmic picture; God is the one in whom, by whom, and through whom the entire cosmic picture exists. "God" is not an answer to a question, a gap-filler, or a debating ploy. God is not that to which believers resort when all else fails. For people of faith, God is not a hypothesis, an inference of logic, or the result of a well-presented philosophical argument. God is the beginning and end of *everything*.

Hence, whether a person of faith makes reference to God in connection with something science cannot yet explain or something that science can explain perfectly well, this reference to God is no trick, no leap of the imagination, no fallback position to prevent the faith from going into full retreat. Rather, when you know God as a personal and abiding presence in your life, you cannot help but make reference to God in all matters. God is the personal presence who encounters people through God's Spirit and calls them back to their Creator. The epistemic avenues by which believers make such claims about God and the knowledge that results from their encounters with God are every bit as legitimate from an epistemological point of view as anything Richard Dawkins could claim for his theories on evolution or for what he sees through a microscope. Intelligent people of faith can therefore encourage science and even cheer it on. The fact that scientists like Dawkins do not believe in God and openly deride those who do is not, strictly speaking, a result of their love of science. The explanation for their cynical unbelief lies elsewhere, perhaps in a recess of the human heart to which science does not have access but about which God's Spirit has been instructing believers for a while now. Science did not create unbelievers; they have been around for a very long time.

But given that physical science has today become so intertwined with philosophical and religious claims, is it even possible to disentangle the a priori, albeit nonscientific, assumptions of some scientists in order to enjoy the fruits of their inquiries? Or do the nonscientific assumptions of some scientists so color (or taint) what they discover that it renders their discoveries useless to people who operate under a religious worldview? Some scholars indicate that scientists who operate with a naturalistic (if not atheistic) world-and-life view may not be trustworthy. Alvin Plantinga, for instance, once wrote that so-called methodological naturalism has tainted scientific research so greatly that we may well need an entirely new approach to science, namely, a theistic science that seeks to understand cause and effect in the physical world but with ongoing recourse to and dialogue with Scripture and its God-informed worldview.[12]

Plantinga is almost certainly correct that a given scientist's religious or a-religious bent will influence at the very least how she interprets the data she discovers. It may also be true, however, that a naturalistic, atheistic set of core beliefs will influence what a scientist looks for in the first place. By way of analogy, consider one feature in quantum physics (which we will briefly discuss in the next chapter): it has been discovered that light beams paradoxically exhibit the characteristics of both particles and waves. If you observe a light beam and ask a wavelike question, you can get wavelike results; if you ask a particle-like question, you see particle-like results. The question you pose apparently can have some bearing on what you find.

Plantinga's point seems to be somewhat analogous: if a scientist asks a naturalistic question, she may well get a naturalistic (and hence nonspiritual) answer. Perhaps this is because the scientist selectively ignores data that might point to a divine influence, or perhaps (à la the light beam) nature can paradoxically look either naturalistic and free-standing or like the handiwork of a divine Creator. Maybe it depends on how you pose the question. If this is true, scientists who pose the question naturalistically will always come up with answers and results with which Christian believers (and perhaps people of any faith tradition) would have to disagree.

I am not convinced, however, that Plantinga's proposed solution of an explicitly theistic science is the best way to proceed. I am not at all certain that one's religious bent *necessarily* molds or infects the data one presents or the discoveries one makes. Surely there are many scientists in the world who are not grinding any particular religious axe, scientists who are neither hostile to religion nor cheerleaders for religion. These scientists would almost certainly see and uncover many, if not most, of the same things as those who do have a definite bias or set of religious convictions.

I also wonder if an explicitly theistic science might not end up doing precisely what one ought not to do, namely, turn God's Word into a kind of field guide that must be checked before, during, and after each look at the physical cosmos. The Bible surely does have a great deal to say about physical reality and its ultimate origin, end, and purpose and about humanity's place in God's design. But although Scripture teaches us the big picture of God, creation, and their relation, it does not necessarily try to establish the boundaries of what we may or may not discover in the course of exploring God's cosmos. The danger is in forcing Scripture to address questions and issues God did not intend his Word to talk about.

For example, Psalm 8 talks about the moon and the stars as God's creations and as reflections of God's own wonder and glory. It does not, however, suggest the best way to measure a star's size or distance from earth, nor does it rule out the vast distances we now know characterize our galaxy and our universe. So in terms of the hard scientific work and the mathematical precision involved in discovering such things as how stars are formed or how far away they are, how would reference to Psalm 8 (or to any other part of Scripture) help a Christian do this work better or more reliably than someone who did the same work without recourse to Scripture?

Of course, astronomy is one thing; matters that touch on evolution (particularly human evolution) are of a different nature and are significantly more controversial. Psalm 8 is also one of many places in the Bible that claim God has crowned humanity with a very special place in the created order. Belief in this tenet of the faith would not necessarily cause a different result when examining how the human brain works, but it would definitely rule out the claim that there is nothing remotely special about the human species over against all others. Even so, it is not clear whether one's belief or disbelief in this tenet would, of necessity, alter significant portions of the raw data.

One's beliefs will of course have a great effect on ultimate interpretations and the spin one puts on scientific data. Clearly, Christians must and will interpret or view science through the lens of theology and Scripture. But that, to my mind at least, is a different issue. Those who advocate a theistic or Bible-based form of science contribute to a notion already present in the minds of many Christians, namely, that it is good to ignore the findings of any and all scientists who do not profess Jesus as Lord. Claiming that you need to be a Christian to be a good scientist seems a little like a heart patient's turning down the world's most skilled cardiovascular surgeon because he is a Hindu and not a Christian. Additionally, the notion that Christians alone can perform reliable scientific research, in ways that non-Christians cannot, runs roughshod over God's providence, God's revelation in the natural creation, and the common grace whereby unbelievers are still capable of producing good and reliable works.

But this discussion raises an important question: Is science ever pure in terms of its findings, irrespective of who does the finding? For instance, much of what I learned about astronomy when I was growing up resulted from watching Carl Sagan's PBS television series *Cosmos*. Sagan was a good teacher who clearly explained to me and to millions of other viewers everything from red-shifted galaxies to nuclear fission within stars. Throughout the series, however, Sagan peppered his lectures with obvious references to his firm belief that the universe he was explaining has no need of a creator and shows no evidence of one, either. To Sagan, the universe was simply the great, churning, implacable, impersonal forces of nature.

Sagan's starting point for thinking about the cosmos is vastly different from mine. I look at the Crab Nebula and see a wondrous "painting" from God's colorful and creative palette. Sagan also sees great beauty, but to him this beauty is no more than a collection of various gases backlit by certain stars that just "happen" to have all come together just so—Matisse made paintings, not God, and nebulae just happened. So does someone like Sagan have anything to teach someone like me? Does the fact that he thinks he has disproved God (or at least has found no useful role for God) mean that I ought to ignore him and stick with only astronomers who speak the language of faith in addition to the language of science?

Here we enter a very snarled area. My answer to the above questions is that *of course* I should apprentice myself as a student to this world's Carl Sagans, even though I use their scientific findings in sermons that declare the glory of God in ways that would doubtless make people like Sagan ill. But if we are not going to insist on an overtly Christian form of science, a Christian perspective on the discoveries of non-Christian scientists will require a thorough, layer-by-layer separation of science from the outer trappings of the philosophical and religious claims in which at least some scientists dress their work. This requires that we do what Sagan (and countless other scientists) failed to do; namely, we must recognize the boundaries and limits of science (and of theology, for that matter) in order to detect where science steps over the line of proper inquiry into the physical cosmos and engages instead in an improper probing of ideas and possibilities that are beyond the reach of even the most powerful telescopes and microscopes.

What we need, in short, is rigorous philosophical work in the area of epistemology that will recognize and legitimate different forms and ways of knowing about reality. We should not privilege science as the only way to gain reliable knowledge about life. But at the same time, Christians should not impugn the right of scientists to present truths about physical reality from science's proper domain. The fact that some scientific discoveries or theories may be disturbing to theologically informed people need not render those findings irrelevant or wrong. Likewise, just because certain theological spins Christians put on scientific findings seem unwarranted to those who wish to deal *only* with physical realities does not render theology irrelevant or wrong. This, however, is a highly complex and nuanced topic. Dealing with it adequately requires skill in philosophy, science, theology, epistemology, and maybe a few other specialty fields. Few people possess knowledge in so many areas, including this author (and as Alvin Plantinga once said, admitting such inabilities is no idle boast!).

John Polkinghorne laments what he perceives to be a lack of theological engagement with the sciences and with people like Dawkins and Dennett. But he also admits he understands why theologians have not been eager to join the larger conversation. "Because God is the ground of all that is, in some second order sense all human knowledge is the concern of the theologian. But books are many and life is short, and much science is formidably technical in appearance, although many of its concepts are capable of at least partial expression in lay language."[13] Hence, what is required for theology to fully engage in the sciences is, according to Polkinghorne, "a bit of intellectual daring" and a willingness to carefully listen to what science has to say and to learn from science.[14]

But as we saw in chapter 1, the starting point for any theological approach to science must remain the recognition of the authority of Scripture, even in a scientifically shaped world. This is what enables Christians to press on in learning from science and attempting to integrate scientific findings into their own worldview without having to believe (or fear) those scientists who make unwarranted statements about the demise of the Christian faith or biblical revelation. It bears repeating that the overarching purpose of this book is *not* to help the scientific academy grant theology its due as a legitimate way of knowing about and investigating reality, though that is a noble goal. My aim is to help the people in pulpits and pews recognize at least the basics of distinguishing between science proper and scientific naturalism so that they can be relaxed when facing the frontiers of science and theology and can recover a healthy appreciation of science's discoveries as part of our delightful image-of-God curiosity. This is no small task. As the statements of Dawkins, Dennett, and others show, the business of separating the findings of science from the trappings of naturalism is far from simple, not least because some scientists clearly believe that it is precisely their physical findings that lead to (and just possibly *demand*) a naturalistic world-and-life view. Nevertheless, taking a cue from Polkinghorne, we plunge ahead in an attempt at a bit of theological (and ultimately homiletical) derring-do and boldness.

Limits: Keeping Science and Theology in Perspective

Some years ago on the Christian television show *The 700 Club*, host Pat Robertson was interviewing a Christian schoolteacher about the effects of Ritalin on children. At one point Robertson asked, "Is it true that Ritalin can actually *make* some children hyperactive?" The teacher replied, "Actually, Pat, the research all shows that this is not the case. But I still believe it is!"

Many non-Christians believe that this science-shunning attitude, one that freely picks, chooses, and abandons research findings at will, is characteristic of all people within Christian churches. Scientists who are not very religious tend to regard people who *are* religious as highly suspect. Unfortunately, there are plenty of representative Christians who daily aid and abet that suspicion.

Through fossils and rocks, science reveals an earth many millions of years old, but some Christians insist it can't be much more than a few thousand years old. Perhaps God created the earth "old," or perhaps geologists have rocks for brains. In any case, many Christians are aware of the findings of geology but blithely proclaim that data to be wrong or illusory. I have also heard others claim there were never real dinosaurs on this planet millions of years ago; God just buried those skeletons in the dirt to test us. Such a view maintains that you can believe what you see with your eyes *or* what God's Word claims, but not both. Again, when astronomy shows us a distant galaxy whose light took millions of years to travel to our eyes (therefore telling us that to look into the night sky is to peer into the very ancient past), some Christians dismiss the literal meaning of such a finding by saying that the universe was created in motion—the whole cosmos popped into being all at once, with the light of that galaxy twinkling in the night sky of earth from the first day. The more scientifically literate among those who wish to maintain a "young universe" theory stretch matters even farther by claiming that perhaps the speed of light was not always constant—maybe in the beginning light traveled so much faster than it does now that it really did not take millions of years for the galaxy's light to reach earth. Most physicists reject this idea as being either impossible or ridiculous. To say that the speed of light was not always the speed of light just because it fits your young-universe theory is like saying that the color purple used to be yellow just because you don't care for the color purple.[15]

Many such examples could be cited. In every case, however, what so maddens the scientific community about such dismissals of their research is that the rationale for doing so has little or nothing to do with scientific evidence and everything to do with long-held theological and biblical beliefs. When a highly sophisticated instrument like an MRI scans a Christian's body to reveal a ruptured spinal disc, few if any Christians respond by doubting the science behind magnetic resonance imaging or the skills of the technicians who read the images. But when a highly sophisticated test like carbon-14 dating shows a rock to be 3 million years old, suddenly both the test and the scientist who interprets it are suspect in the eyes of some believers. The reason for this difference in response is obvious: no one believes the Bible talks about the condition of a person's spine, but many Christians believe the Bible *does* talk about the "how" and the chronological "when" of creation's origins.

When Christians tell scientists that they are not seeing what they are so obviously seeing through their telescopes, the scientists get upset. When scientists tell Christians that telescopes have never been able to locate the Holy Spirit brooding over the cosmos (and so he must not be out there), Christians get upset. Both groups are frequently guilty of an equal but opposite error: using their own valid way of knowing to set aside the other's equally valid way of knowing. Neither group, on its own, knows everything. But when science dictates the limits and content of theology, and when theology dictates the limits and content of scientific research, each side diminishes the other. As Ian Barbour has pointed out, the notion that science and theology are inevitable and perennial enemies is fostered equally by the extremes in the church and in scientific circles. For every Richard Dawkins who declares he has absolutely no use for religion, there is at least one Christian who dismisses science and its findings in the name of biblical purity. Both extremes are unhelpful.

Scientists who dismiss faith can be excused, however, because they so clearly lack a faith-informed perspective on life that could perhaps lead them to a wider vision. The same cannot be said of Christians. Blatant dismissals of what science teaches us about God's world cut against the grain of the broad world-and-life view that faith ought properly to give us. Believers unwittingly undermine the very God they wish to proclaim if they essentially tell scientists, and everyone else, that the universe is an odd house of mirrors. Believers that dismiss science in this way are in effect saying: God buried skeletons to trick and test us. Find a skeleton of a horse and we know that once upon a time some stallion dropped dead on that spot. The skeleton of the brontosaurus you found, however, is not real. The horse skeleton was once covered with muscle, flesh, and fur. The brontosaurus never was; it was *created* as a skeleton. Or perhaps some things only *look* old; perhaps God tricked us by making us intelligent enough to figure out how old rocks are but failed to tell us that, by the way, God has stacked the geological deck so that we can never really know how old things are after all. Is this really the God whom Christians wish to present—a God of feints and shadows who made a world that both does and does not yield reliable information when the same methods of investigation are used?

The problem with such an approach is that it pits God against Godself, God's Word against God's world. If Christians take this approach, how can we *ever* believe what we see in the physical world? It seems inconsistent to claim that the physical world both does and does not convey accurate information. A Christian cannot debunk old rocks as being unreal but yet hold up some other beautiful facet of the universe—say, a gorgeous jewel or the wonder of an infant's perfectly formed little hand—and claim that in *this* case we can reliably see things that tell us something about the good Creator God, whom we praise for creating this physical cosmos. Why would God want to "set us up," so to speak, by simultaneously giving us the mental and spiritual abilities to investigate the world and inserting here and there features designed to trip us up and make us look foolish? Such a God would be arbitrary, perhaps even trying to goad us into error, and would not seem to resemble the God Christians proclaim as loving, gracious, compassionate, and eternally reliable.

Conversely, however, do scientists really wish to present a front so presumptuous as to say that there is nothing in heaven or on earth that cannot be discovered by them? As already noted, there are a few scientists who seem to claim this. But if they cannot locate a human soul through neural connections and their interactions, does it follow that there is none? Even if cognitive neuroscientists like Steven Pinker could one day manage to suggest precisely how the neural wiring of the human brain gives rise to a sense of personal consciousness, would it necessarily follow that nothing more could be said about it on a spiritual level? How much, if anything, can science rule out from the realm of ideas, thought, dreams, and invisible realities like angels, demons, or ultimately the Triune God? Christians have believed from the beginning that the Creator and the creation are not the same thing; indeed, confusing the two was long ago declared heresy. The Bible consistently makes it clear that although God can, if God so chooses, take on a visible form, God is not typically visible and does not live "inside" this universe in the way all other life of which we are aware so clearly does. Science investigates what exists within the "bubble" of the universe. To prove reliably that there is or is not anything outside or beyond the physical universe would require science to be able to get outside the very realm that defines humanity and its scientific efforts. Until it can be shown that science has found a way to escape the universe and probe other

dimensions, scientists should maintain a respectful silence on what may
or may not lie beyond our universe.[16]

Of course, scientific naturalism, or even just plain old garden-variety
naturalism, can itself count as a form of religion. If scientists who have
adopted naturalism as their metaphysical or religious position wish to
make declarations based on that position, they ought to be as free to
express such views as any other person of faith. Christians should keep
in mind, however, that such declarations do not stem from science per se
or even from a scientist's faith that science can reliably reveal this world
to us; rather, such declarations stem from a philosophical orientation of
the heart that is at variance with other faith-based orientations. But as
such, these declarations are faith claims that ought to be judged on the
same basis and stand on the same level as other faith claims, including
the claims of Christianity. If adherents to scientific naturalism wish to
allege that Christians cannot empirically prove something like God's
existence or Christ's resurrection, they may do so. But if the faith dimension
of scientific naturalism is clearly in view, it seems only proper that Christians be allowed to reply to such scientists that, strictly speaking, science
likewise cannot empirically rule out God's existence or the possibility that if
a God exists, he could interrupt the normal progression of things and raise
a dead person back to life, even to an eternal life. As John Polkinghorne
and Michael Welker have pointed out, when Christians and scientists find
themselves dialoguing in the realm of metaphysics and theology, the need
for *both* groups to validate such claims is indeed, and properly, a two-way
street. Sauce for the goose, as it were.

Carl Sagan once gave an illustration that can serve here as a reminder of
why the realm of science, whether or not scientists will admit this, should
properly confess a certain agnosticism about the reality of God, in that
science cannot say much on the subject one way or the other. Imagine,
Sagan suggested, a universe of beings who are only two-dimensional.
Each creature in this flat universe (let's call it Flatland) is perfectly flat,
having no thickness at all. And imagine that these creatures, therefore,
have absolutely no sense of up and down or of any direction or possibility other than forward, back, and sideways. Imagine that it has always
been so in Flatland and will always remain so, within the confines of this
perfectly flat, edgeless, thickless world.

But suppose, Sagan suggested, that another dimension exists beyond
Flatland: a third dimension in which, in addition to forward, back, and
sideways, there is also a true sense of depth—of up and down. Suppose
further that a creature from this three-dimensional universe could somehow get "underneath" one of the Flatland inhabitants and waft this wafer

of a critter up into the third dimension, bringing him to a place "above" Flatland, out beyond the only world he had ever known.

What would follow were such a scenario possible? Several things: First, this creature would vanish from the sensory possibilities of the other inhabitants of Flatland, who lack any vertical awareness. A second possible consequence of this situation is that the Flatland creature who got lifted up would become completely disoriented. He would certainly have no idea where he was and, even assuming he could look "down" on his Flatland world (which he would not be able to do without outside help, since by definition he has no vertical abilities or senses), he surely would not recognize a thing. A miracle of intervention would be required to install into his mental hardware the very ability to look down (and even to know he *could* look down), and long and patient instruction on the part of some three-dimensional being would be required to explain to him that what he was now seeing is Flatland from above. If it were even possible to make him understand all of this well enough that he tried calling out to his comrades below, they in turn would be disoriented, having no possible way of knowing where the voice was coming from and no ability to locate it. If they searched for their comrade within Flatland, they would never find him.

The point of this extended analogy is clear: science cannot escape the bounds of this universe. We are simply incapable of discovering (or of ruling out) other possible dimensions. Sagan's intent was to suggest that there could be other dimensions of which we three-dimensional creatures cannot be aware, and even if it were possible for us to enter another dimension, we would not know what to make of it. My purpose in using Sagan's analogy is to suggest that Christians have known and declared from the beginning that God and his hosts exist in just such an "other" dimension. This does *not*, however, rule out the presence of God in our dimension of time and space. The analogy ought not to be interpreted to mean that God is always beyond us and the life we know. Rather, this analogy recognizes the hermeneutical circle: the way that something can be known will accord with its nature. God is, by definition, a very different being than a red-tailed fox. The existence of God is a very different subject than the existence of an electron. So *how* one would know about God must accordingly be very different from how one would discover or learn more about foxes and electrons.[17] (Obviously, it is also true that the way one would know about a fox is different from the way one would know about an electron.) The nature and reality of God is something science cannot probe. Nor do Christians claim that on their own they can have knowledge of God, but rather that such knowledge and awareness is a gift of faith. We believe that God is able to reach out to us in our dimension of the universe to suggest to us that there is more than our eyes can see and our minds can understand. Further, our Spirit-given faith tells us that what lies beyond the limits of our senses is love and grace, goodness and mercy, and a new creation just waiting to burst one day into this fallen and decaying creation.

Christians should not tell scientists what they may and may not see within this universe, at least not in terms of physical matters such as what appears at the end of a telescope or the result of a carbon-14 test to determine the age of a rock. Christians *may,* and must, contradict scientists, however, if and when science strays into spiritual realms of thought, claiming that their not seeing the Holy Spirit proves there is no such being. In that case, which has less to do with what scientists *see* and more to do with the metaphysical spin they put on their work, Christians can rightly contradict scientists. This, however, is quite a different matter than a believer's impugning or simply ignoring the mathematics by which astronomical distances are calculated or the chemistry that reveals our planet to be millions of years old.

Of course, we ought not to discount the possibility that even within the strictly physical realm, faith may at times need to contradict science. If some scientist were to declare that he had found the skull of Jesus and that this skull indicated Jesus had died an old man as a result of a blow to the back of his head, then faith would have good biblical reasons to disagree—that is *not* the skull of the one whom we know is the resurrected Lord Jesus. Also, anytime science claims to "prove" that water can never be instantly turned into wine or that instant healing can never happen, faith rightly contradicts such claims, even though these claims are located within the physical sphere to which science has access and within which science does its work.

So it could be alleged that my attempt to keep faith's spiritual claims in a different "dimension" from science's physical findings is too simple. I would suggest, however, that clashes stemming from physical findings, and not from science's willfully straying into the realms of religion and philosophy, are not typically going to result from the normal operation of the physical sciences. Obviously, science, investigating as it does the ordinary operations of the universe, will *always* claim that miracles of any kind cannot be scientifically established, because miracles represent at the very least a deviation from the norm. This is no surprise to a believer, however, since if the event in question were *not* a highly unusual and thus wholly unexpected event, it would not count as a miracle. We call them miracles precisely *because* they are unusual and unexpected.

Believers factor God into their world-and-life view and hence hold out for the possibility that God, being God, could shape and influence events to bring about nontypical, novel, surprising events in the service of some higher purpose and goal toward which God is working. The resurrection of Jesus from the dead is the premier example of such an event because Jesus' resurrection is the necessary linchpin in God's larger efforts to bring the universe from death into life. But if a person does not believe in God in the first place, she would expect the "normal" to rule always and without deviation—at least without any deviations that could not ultimately be explained by physical laws operating in some understandable, and therefore ordinary, manner. The point here, however, is that this kind of clash between faith and science on the purely physical level is not typical. Insofar as science investigates physical reality accurately, it will not ordinarily conflict with the theological viewpoint of faith or with scriptural revelations about the nature of God, God's love and grace, and the gospel plan of salvation through Christ Jesus the Lord.

But if believers are generally willing to grant broad credence and credibility to the average physical discoveries that emerge from the scientific community, scientists should show a similar respect for the realms to which faith has access but strictly proscribed empirical science does not. Science should not tell Christians that it is impossible that they are "hearing" a divine voice from a dimension that is simply beyond science's ability to probe or that the Holy Spirit is not already in our dimension, taking up a real residence in our very hearts, whereby we have access to knowledge of God. Christians should want scientists to know that the God we hear calling to us is a reliably good and wonderful God who does not wish to deceive anyone and that the physical findings of science reliably discovered within the universe God created are truths already known by God and can therefore be embraced by Christians, even with gratitude to the scientists who keep enlarging our appreciation for the wonders of God. Scientists should respond to this invitation by forthrightly presenting what they have discovered and what they think it means without sullying those findings with theological and philosophical pronouncements that have very little to do with their field of inquiry. As Polkinghorne notes, "Science and theology face similar problems in relation to the public's perception of them. Yet they share one fundamental aim that will always make them worthy of the attention of those imbued with intellectual integrity and the desire to understand: in their different ways and in their different domains, each is concerned with the search for truth. In itself, that is sufficient guarantee that there will continue to be a fruitful developing dialogue between them."[18]

Forging a Relationship Model

By now it should be clear that our discussion raises many other important issues on the science-and-theology front, chief among which is the question of just how theology can positively acknowledge something like contemporary cosmology. A range of possibilities exists, and some would claim a very large range of possibilities at that. One of the best-known writers to categorize the various possibilities for the interaction of faith and science is Ian Barbour, whose fourfold scheme is both used and criticized by a great many other writers on this subject. Barbour himself admits that his scheme is by no means the only system available. Ted Peters has presented an eightfold classification, Willem Drees proposes nine categories, and some writers, such as J. Wentzel van Huyssteen, suggest that in our postmodern context all attempts to categorize or classify the discussion between theology and science may be too simple to capture the epistemological nuances of our time. Van Huyssteen claims that though Barbour's taxonomy is potentially helpful, his four categories, and one would assume most any attempt to make the parameters of the theology-science discussion neat and tidy, are now "too generic, too universal . . . to catch the complexity of the ongoing exchange between these two dominant forces in our culture."[19] I will deal with van Huyssteen's observations more fully below, even granting that he may well be correct that the postmodern ethos resists neat categorization or summary. Nevertheless, I would like first to summarize Barbour's taxonomy so as to lay the groundwork for my own suggestion, which I will draw from two of Barbour's four categories.

Though admitting the great complexity that attends the science-and-theology discussion, Barbour believes the basic approaches can be lumped under the four headings of Conflict, Independence, Dialogue, and Integration. Those in the Conflict school include, ironically, both religious fundamentalists and scientific naturalists (whose attitude toward science could be described as a kind of fundamentalism all its own). Both groups seem to believe that at bottom science and theology are opposed to one another—conclusions about the universe that are based on faith will *always* be different from what science thinks is true about reality. On the religious side of the Conflict category are those who believe that the Bible alone is our best, if not only, guide to the nature of the universe, the nature and timing of its origin, the nature of humanity's formation, and so on. The Bible, in other words, is the bottom line and the final arbiter of all matters related to the physical universe; indeed, in such matters Scripture is accurate and detailed enough to be able to impeach the apparent findings of science, no matter how much ostensible physical evidence the scientific community marshals. On the science side of Conflict are the Richard Dawkins and Daniel Dennetts of the world, who believe that religion is at best a naive attempt to explain the world and that religion has perennially been a worldview founded on silly superstition and folk cosmologies that have now been discredited by the advance of science. The Conflict model is, of course, the least helpful and least hopeful way to view science and theology, essentially boiling down to an attitude that says each field of inquiry not only *could* get along just fine without the other but that each field *must* proceed by ignoring the other because it is impossible that both could be correct. Take your choice: what science claims to discover physically or what religion claims is physically findable.

It is difficult to know precisely which of Barbour's other three categories would constitute the opposite of the Conflict model. On the one hand, it could be said that the second category, Independence, would be the opposite in that it applies to those who believe that as long as science and religion keep a safe distance from each other and do not stray into one another's unique way of knowing about and investigating the truth of reality, they can coexist just fine. Each is right, neither is wrong, and as long as they stay away from each other, all will be well. If the overall reality of the universe were like some broad boulevard, science would work on one side of the street, religion on the other; science seeks to walk up the street, religion walks down the street. But the main feature of Independence is the claim that neither area of inquiry should ever *cross* the street, and perhaps there need be no shouting out to one another, either. So science explores facts, theology reveals values, and each possesses its own kind of valid truth. In one sense, if theology were to grant that science does indeed find truth and science were to grant the same for theology, this would be the opposite of Conflict, since in the Conflict model each side asserts the utter falsity of the other side.

On the other hand, it could also be said that Barbour's Integration model is the opposite of Conflict, because this category claims that only by throwing the best of *both* scientific and theological insights into the epistemological blender can we whip up a frappé of unified truth. On this model, theology and science are not enemies but are in fact partners who can achieve a larger, more comprehensive truth by coming together, nuancing one another, and accommodating one another's findings into their own. The Integration and Independence models are alike in that theology grants science access to the truth and science does the same for theology. The difference between these models lies in what each field does with its truth: the Independence camp keeps religious and scientific truths separate (perhaps fearing cross-contamination or confusion), whereas the Integration camp says the real, larger truth can be found *only* by cross-fertilization and blending.

The category that most clearly lies in the middle of the spectrum is Dialogue. Like the Integration camp, those who opt for Dialogue acknowledge the valid truths found by both theology and science and are willing to talk across the epistemic boundaries in order to borrow meaningfully from each other (where this seems possible) and so together perhaps to sharpen what each knows. This, however, stops short of the blender approach of Integration. Those in the Dialogue camp believe that theology can nuance science, or at least keep it from straying into the area of religio-philosophical pronouncements, and science can perhaps help Christians read the Bible and understand God's handiwork a bit more accurately, but it is uncertain how fruitfully the two fields could be combined.[20]

Such is Ian Barbour's fourfold taxonomy, although when detailing this in his book *When Science Meets Religion,* even Barbour cannot resist giving each category two or three subcategories, thus highlighting once again the slippery, dicey nature of delineating the science-theology discussion. Barbour clearly favors some version of the Integration model, making his own case for what he calls a "theology of nature" (as opposed to the "natural theology" of the Christian theological tradition). Barbour's theology of nature would seek less to describe God based on what is found in the physical cosmos (which is the tack taken by natural theology) and instead to speak of religious belief from within a context where the findings of science are acknowledged and positively utilized. In some ways this is also my own approach, but before delving into that in greater detail it would be useful to consider van Huyssteen's overarching wariness of any attempt to classify the larger relationship of these two fields of inquiry too neatly.

Van Huyssteen's primary argument against a reduction of the science-and-theology relationship into identifiable categories or models stems from his views of postmodern pluralism. "Many stereotyped ways of relating theology and science, through models of conflict, independence, consonance, harmony, or dialogue will be revealed as overly simplistic generalizations about the complex relationship between these two dominant forces in our culture. Postmodern pluralism makes it very difficult even to speak so generally about 'rationality,' 'science,' 'religion,' 'theology,' 'God,' or 'divine action' today."[21] By detailing the multivalent pluralism of viewpoints even *within* theology, as well as within science, van Huyssteen believes he has shown that it is impossible to approach either field, much less any interaction between the two, in general terms. In a day when feminist theologians, for example, sometimes seem to speak a different language altogether from evangelical or liberationist theologians, how can we step back and ponder what theology has to say to science when it is not even clear what theologians want to say to each other?

Similarly, van Huyssteen says that science is not some monolith of insights that can be approached as a single enterprise. What science has to say to the world (and therefore to the religious world) and how you may wish to reply to what it has to say depends on whether you are talking to a cosmologist, a neurobiologist, or an evolutionary biologist. In short, the plurality of viewpoints, disciplines, and subspecializations in both theology and science make a one-size-fits-all model for dialogue naive at best and fruitless at worst. Van Huyssteeen comments:

> The fundamental question is, "Is postmodern religious dialogue possible today?" This now translates into an even more complex question: is any meaningful dialogue possible or does the pluralism and localization of postmodern discourse throw theologians, philosophers, and scientists, who are supposed to share some common quest for human understanding, into near complete epistemological incommensurability? . . . For theology the shift to postmodern thought will immediately mean that central theological terms like religious experience, revelation, tradition, and divine action can no longer be discussed within the generalized terminology of a metanarrative that ignores the socio-historical location of the theologian as an interpreter of experience and an appropriator of tradition.[22]

Van Huyssteen is certainly in touch with epistemological and pluralistic issues that ought not to be ignored. Our global awareness of the variety of opinions, viewpoints, theories, and religious beliefs truly does force us to recognize, in ways that would perhaps have been inconceivable in prior generations, the coloring influences that time, place, and situation exert on how one pursues many different forms of thought, including theology and science. It is also true that the tradition in which a person was raised, where he or she was educated, and perhaps also the political climate of one's homeland can pour new and different content into old words. What I mean by the word "revelation" may be quite different from what another person from another part of the world means when he speaks the same word, even from within the same broad Christian tradition.

In such a pluralistic climate it is paramount that dialogue partners listen to and learn from one another. It may well be true today that constructive dialogue cannot even begin until we have carefully listened to each other to ensure a common vocabulary or at least an awareness of what other parties mean when invoking the same words. I would agree with these statements. However, I still resist granting too broad a credence to the idea that because this kind of diversity and plurality exists today, it is difficult, if not ill-advised, to suggest general approaches to something like the debate between Christianity and modern science. True, neither Christianity nor modern science is a monolith of univocal opinion on the strata and substrata of its area's ambit of thought and expertise. But although there are indeed many divergences among, for instance, evangelical theology, Roman Catholic theology, and liberation theology, surely there is also a sufficient overall convergence of what the Christian tradition, broadly speaking, stands for. Certainly the various Christian groups would have more in common than would, say, Christians and Buddhists. In short, I believe that despite the various differences that weave through Christianity worldwide, Christians have enough in common that the question of *Christianity's* relationship to the scientific enterprise is a viable one to pursue. Surely our postmodern pluralism need not completely balkanize academic discussion and inquiry, even though this has already occurred in many quarters.

Having provided the background of this discussion, I will now return to Barbour's categories in order to cobble together my own approach—an approach I recommend for preachers, or at least for preachers to bear in mind (particularly when later we begin delving into specific preaching strategies by which pastors can allude to science while preaching). In general I propose approaching the relationship of science and theology through a combination of the elements Barbour identified in the categories of Independence and Integration. My suggestion to combine these two approaches may seem contradictory, if not incoherent, since Independence insists on letting each field do its own thing without ever touching the other (and maybe even without ever *talking* to the other) and Integration seeks to move beyond dialogue to an actual blending of science and theology.

Combining any elements of Independence and Integration is, some would allege, a little like mixing oil and water—even if they are in the same glass, they stay separate. But sometimes oil and water can be fruitfully combined. If you combine them correctly and in proper proportion—and if you don't mind having to shake the container when you want to use it—then a skillful blend of oil and water (or in this analogy, vinegar) can yield a zesty vinaigrette to liven up a salad. So also with Independence and Integration: though there are divergent, if not oppositional, elements in these two categories as Barbour defines them, they nevertheless can go together to create a third approach.[23]

My rationale for suggesting this combination stems from my agreement with some of the elements of each category. From Independence comes the insight that science and religion do have different ways of knowing that ought not to be collapsed into one another or impeached by one another. In part this insight acknowledges the hermeneutical circle referred to earlier: how a thing can be known is largely determined by what that thing is. So how God is known (through God's own divine revelation) is perforce different from how an electron is known or how water is known. C. S. Lewis once wrote that if you wish to pursue the study of geology, go out, find a rock, and study it. Science proceeds on the assumption that there is a real world out there, that it is available for us to capture (on film, under a microscope, in a sample bag), and that our minds and rationality are such that once we do this, we may begin to unlock this universe's secrets.

But if you want to pursue theology, God has to find *you*. God is not some finite object available for our cold, impassive scrutiny the way a rock is. God has to take the initiative. Christian theology asserts that God has already done just this. God has revealed himself to people throughout the long history of humanity. God has left vestiges of himself in the designs and glories of the physical creation. Still, accessing divine truths (particularly specific truths regarding salvation, Christ Jesus, and the like) is perforce going to require a different methodology than that used by a scientist exploring the extant physical world.

So the Independence side of the equation maintains the useful and necessary distinction of the different and separate ways of accessing truths about the universe. Science and theology have different objects in view, and science, via its normal empirical and theoretical methodology, is neither going to confirm nor disconfirm the articles of, say, the Apostles' Creed. When science, via scientific naturalism for the most part, does try to gainsay faith, conflict arises, and the possibility for fruitful, nondestructive exchanges seems remote and perhaps impossible.

The Integration model is desirable and necessary because the integrity of creation and the reliability of the Creator God (who will not deceive us when we carefully study God's handiwork as God designed us to do by giving us the divine image) demand that religion respect what science uncovers and seek to view it as God's truth about the creation. Some of the claims of God's revelation in Scripture demand that believers have respect for science. The very same Bible that religious fundamentalists in the Conflict camp use to smash science actually tells us that the Bible alone will not tell us every truth there is to know about the universe! Scripture points beyond itself. True, a tenet of traditional Christian faith is that the knowledge about God and the creation that we gain in extrabiblical pursuits of truth will not trump or invalidate what the Bible reliably reveals about the nature of God, sin, and salvation. Instead, revelation knowledge will supplement and add to the larger picture of the cosmos that God wants us to see (and that Christian theology says we can gain by making full use of our God-given rationality, which therefore includes scientific rationality and inquiry).

The two ways of knowing about the larger picture of reality are distinct from and in a real sense independent of one another. Yet within the Christian church there is also good reason to look for some integrating of the two as well. It is precisely the belief in divine revelation via Scripture, conjoined with the belief that there is a Creator of all who endowed the universe with purpose and who endowed us with the ability to study the universe, that allows us to accept the science of non-Christians, make use of their discoveries, and rejoice in the truths that science uncovers for us as an indirect but definite gift of God.

In the history of my particular branch of the larger Reformed tradition, a furious controversy raged one hundred years ago on the question of whether there is any such thing as God's "common grace." The doctrine of common grace asserts that despite humanity's condition of being mired in sin, the vestiges of God's original grace in creation (which, among other things, endowed humanity with the image of God) are such that Christians may well learn from, esteem, respect, and enjoy the good fruits of non-Christians who work in the arts, sciences, and all other fields. Some in my tradition disagree with this, claiming that the only grace about which one may legitimately speak is *saving* grace; unless a given person has been granted saving grace through Christ, one ought not to speak of God's grace in his or her life at all. Those who resist the idea of common grace often also assert that unbelievers cannot produce anything that will have much connection to God.

Such was the controversy of a century ago, which led to a schismatic split in my denomination. But a friend of mine, with an impish grin and a gleam in his eye, likes to say that we can still be friends with these Christian brothers and sisters, and if they wonder why this is so, we can say to them, "We love you because common grace helps us to respect all people!" Curiously, a similar irony may apply to theology and science, although the more hard-bitten, anti-religious types in the scientific community might not like to hear it. Still, there is a sense in which Christians may legitimately say to people of science, "We respect and love your work because God's Word tells us to!" Such a statement reflects a core truth of the Christian tradition—but one, alas, that seems to have been largely forgotten in much of the contemporary church world.

My approach to the interaction of faith and science implies that theologically informed, biblically serious Christians should also take some measure of joy from being scientifically informed about the wonders of the world, which we believe God not only made once upon a time but continues to make and sustain and shape. Such a stance does not necessarily mean that Christians must accept every scientific theory that comes along. Christians who have good *scientific* reasons for doubting the validity of a given theory about the physical world may and should disagree with those promoting the theory, and if they are able to do so, they can and should propose a countertheory based on the evidence as they see it. Even those who are not scientists but perhaps philosophers should be free to dialogue meaningfully, and sometimes critically, with the scientific community if they have good reason to suspect that the argumentation in favor of a theory has logical holes in it, is internally incoherent, or has simply not been verified on the basis of the scientific evidence at hand.

In other words, I believe that bringing together theological and scientific truths ought not render the Christian community mute, as though respect for the scientific field dictates a blind acceptance of everything that comes along. And some Christian thinkers are now speaking up on the scientific front. Writers like Michael Behe, William Dembski, and others in the Intelligent Design movement (who argue from creation's irreducible complexity to the necessity of a designer) are engaged in an enterprise that can properly be respected by people both in the church and in the scientific academy—at least they are trying to address science in scientific terms, although it cannot yet be known whether they will be proven correct scientifically. It is not my intention here to delve into the specifics of those debates or render a final opinion on them. I will, however, state my contention that if Christians want to argue science with scientists, they may of course do so, but they ought to pursue the discussion on the basis of physical evidence and the methods used to uncover them.

So if a scientist claims to have discovered element X in the universe and a Christian has doubts or questions about this finding, then those doubts and questions should be expressed, but from a scientific standpoint (unless element X were something that would cut into vital articles of faith, like someone's claiming to have found the skull of Jesus, as mentioned earlier). Was the experiment that led to X done correctly? Does the evidence support X or is it an as-yet unsubstantiated inference? Has the data been manipulated or is it clearly straightforward and convincing? If Christians wish to discuss physical findings, they should do so based on the physical sciences, but it won't do for a Christian to raise questions about the discovery of X solely because he believes that a verse somewhere in Deuteronomy rules out the existence of element X. A Christian may quite properly use the Bible against the naturalistic worldview espoused by some scientists. However, when Christians promote the Bible as a kind of quasi–field guide for physics, botany, or biology, thereby dictating what may or may not be discovered by scientific explorations, there is good reason to question how appropriately Scripture is being used.

By way of a rather simple analogy, although the Bible talks a lot about bread and fish, no one has ever claimed the Bible should be brought into the kitchen as a cookbook. Just because King David was a shepherd and the apostle Peter was a fisherman, few if any have ever hauled the Bible into a pasture for guidance on sheep farming or into a boat to learn the best way to land a bass. Likewise, the fact that the Bible has many descriptions of stars, the moon, mountains, and the human body does not mean it is proper to haul the Bible into a laboratory or observatory as a scientific textbook to dictate the limits and parameters not only of what exists but of what is discoverable by the methods of science. Great caution needs to be exercised by believers and very careful biblical work and interpretation needs to be carried out before we can conclude that the Bible does indeed rule out some past or present element in the physical cosmos.

But of course it is not that simple. Science itself is, as van Huyssteen points out, a value-laden activity. The "facts" that go into any model of the universe seldom fall into place in perfect, logical order for a scientist. There are almost always gaps that need to be bridged and details that need to be filled in with plausible speculation. Even if a theory is nicely supported by various discoveries and facts, what the theory *means* or implies can rather quickly lead a scientist from the strictly physical realm into metaphysical realms. If the philosophical naturalism that reduces all of reality to only the physical world accessible to science were always as obvious as it is in the work of people like Richard Dawkins or Carl Sagan, assessing science from a theological standpoint would be significantly easier than it in fact is—all a person of faith would have to do is shuck the naturalistic shell and examine the purely physical, scientific kernel in the middle. But all science is at least a little colored and influenced by the philosophy, religion (or lack thereof), and worldview of the scientist doing the work. Separating such influences from the actual facts is less like shucking a shell to see the kernel and more like peeling an onion: you peel layer after layer until there's nothing left, and then you wonder at what point you should have *stopped* peeling!

Some today go so far as to say that the entire scientific enterprise ought to be chalked up as just one more belief system among other belief systems. In that case, science would never be a merely physical enterprise but would always contain elements of faith—tenets that would likely conflict with different faiths in the way that Judaism differs from Shintoism, Christianity, and Taoism. Such a view of science, however, may well go too far. If the very practice of science necessarily represented a different religion, how could a person of faith (be it Christian faith, Muslim faith, or any other belief system) ever be a scientist? In that case, a person of faith's engaging in science would be an act of religious compromise or dishonesty, rather like claiming to be a Buddhist Jew.

Still, as van Huyssteen notes, it has become increasingly clear that even if the enterprise of science is not a religion or belief system all its own, scientists do indeed approach their work from a particular vantage point, which may have little to do with scientific methodology but will almost inevitably influence the interpretation of scientific results. Gone are the days of positivism, in which scientific findings were said to be empirically proven facts completely free of any extrascientific interpretation or spin. Just as theology sometimes strays into making scientific pronouncements (much to the annoyance of scientists), it is increasingly recognized that science likewise regularly bleeds over into other fields in its rejection of any authority other than its own and in its resistance to the notion that there may be a larger "story" to explain the cosmos and its history than the purely physical, evolutionary tale that is spun out from physical scientific data.

This highlights once again the enormous challenges facing preachers and theologians, not to mention lay Christians everywhere, in navigating the headwaters and crosscurrents of the science-and-theology discussion. The boundary lines and where various disciplines cross over those lines into other territories are not always clear. Dealing with clear-cut examples of illegitimate meddling in one another's epistemic fields can be difficult enough, but most often matters are significantly foggier and more formidable.

I return to van Huyssteen's point with which I disagreed earlier, namely, that our world today is so pluralistically diverse that making generalized theories or pronouncements is impossible. Though I believe we can legitimately speak in general terms about an overarching relationship between faith and science, we do need to acknowledge the diversity and difficulty just mentioned. Clearly, this is an area in which snap judgments from either side of the discussion are ill-advised and in which careful, open listening is not merely a courtesy but a necessity. Those who believe that their field alone has or one day will have *all* the answers, to the exclusion of every other way of knowing, not only demonstrate by their stance an unwillingness to be open to learning from others but also reveal a nearly wholesale unawareness of the rich diversity and supple complexity that exist in this world.

Christians Talking Science: An Analogy

Perhaps it would be helpful at this point to illustrate more specifically how Christians can approach science based on the model I have suggested. I note once again, however, that the purpose of this project is to demonstrate how Christians can take science into account when thinking theologically—indeed, even more specifically, the purpose is to goad pastors into reflecting an appreciative awareness of science throughout their preaching. This aim is quite different from trying to find ways to help scientists take theology into account. Hence, what follows is an analogy of why and how theology can appropriate science within the realm of faith. What is it like when Christians talk about science in distinctly Christian ways? Is it similar to how other nonscientific fields talk about science? It is my contention that when Christians speak of science with a strong theological accent and in recognizably faith-informed ways—mingling the findings of science with various articles of faith—it is actually very similar to how other nonscientific disciplines talk about science in forms of speech quite different from the technical language of scientific description. These other modes of discourse are not considered illegitimate just because they are not scientifically technical or precise or because they blend science with another field of knowledge (the tenets of which would have been arrived at via different epistemic avenues than those traveled by scientists). I further contend that if it is natural for other disciplines to use nonscientific modes of expression when reflecting on science, Christianity's *spiritual* way of reflecting on science ought to be seen as equally valid and natural.

Let us begin by considering Tom Stoppard's play *Hapgood*. In this highly creative and intentionally confusing drama, Stoppard presents what appears to be a story about international espionage. The main characters of the play are spies who are frequently in radio contact with each other as they attempt to track a certain Russian who keeps appearing and disappearing in baffling ways. In the end the two chief spies, characters named Hapgood and Kerner, conclude that the paradoxical and mystifying movements of the Russian could be explained by the Russian's having an identical twin. That would account for how the Russian appeared now here, now there, yet apparently without having actually moved from point A to point B. The movement of the play mirrors the larger confusion and uncertainty of the story line. The lines spoken by the characters are chock-full of espionage jargon, and frequently two or three different topics of conversation weave in and out of each other in jarring ways.

In the end, however, *Hapgood* is not really about international intrigue but about the quantum universe of atoms, electrons, and their curiously unpredictable, paradoxical movements. In preparing to write this play, Stoppard had studied the physics of quantum theory, reading technical scientific manuals and other volumes that attempt to explain the maddeningly complex world detected by Einstein and further explored by Einstein's twentieth-century successors (Heisenberg, Bohr, Hawking, and others).[24] Stoppard imported what he had learned in his scientific studies into his own realm of the theater. In this setting the playwright adopted the dramatic metaphor of intrigue and espionage and used this metaphor to convey the quirky behavior of electrons and other particles that scientists have observed at the subatomic level.

The resulting play does not, of course, read like a science textbook, nor does Stoppard necessarily strive for the kind of precision in description that a scientist would strive for when composing an article for a science journal or when writing a book on physics. Instead, Stoppard at times lets the metaphor of espionage carry and deliver the quantum freight even as he at other times more directly points to science, albeit through poetic language and imagery. Consider this passage, where the character Kerner tells Hapgood about the nature of an atom: "The particle world is the dream world of the intelligence officer. An electron can be here or there at the same moment. . . . Its movements cannot be anticipated because it has no reasons. It defeats surveillance because when you know what it's doing you can't be certain where it is, and when you know where it is you can't be certain what it's doing . . . and it's all done without tricks, it's the real world, it is awake. . . . And you don't know how small things can be, you think you know but you don't know. Make a fist, and if your fist is as big as the nucleus of one atom, then the atom is as big as Saint Paul's, and if it happens to be a hydrogen atom then it has a single electron flitting about like a moth in the empty cathedral, now by the dome, now by the altar. . . . Every atom is a cathedral."[25]

So what we have in Stoppard's play is the quantum world spoken of through the medium of theatrical drama and in the language of analogy, poetry, and metaphor. *Hapgood* would not be the thing to read if you were interested in a thorough and accurate education in quantum physics. Nor would the language of this play pass strict scientific muster—what physicist in the world would want to present a formal seminar paper before her highly educated colleagues in which she could do no more than say "every atom is a cathedral, and electrons are like moths"? Still, does Stoppard's dramatic and metaphorical utilization and presentation of science do harm to the scientific enterprise? It may be an incomplete and poetic picture of the quantum universe, but does that mean that such a play serves no purpose and ought to be shunned by all serious-minded scientific thinkers? Clearly, very few scientists would claim such things.

At least part of the reason *Hapgood* works and is acceptable as a fanciful portrait of quantum physics is because it does not pretend to replace serious science. Nor does the play communicate any negative sentiments about the science on which it is based; the fact that Stoppard does not talk in strictly scientific terminology does not mean he thinks that those who *do* are foolish or unnecessary. Instead, a drama like *Hapgood* can coexist very peacefully with professional science in that neither the medium of theater nor the field of science is seeking to undermine or impeach the validity of the other. There are multivalent ways to talk about a great many features of life in this universe.

A more recent play that makes a similar metaphorical and analogical use of science is *Copenhagen*, by Michael Frayn. This three-person play dramatically speculates on the content of a conversation held in 1941, when the German physicist Werner Heisenberg paid an unexpected visit to his old friend and teacher Niels Bohr in Nazi-occupied Copenhagen. The dialogue of the play makes frequent and at times extended reference to Heisenberg's and Bohr's scientific work in theoretical physics—work that ultimately helped make the atomic bomb possible. But the stage is as intriguing as the dialogue. The play is presented on a slightly tilted, elliptical stage designed to look like an atom. One actor is always the nucleus of the atom, and the other two are like electrons orbiting that nucleus. The dramatic import of this 1941 conversation is high; Heisenberg was involved with Hitler's failed nuclear program, and Bohr eventually escaped from Denmark and helped the Allies with their ultimately successful nuclear program. So what did these two people say to one another? No one is certain, so Frayn's play presents four different versions of that evening, each a potential possibility, but none of them *the* way it happened. Hence, Frayn's clever dialogue as well as the staging of the entire play mirrors the world of Heisenberg's famous uncertainty principle: the quantum world seems to be more potentiality than actuality; we can never be completely certain what the true state of a particle is. If we know where it is, we can't tell what it is doing, and vice versa. Again, like Tom Stoppard, Michael Frayn has imported elements of science into the genre of drama. The resulting play is not science exactly, but it borrows freely from science to make a larger point.

Similarly, a poet could, if he so wished, compose a poem about the behavior of a helium atom's dual electrons. Like Stoppard's and Frayn's plays, such a poem would not sound much like a science textbook, but that would not render the poem invalid, useless, or misguided. Poetry simply uses a different mode of speech and a different perspective to express the truths of the universe as we know them. By way of further analogy, picture a beautiful mountain lake. There could be any number of ways to describe this lovely scene: geologically, environmentally, narratively, poetically, theologically, scientifically. A person observing this lake might convey the aesthetic wonder of the scene through no more than a gasp or a whispered "Wow!" Then again, if you were trying to describe the scene to a blind person or to someone far away on the telephone, it would not be enough to murmur a few appreciative comments. You would have to dive a little deeper into your thesaurus to come up with the words needed to sketch out the scene for the person who cannot see it firsthand. A religiously minded person could compose a spiritual ode on a par with Psalm 104 and describe in detail the color of the water, the beauty of the trees, and the grandeur of the mountains with constant reference to the God whose power, might, and goodness created this vista. Finally, the same scene could be accurately described by a park ranger as she might talk about it to a tour group, detailing how the movements of the glaciers carved out this lake, deposited certain sediments that allowed for unique forms of vegetation, and pushed up the mountain peaks whose grandeur we now enjoy.

Each of these descriptions would be valid. It could even be alleged that no one of them alone is sufficient to convey fully all aspects of such a beautiful scene. But though each form of discourse is valid and helpful, no one of them tries to undo any other. What would we think of a park ranger who, upon hearing someone in a tour group utter a wonder-filled "Wow," told this person, "Well, I really don't think that is a necessary or appropriate thing to say, madam. The real thing to think about is glacial movement in the last ice age. If you come to understand *that,* my dear woman, then your 'Wow' will properly dry up!" Similarly, were a poet to compose a sonnet or a haiku to capture something of the grandeur before him, it would be a poor scientist who scorned the resulting poem because it failed to mention any data from the geological or horticultural sciences. Conversely, what poet would reject a geological article about glaciers and sediments because it didn't rhyme?

These illustrations are intentionally rather absurd, but they help us to see that when we step back to take in the big picture of reality, and when we take into account the multiple legitimate ways by which human beings are able to experience and describe that reality, clearly no one medium of expression and no single form of discourse suffices to cover it all. A comprehensive view of life requires, and even lends itself to, many different forms of perception and expression. As long as each field, operating with its own mode of discourse, tries by and large to get it right and to be accurate—and as long as a poet does not scorn the scientist for not being poetic enough and the scientist does not dismiss the poet for not being rigorous enough in precisely detailed descriptions—then all these ways of talking about the same physical phenomenon have their place and are indeed necessary to the larger picture.

The approach I have suggested in my relationship model is similar. Christians can talk about and reflect on science within the modes of discourse and within the theological framework that properly characterize the spiritual realm of faith. When Christians talk about or reflect on science, they should do so with all due acknowledgment of science's legitimate way of knowing about and investigating the cosmos. This is the part of my model that is drawn from Barbour's Independence category—both science and theology have their valid ways of discovering truths about life and the larger universe in which we live. Drawing from Barbour's Integration category, I suggest we recognize that even though we have different ways of describing reality, we are talking about the *same* reality and the *same* universe. Scientists will speak in the language of precise scientific description, and theologically minded people of faith will talk in the cadences of Christian belief and spirituality. Similar to how Tom Stoppard used science in dramatic and metaphorical ways, Christians will read and think about science in theological ways and reference the findings of science to God's divine revelation in Scripture. But even as Stoppard was not scorning science by turning it into drama, Christians should not be seen as scorning science when they meld it with their belief in God as Creator, Sustainer, and Savior of all that exists.

Of course, I recognize it is not quite this simple. Most scientists have no problem with the medium of the theater; they understand it, appreciate it, perhaps even applaud it. When their own field of science gets dramatized on the stage, most scientists would find it an acceptable and maybe even enjoyable spectacle to watch (and anyway, theater is just fiction). But at least some scientists do not grant the same acceptance to theology or religious belief in general; they do not appreciate it, do not applaud it, and even reject it as a corrosive fantasy that inhibits a true understanding of the world. When science is imported into the realm of faith and talked about in theological ways, such scientists see this as a threat to what they stand for—or at the very least they see it as an inappropriately quirky way to talk about science, perhaps on a par with an adult who thought it necessary to reduce science to the genre of nursery rhymes even in the company of other grown-ups. Why, some scientists wonder, might a mature person want to do *that?*

Clearly, this is what at least some scientists think about religion. That is their problem, however. This is a book for people who have faith and who seek to add to that faith understanding. For our part, I suggest Christians grant science its epistemic due: science can and frequently does get things right. We can learn from science, appreciate what it reveals about the world, and unabashedly reflect on such matters with direct and overt reference to our beliefs based on God's Word. Like a poet who describes a mountain lake through a sonnet or a park ranger who describes it through a lecture about glaciers, Christians will use their particular language to describe the world. Our particular language is faith based and theological and is the mode we use to reflect on the world and to discuss almost everything that is "out there" in the wider universe, including the information uncovered by science.

This approach does not, however, rule out disagreements with various scientific theories or findings if and when Christians have serious reasons to believe that there is a direct conflict between what a certain scientist is saying and what God reveals in Scripture. But there is nothing improper or odd about Christians thinking theologically about science. Indeed, it is a wholly proper and natural thing to reflect on science through the mode of expression particular to our field—something that is likewise done by many other nonscientific fields.

Thus far I have suggested that it is good for Christians to recognize and acknowledge the legitimacy of both science's way of knowing about the universe in physical ways and Christianity's way of knowing about the universe in spiritual and theological ways. We have also come to see the legitimacy of other disciplines reflecting on and talking about science from a variety of perspectives and forms of language and speech, through which science becomes part of a larger, more complete portrait of reality—a comprehensive picture that is informed not by any one field alone but that is enriched through multiple perspectives and ways of talking. We have now cleared the way for casting a more appreciative glance on scientific matters.

As we continue toward a more direct consideration of how pastors can model a positive attitude toward science in their preaching, we now turn from the necessary groundwork to a more direct and concrete engagement with contemporary science. We will reflect in a somewhat cursory yet wonder-filled way on current physics, cosmology, and biology before turning in chapter 5 to theological reflections on some of what we think we know about the universe that we call our home and God's handiwork.

4

Learning from Science

Relaxing

At one time or another we have all met people whom we frankly find to be disagreeable. Chief among the people many of us find hard to take is the so-called know-it-all. It matters little what the topic of conversation is, the typical know-it-all will make ironclad pronouncements, often couched in insufferably long diatribes, which seem calculated to stifle anyone else from venturing his or her own opinion. But because few people are so brilliant as to be able to speak authoritatively and accurately on all subjects, the know-it-all frequently expresses comments that at least some others in the circle of conversation know to be inaccurate. The subject may be the history of the United States, and the know-it-all is holding forth on the exact inner thoughts that motivated Thomas Jefferson. But suppose you are a well-informed historian and know with a high degree of certainty that the opinions being expressed about Mr. Jefferson are flat-out false. You could in such a situation proffer a corrective, though this has little effect on most know-it-alls. Fools, as the old saying goes, are often in error but never in doubt. And so perhaps many times the wiser approach is simply to let it slide. If you are confident in your own education and knowledge, you can relax and suffer fools gladly. It is simply impossible to go around in life and successfully correct every false opinion or outshout every know-it-all you happen to run across.

Similarly, as long as there are scientists who do not believe in God, there will likely also be scientific papers, books, and articles that subtly or overtly proclaim that atheism has been validated by science. Some scientists clearly believe science knows all, and since scientific methods are not able to discover anything about God, they therefore believe theology is necessarily false. But as we saw earlier, Christians have very good reasons to believe that such a privileging of science's way of knowing as being superior to all other forms of knowledge is simply bad form. If all the beliefs to which we firmly hold had to pass scientific muster, we would have to part company with a good many of the everyday assumptions and memories that we need in order to function as sane people. Not every scientist is a know-it-all kind of person, but some are. When we encounter the scientific know-it-alls of this world, we sometimes need simply but quietly to disagree and move on. Christians should stop fighting battles they cannot win, or more properly construed, that may not be battles at all. As we have seen in previous chapters, Christians can ease some of the tensions in the science-and-theology relationship and can begin to approach science in a more relaxed, positive, and constructive way. Few North American evangelicals and fundamentalists, however, could be characterized as "relaxed" when it comes to the findings, theories, or pronouncements of science.

The reasons for this are many and varied. Some believers perhaps fear that science really is rolling back the credibility of believing in God, exactly as certain scientists claim. Others have perhaps for too long unwittingly operated under a "God of the gaps" mentality, which tacitly holds that as long as some mystery is left somewhere within the confines of the physical universe, that must be where God "lives" (or must at least be a window through which to glimpse God). This line of thought, of course, is a sure formula for future despair. Science is a tentative enterprise always open to revision; in the future it is all but certain that some contemporary theories and models will be revised and perhaps even discarded. But science does tend to advance. In the future it may well be that our understanding of quarks and gravitons will vastly change our understanding of the nature of water. What seems exceedingly unlikely, however, is that the prior discovery of water's being made up of hydrogen and oxygen will be completely discredited. Science textbooks may get longer as more understanding is amassed, but they are unlikely to get shorter. It seems most unlikely that everything science has already discovered will one day get discredited such that the universe will be nothing but mystery again. Science tends to fill in more gaps and accumulate more knowledge as time goes by. Hence, those who try to maintain God's presence in the cosmos by pointing to the nooks and crannies that science has not yet figured out will forever be on the run as science keeps tidying up those nooks and crannies. The Intelligent Design movement, which argues for the existence of God based on "irreducible complexity" that necessitates a designer, may be inherently vulnerable to this. The problem with this argument is that science may well find a way to demonstrate that what we now deem complex is actually less complex after all.

So how and why should Christians relax in their approach to science? Perhaps thinking of our earlier Flatland analogy can help to make this clear. Although it may seem like a cop-out to remove God from the physical cosmos by placing him in some other dimension, as implied by the Flatland analogy, or to claim that God's presence in our cosmos, though real, is by definition different than that of all other creatures in this cosmos, this thinking is wholly in accord with traditional Christian thought. True, for many centuries Christians affirmed a three-tier model of the universe that held that our flat earth floated on a vast sea. Below the earth was the realm of the dead; above was where God and his hosts dwelled. This is a very naive portrait of the universe, of course, though an understandable one given the limits of how far people could see into the cosmos at that time in history. But even when that primitive view of the cosmos prevailed, few if any thought it was possible for humans to punch through the firmament's glass ceiling to fetch God and prove his existence. Few if any thought that if they stared long and hard enough up into the firmament, they might eventually catch a glimpse of God strolling past, the same way you can sometimes glimpse your neighbor walking past his kitchen window.

Jews and Christians have always believed, albeit to varying degrees of sophistication, that God was the wholly "Other," who dwells in realms beyond our ordinary access. So if science says it cannot locate God, believers should respond, "Who ever said you would?" Science will neither find God nor be able to rule God out. Even if it were possible for a scientist to enter another more spiritual dimension—and it appears not to be—she would be as disoriented and as wholly unable to account for this other dimension as was our hapless Flatland inhabitant when he was whisked into a dimension that he had no ability to sense or comprehend.

Christians too often feel as if they are on the run from a dangerous science that is overtly out to get them and their God. Science cannot, however, chase believers out of realms to which it has no empirical access. But what about the realm to which science *does* have access, namely, the entire physical cosmos? Why don't, or why can't, more scientists clearly see the subject matter of their investigations as the handiwork of God? Christian theology has a built-in answer to such a question: we live in a fallen universe, and the effects of sin are everywhere on display. Chief among the effects of sin are the so-called noetic effects that obscure human thinking and keep people from seeing or understanding the physical world in the fullest sense, including a theological sense. It could well be alleged that if every person who ever peered through a microscope had understood that each mitosis of a cell is the result of a loving God's intricate designs, there would have been no need for God's Son to come to this planet to die for our sin. So if a scientist looks at the same physical wonder as a believer but does not draw the same conclusion from it, a theologically informed Christian will know that there is nothing remarkable about this whatsoever and, therefore, nothing threatening, either.

Earlier it was asserted that it is both proper and prudent to pursue wisdom and that, furthermore, this pursuit relies on our ability to draw keen observations on how things work in God's universe. But if sin has a strong noetic or mental dimension, does that rule out the human ability to gain wisdom? In a sense, the answer to that question is both yes and no. On the one hand, short of the regeneration and renewal of heart and mind brought about by God's Holy Spirit, people will not attain a full knowledge of God and his salvation, nor will they be wholly successful in discerning the breadth of wisdom as Scripture defines it.

On the other hand, however, the noetic effects of sin are not total. One does not need to be a regenerate Christian to attain a certain degree, in some cases a high degree, of street smarts and wise savvy about how life goes, nor is being a Christian a requirement for learning a great many facts about this universe. Hence, although non-Christian scientists may miss making spiritual connections to God and to God's creation designs in the course of investigating the world that Christians regard as God's handiwork, that does not mean that scientific discoveries about the physical cosmos are invalid, nor does it mean that *only* believers can make reliable scientific discoveries. This point was made more extensively earlier, when I summarized Alvin Plantinga's notion that the best science for Christians to embrace is a theistic science that investigates the physical world with reference to the Bible. The claim that sin has a noetic dimension says only that the full truth of the universe, starting with the reality and character of God and including God's plan of gracious salvation, is no longer plain to see, as would be the case were there no sin.

Awareness of sin's noetic effects, however, can allow Christians to be more relaxed when reflecting on what science has already discovered and what it will yet discover. Faith informs Christians that everything is the result of God's work. The philosophy of religion has long claimed that a workable definition of divine omniscience is that God knows every true proposition that is knowable. If science uncovers a truth, therefore, God has known it all along, no matter how novel the discovery may be for us.[1] Conversely, if the discovery in question should prove false, God knows this already as well, and because we believe God has endowed us with the ability to investigate the physical cosmos in the first place, we can have some measure of confidence that false scientific claims or erroneous discoveries will some day be found wanting by the same scientific methods through which all else that is known about the physical universe has come to us.[2]

Because science has moved forward so swiftly in recent decades, it seems many fear a day will come when everything will be explainable in secular, naturalistic fashion. If this happens, some appear to reason, God will be squeezed out; it will truly be the case, as biologist Richard Dawkins once alleged about life after Darwin, that it is now possible to be an intellectually fulfilled atheist. Similarly, in more recent years neurobiologists like Steven Pinker have claimed that our increased knowledge of how the brain functions has rendered moot the very notion of each person's possessing a soul. Consciousness, Pinker and others claim, is a by-product of the extremely complex interactions of our trillions of brain neurons and is purely a physical phenomenon. This is the kind of talk from scientists that makes it sound as if a day will come when science will have rendered all spiritual phenomena inoperative and useless. Many scientists certainly think they have God on the run. So are believers justified in feeling the same way? If Christians focus too much on the physical findings of science (even if we do manage to separate such findings from the naturalistic trappings with which many scientists cloak their work), will this diminish our spiritual sensibilities?

Perhaps a simple historical comparison will help to head off this fear of science. Believers might do well to ponder what effect, if any, our current level of understanding regarding the physical cosmos has had on faith and on the overall beliefs of the faithful. Compared to the majority of human history, our current understanding of the universe is vast. Indeed, it seems probable that we learned more about reality in the twentieth century than in any prior century, or perhaps even in all prior centuries combined. Large areas yet remain for us to explore, though some people have contended that all the really great discoveries of science are already behind us, which seems unlikely given that even the world's most brilliant theoretical physicists profess complete mystification about the microlevel of quantum physics. As the human race adds to its knowledge bank, does it therefore follow that the bank of faith will be concurrently emptied; is this, in other words, a kind of "zero sum" game, where if one gains, the other necessarily loses?

For instance, has our heightened understanding of human biology and reproduction led Christian couples no longer to pray about their desire to have a child? Does the availability of ultrasounds that can reveal the fetus to couples months before the baby's birth mean a couple is less likely to commit their child's well-being to God than was a Christian couple in Antioch eighteen hundred years ago? Does our increased knowledge of outer space, the composition of stars, and the nature of their hydrogen-helium fission make Psalm 19 meaningless? Do believers today, armed with tremendous amounts of astronomical knowledge, look into the night sky and conclude, "Well, I guess God wasn't involved in all that after all, seeing as we understand it so well now"?

The artificial way in which I am placing these questions reveals the answers. Science has from its inception been plugging the holes in our knowledge of the universe and now is filling the gaps in even our self-understandings and cataloging life-forms of which we were totally unaware prior to the advent of the powerful tools that have allowed us to plumb below and beyond the depths of what can be seen by the naked eye. Yet despite all this, most believers' religious sense has not waned, much less been snuffed out. Many people today do not believe in God and regard with derision those who do. But when in history has this not been the case? That some now use science as the excuse or as the launching pad for this derision may be a historically recent phenomenon, but unbelief has perennially found some kind of an excuse for its agnosticism or outright atheism. In the early days of the church it was Greek philosophy. In the course of subsequent centuries it has been rampant cynicism or economics or politics or apathy or any number of other phenomena that have fueled unbelief or have been co-opted as partners in unbelief. Science did not create unbelievers. Nor, as we have seen, does science inherently make unbelief more or less likely in any given person. Dawkins may be correct that Darwin helped to create intellectually fulfilled atheists. But the subtext of that remark indicates that such people were atheists from the beginning, albeit perhaps intellectually unfulfilled ones.

Science can, may, and should continue to advance in its investigations of God's handiwork—although many scientists would not, of course, characterize their work in this way. Believers can, much of the time at least, follow scientific discovery, marveling at the truths science reveals to us and praising God for giving us so interesting a cosmic home. When science begins to speak theologically and philosophically, believers can recognize the blurring of the boundaries between science and theology—a blurring that may reveal much about the scientist who says such things but very little about what the Holy Spirit has to say to God's children through faith alone. And if a scientist should claim he can physically disprove miracles reported in Scripture or rule out the possibility of Jesus ever having existed, then Christians may politely beg to differ on the basis of their faith and on the valid way they receive knowledge of God through God's Word. Such occasional disagreements, however, are quite different from a wholesale impugning of all science, much less claiming that these occasional disagreements prove that Christians are best off *never* taking science seriously.

But even given the errors that science has made and still makes in moving from physical descriptions to theological implications, the Christian church, recognizing that theological beliefs led to science's rise in the first place within the bosom of the church, should take science seriously and address the specifics of science with great care. Philosopher Nicholas Wolterstorff recently summarized an ethics of fair intellectual exchanges he believes the Christian community should follow: "Thou shalt not take cheap shots. Thou must not sit in judgment until thou hast done thy best to understand. Thou must earn the right to disagree."[3] In the case of Christian attitudes toward science, believers should delight in earning this right, especially when we recognize that a better understanding of science may give us a clearer understanding of God's handiwork. When this point of view is coupled with the recognition that it is God's very image within us that allows scientists, and all of us, to explore and learn about this world, the carefulness with which believers will discuss matters of science should quite naturally increase.

True dialogue, however, is a transformative process. Genuine give-and-take requires that both parties engaged in the discussion are willing to be challenged and perhaps even changed by what they learn from one another. There may well be times when both theology and science will have to admit errors—occasions when each strayed out of its respective field and made claims or counterclaims it could not properly substantiate, as Pope John Paul II acknowledged in 1992, when he issued a kind of apology for the church's treatment of Galileo some 350 years earlier, saying, "A tragic mutual incomprehension has been interpreted as the reflection of a fundamental opposition between science and faith."[4] But the Pope could make that statement only because the church had been willing, at long last, to engage in the transformative process of dialogue with science. For Christians to dialogue in this way requires both courage and humility: courage to open oneself up to change, and humility to make those changes if need be. Both traits, however, are proper Christian virtues founded on Scripture. People of faith who have confidence in God and in God's revelation can enter into this dialogue without fear that their faith will be smashed as a result. But a humble openness to the Holy Spirit who brings us God's Word may also position believers to understand God's Word even better—a development for which believers could be truly grateful to God and to his Spirit, who is never finished leading God's people into all truth.

Perhaps a brief explanation of the particular way I am using the word "relax" is needed. I do not mean that when it comes to the relationship between theology and science Christians should "relax" in the sense that they simply ignore these issues, as if I were saying, "Relax! Don't worry about it; somebody else is taking care of it." Nor do I mean that Christians should relax in the sense of letting their intellectual guard down or of being so mellow that they do not pay careful attention to what is going on—these are, after all, difficult issues that require careful thought. Instead, what I have in mind is the image of someone at a party who is so fearful and uptight that she is unable or unwilling to relax long enough to mingle with the other guests and just possibly have a good time. If a person at a party felt she were in the company not just of strangers but indeed of enemies, the social and mental tension generated by this feeling would prohibit any chance of fruitful conversation. Assuring her that she need not fear the other guests and that she can even interact with them with a measure of confidence would help her to relax enough so that conversation could begin. She could then, so to speak, at long last "join the party."

A further word should be said about the source or the rationale behind a Christian's relaxed approach to the science-and-theology relationship. First, the reason to relax is *not* because the Bible is so superior a form of knowing about almost anything that we will never learn anything new from other sources—or in other words, that because "the Bible tells us so" we can safely listen to science with an amused smirk on our collective face. If it is wrong for Richard Dawkins and Daniel Dennett to privilege the scientific way of knowing as superior to all other epistemic avenues, it is equally wrong for Christians to think that science routinely gets things spectacularly wrong in ways that *only* Christians can point out (based on Scripture alone rather than on any counterevidence from the physical world). Second, the reason to relax is *not* rooted in any kind of a "God of the gaps" mentality. The source of a Christian's relaxed attitude should not be the thought, "Well, there are still *lots* of things science doesn't know, so God must still fit in there *some*where after all." Similarly, a relaxed attitude should not be forged by impugning contemporary cosmology, physics, or biology to make "space for God," thereby essentially reestablishing *former* gaps that science has now filled in.

The source of a Christian's relaxed attitude toward the science-and-theology discussion stems neither from the idea that believers already know it all nor from positing God in scientific gaps. Rather, this relaxed attitude stems from a broad and comprehensive view of God and creation—something suggested by the traditional theological tenet of *creatio continua*, which refers to the idea that creation is an ongoing, continuing work of God and not simply a once-for-all accomplishment that God finished eons ago and never touched again. This sense of God's abiding presence and the valid source of Christian beliefs is the firm ground on which believers can stand when considering issues and questions related to the interaction of theology and science. Taking a cue from theologian Roland Frye and others, churches should begin once again to take seriously a belief that is deeply embedded in the Reformed heritage, namely, the idea of the "two books of God," which reminds believers that much can be learned about God and his handiwork through careful study of creation's endlessly rich tapestry. Within the Reformed tradition, this idea was stated in the Belgic Confession, Article 2: "We know [God] by two means: First, by the creation, preservation, and government of the universe, since that universe is before our eyes like a beautiful book in which, all creatures great and small, are as letters to make us ponder the invisible things of God." But where is such careful study of what we could call the ABCs of God's created universe pursued more than in the physical sciences?

Earlier I mentioned how much I have learned from astronomer Carl Sagan. He was a lucid teacher and a first-rate scientist who was, alas, also prone to make religious pronouncements with which few Christian believers could agree. But near the end of his life Sagan made what may well be one of his few religious judgments that I can largely accept. Sagan wondered why hardly any major religions or religious thinkers had ever looked upon the wonders that science has revealed about this universe and then responded, "Why, this is better than we thought! The universe is much bigger than our prophets said, grander, more subtle, and more elegant!" Instead, Sagan lamented, people of faith alternately ignore science or shun it, insisting that they prefer to keep their view of reality smaller, more confined, more manageable (and perhaps more in accord with the way they believe the Bible presents the physical cosmos). On this particular point Sagan may well have been all too accurate in his assessment of the way many believers, past and present, conduct themselves.

This chapter aims to be a very small beginning in redressing this situation. Believers, as I have suggested, can bring science into conversation with their faith and can reflect on science and talk about its findings in ways that are not strictly scientific. I suggest that learning from science will in many ways enhance our Christian sense of awe for God's creation and will provide us with the opportunity to ponder imaginatively the clever and marvelous ways God works in this universe. In fact, at least a few recent discoveries in quantum physics have, ironically, answered or rendered moot some of the arguments that atheistic philosophers of past centuries made *against* the existence of God or the possibility of God's ever performing a miracle.

Since the overarching goal of this book is to encourage a positive use of science in the pulpit, I will model this practice by highlighting some of the more wondrous things science now tells us. But before turning to this survey of scientific wonders, a few matters need to be clarified. These matters are key principles for preachers to bear in mind anytime they find scientific facts or issues arising naturally as they attempt to bring God's Word to bear on this world. First, although I will suggest that the presence of God, his providential superintending of the cosmos, and the possibility of miracles are perhaps easier to see from a quantum standpoint now than had once been true, I do not thereby intend to reintroduce a "God of the gaps" mentality. I am not plugging God into only those places where science seems uncertain, nor am I saying that God can be detected only here and there, now and again. The presence of God is all-encompassing. My belief that this is so, and thus my ability to see God almost everywhere, is not dependent on any scientific theory, much less on any gap in scientific theories. In short, in our survey of scientific wonders I will indeed mention God in connection with a few facets of the universe as we now understand it scientifically. I will do this not because I think these are the *only* places to see God at work but because I see God's hand everywhere. The specific facets I will highlight and suggest are therefore merely examples of the myriad of ways God is constantly active in the universe. I make this point to head off any who would construe my comments as being no more than an attempt to sneak in the name of God every time a scientist stops to scratch his head. To be perfectly clear on this matter, I present the following example.

Whereas not so long ago most people held to some version of Newton's mechanically driven universe of straightforward, and possibly predictable, cause and effect, scientists have in recent decades come to understand that our universe is vastly more complex, subtle, and integrated than they ever thought. Many now see our universe as an interwoven whole driven by indeterminate forces whose overall interrelationships are nearly impossible to map out, pin down, or even predict. There is still a sense of cause and effect, but we now know that a single observable cause may well contain a myriad of tiny, invisible subcauses, even as the resulting effect may take on a surprising shape in regions far removed from the locus of the cause. As it turns out, minute changes made in one part of the world may create very large effects in places one would not expect. The classic example of this is the flutter of a butterfly's wing in New York City's Central Park contributing to a typhoon over Bangladesh some time later, which, by the way, is *not* a silly exaggeration! I suggest that this new understanding of the universe lets us realize that God's ways of interacting with this world (even when bringing about what we would regard as miraculous) may likewise be filled with diverse and subtle influences.

This suggests the possibility of a very different way of divine operation than anyone could have guessed back in the days when atheist David Hume alleged that miracles were impossible because they would require an awkward "violation" of the laws of nature. To Hume and many other thinkers in the eighteenth and nineteenth centuries, divine action in the universe would have required God to meddle in a heavy-handed way with the very laws of nature and the laws of straightforward, mechanically predictable cause and effect. The scientific picture of the universe now, however, looks much more subtle and complex, hence undercutting what Hume and others regarded as solid arguments against the possibility of God's activity in the world. We have now begun to realize that a myriad of factors and influences affect most any observable event, so that Hume's narrow definitions of what God would simply *have* to do in order to bring about a miracle (namely, interfere with and so violate the laws of nature) now seem very far off the mark.[5]

Well and good, but I want to be clear that by thus positing God within the picture of our quantum universe, I am not doing so in a stopgap way. I am not suggesting that God *must* perform his miracles through subtle influences on the quantum web, nor am I saying that as long as there are indeterminacies and uncertainties about how quanta of energy (subatomic "packets" of energy) interact, believers can rest assured that *this* is the place where we can still infer God's presence and work. If the current picture of the universe is correct, this quantum cosmos is the handiwork of God as is everything else, and it may well be that God's interaction with the universe would indeed be made through quantum influences, as I will suggest. But if one day in the future quantum physics goes the way of the ideas of Ptolemy and Newton, getting discarded or significantly revised in favor of some new view, this may say much about our human propensity to get things wrong, even spectacularly wrong now and again, but it will not undercut God. All I or anyone can reasonably do at any given point in history is to suggest *possible* ways by which God may work based on what we think we know about the nature of the world God made. So if the quantum view of the world turns out to be false—and hence the notion that God works through quantum influence would likewise be false—this would only mean that God works some other way; regardless of *how* God works in this universe, faith tells the believer that God *does* work! If, on the other hand, the quantum picture of the cosmos is completely accurate, my suggestions on how God may influence and work with quanta of energy could nevertheless be wrong or be only one small sliver of the richly diverse ways God operates. Even if the universe is a quantum reality exactly as science now suspects, it may be that God can and does work out his purposes and perform his miracles over, above, beyond, or quite simply *without* any quantum realities! God has no box, and I do not intend to put God into one, either.

In short, God will "fit" with and be sovereign over the whole of reality, whatever the most fundamental structures of the universe turn out to be. And even if we ever reliably discover what those fundamental structures are (and it's possible, of course, that starting with Einstein we have been reliably uncovering those very structures for the past century), God will forever be grander than even the grandest physical truth science could ever show. This is one reason why Stephen Hawking is so sadly off base in his assertion that if ever we could achieve a grand unification theory, we would "know the mind of God."[6] No, all such a theory would achieve would be the same thing that new and valid scientific theories have always achieved, namely, it would help us to learn a bit more of what God himself has always known.

But learning *some* of what God already knows is a far cry from ever learning *all* that God knows! And if, for instance, via the epistemic avenue of faith, Christians are right to assert the mystery of the Trinity, but if physical science cannot discover something like the Trinity, then God as Trinity would be at least one significant part of "the mind of God" that a grand unification theory would miss. But if being triune is constitutive of who God is (and if God is indeed one God in three persons, one would have to call that fact quite constitutive indeed!), the grand unification theory's claim to know God's mind while it misses the concept of divine Trinity would be a little like claiming to know "the mind of Lincoln" while being ignorant of the fact that he once freed slaves (or maybe missing the little fact that Lincoln had run as a Republican). So much for science's discovering "the mind of God."[7]

God accords with the universe he created, yet not in an occasional way but comprehensively and in every way. This brings us to the second point I wish to establish up front, and that is my stance of "faith seeking understanding." In other words, we are not trying to establish our faith but rather we begin from faith and see the world through it. I believe a strong case can be made for God's role, and even for God's necessity, in the evolutionary universe that science is more and more uncovering. The so-called anthropic principle, which we will explore below, is a key place (perhaps *the* key place) where the probability, if not utter need, of a loving Designer's presence can be quite logically posited. But the aim of this book is not to mount a case that could convert hard-boiled skeptics. Christian believers who know that their faith provides them with a perfectly valid way of attaining true knowledge about reality need not be ashamed both to begin with this faith and subsequently to view everything from its vantage point.

So as an exercise in faith seeking understanding, the remainder of this chapter and the whole of the next will explore how scientific data often nicely accord with many of our beliefs about God, even as the presence of God helps us to make sense of what we know scientifically. Reality hangs together, as do all the many sources of our knowledge about reality, in this case the specific sources of faith and science. But as we turn now to our survey of some of science's more startling discoveries of the past century, we should have no delusions: if someone does *not* start with faith and view the world through its lens, my bringing God into the picture not only will be unconvincing but may even be seen as ridiculous. So be it. But for those of us who do possess the precious gift of faith, seeking to see God in the details and seeing the details as God's work is a proper exercise in gratitude to the gift-Giver. Let us begin.

Science's Story

"In the beginning was the singularity." Though some scientists might protest, one could just as easily say, "In the beginning was the mystery," because "the singularity" is the name that some cosmologists and physicists have assigned to what they do not know but only infer based on what they do know. The singularity is, physically speaking at least, all that existed the moment before the big bang exploded this present universe into existence.[8] At that particular moment, referred to as $t = 0$, every single atom that now exists in every far-flung corner of this unimaginably vast (and still-expanding) universe was contained in the singularity. Every spark and speck of energy that ever eventually became a galaxy, a star, a moon, a daffodil, an ocean, a human person, was jam-packed together in what some scientists describe as an infinitely dense yet dimensionless wad that, for reasons unknown to science, ignited, expanded at a colossal rate of speed, and has been spreading out and cooling off ever since.

As this vast sea of expanding energy raced out from the "center" that had once been the singularity, one of the first things to happen was the high-speed collision of particles, which thus produced hydrogen and helium. Over time (a lot of it) suns formed, blazed their light into space, and then died, creating heavier elements such as carbon, which ultimately (over a lot more time) made possible the formation of planets and biotic life-forms of all kinds. The Genesis account says that God created humanity out of dust, and the scientific story tells a similar tale of our carbon-based existence being made of the ashes of long-deceased stars. We are stardust beings, luminous in our own right, yet in some sense we are also the reflected glory of suns whose light has passed into our life.

But despite this neat and tidy telling of the cosmic story, scientific investigation into what existed prior to the big bang routinely hits a brick wall. The problem for science is in using existing models dependent on the laws of nature to theorize about a time when no one is certain what, if any, laws were operative. The singularity—if it did indeed exist in a solitary state—and whatever made it explode into new life and new possibilities are by definition nonrepeatable, nonobservable events. As William Stoeger has said, you can call the big bang the "beginning" of the universe only in a limited sense. All models break down long before science can get anywhere near the essential nonexistence of all that now exists. Or as van Huyssteen puts it, "Even if the singularity did represent what actually occurred, it is not an origin or a beginning in an absolute

sense. . . . Long before reaching it, we will gradually lose our ability
to make observations or perform experiments that directly test these
extreme epochs. Because of the fact that the very laws of nature here
cease to exist, this is the point where we reach the limits of scientific
rationality."[9]

But clearly *something* happened, since we are, after all, rather undeniably *here*. There is now something rather than nothing. And it may well
be as logical to argue in favor of there having once been that infinitely
dense wad of energy called the singularity as it is to argue in favor of
there having once been nothing at all save for a God who created our
something out of quite literally nothing. But the question that has
perennially nettled me about either scenario is whether or not we can
escape the sense that there is something "outside" or beyond the physical
universe we know. The ancient Hebrews, whose creation stories were
enshrined in Genesis 1 and 2, believed that the physical reality to which
humanity had access and in which humanity was restricted was a kind
of bubble floating in a vast, chaotic sea. This ancient view of reality says
that beneath one's feet is the flat earth, stretching out to the horizons
for an unknown distance (though eventually the plane of the earth had
a clifflike edge to it, they were sure), and above one's head is that thing
that Genesis calls "the firmament," which was believed to be a kind of
vast dome or ceiling enclosing the universe.

In a way, this picture is similar to those little water-filled glass globes
you can find in gift shops. Inside the water-filled globe is perhaps a
snow-covered house and yard. When you shake the globe, you stir up a
flurry of little fake snowflakes, thus creating the illusion of gently falling snow landing on the roof of a wee house and yard. So also with the
Genesis view: we exist inside a globe of glass, with a pedestal of terra
firma beneath us. The water, however, is not inside the globe but outside
it. The bubble of the universe floats, as it were, like a submarine within
a vast sea of water. Only the good creation providence of Yahweh holds
at bay the waters above the heavens and the waters beneath the earth,
through the twin protective layers of the earth and the firmament (hence
the many references in the Bible to "the waters below the earth" and the
depiction in the Noah story of the floodwaters both coming *down* from
the skies and welling *up* from the earth. For the flood, God temporarily punched a few holes in both the firmament's roof overhead and the
earth's floor below).[10]

Although we today find such a depiction of the universe to be naive,
albeit picturesque and creative, it nevertheless contains at least one element that most people cannot resist pondering, namely, the possibility of

there being something beyond the "bubble" of this cosmos. Even if the singularity posited by contemporary cosmology did once exist in that intense wad of energetic essence, can our minds escape visualizing that ball of energy as being somewhere? Did the singularity necessarily have a location? Was there something beyond the singularity? In these matters we are, as van Huyssteen noted, so clearly at the conceptual limits of thought and language that such questions are either sublime or silly. Wondering if there is now and was in the beginning anything beyond or outside this universe is a line of inquiry either very near to the heart of everything or so tainted by the perceptual limits of creatures who are physically and mentally "trapped" within a spatial universe that such questions are meaningless chatter.

In any case, science is beyond its ken in these matters (recall the earlier Flatland analogy). If science cannot plumb the physical reality of the singularity, it surely cannot prove or disprove anything's having been beyond, outside, or prior to the singularity. And if science cannot see into the singularity, much less empirically show that there was nothing beyond it, neither can it say with any certainty that the singularity did not lead to something beyond this universe. In short, the questions of whether there was anything prior to or beyond the singularity and whether there is anything beyond what the physical sciences have access to today are properly yoked questions. These two questions will have the same answer, but science seems unlikely to provide it. After all, science depends on having access to some manner of hard evidence, and the absence of such evidence makes scientific investigation difficult, if not impossible.

But I said earlier that this chapter would be an exercise in faith seeking understanding, and it should be patently obvious that Christians will adopt the perspective that there was in the beginning, as there is now, a reality, a divine reality, beyond our physical universe. I believe that this is a more commonsense view than the, in my opinion, counterintuitive idea that if the singularity once existed, it was itself nowhere, existed nowhere, came from nowhere, "floated" nowhere.[11] We are spatially limited creatures and can scarcely conceive of nonspatial extensions or existences. Still, nearly all cultures in human history have had at the very least a *spiritual* sense of beyondness. On the one hand, this may simply mean that as by-products of a spatially extended universe, we cannot help but think in terms of inside and outside, and so we naturally assume that if we are *inside* the universe, there must be some place *outside* the universe.

On the other hand, it could also be argued that this human tendency to embrace a realm beyond the purely physical may be an eloquent witness to a deeper truth: there really is more in heaven and on earth than is dreamt of by any philosophical system or, I would add, than is accessible to any science. The Christian faith claims that the whole process of creation had a Designer and a purpose greater than merely creating something rather than nothing. The notion that there is something beyond this physical universe is best seen not in some attempt to visualize a singularity with or without an extended location. Rather, we gain our keenest sense that there is something, if not *someone*, beyond us by considering the ultimate outcome of the big bang (or the big whatever), not the least of which is humanity, through which, as John Polkinghorne likes to say, the universe has become aware of itself.

Bertrand Russell once said he didn't find much in humanity worth bragging about. "If I were granted omnipotence, and millions of years to experiment in, I should not think Man much to boast of as the final result of my efforts."[12] Many things could be said in response to such a critical assessment of the human race. From the Christian viewpoint, one could point out that theologians have never claimed that humanity in its present state is the "final result" of God's efforts. Today some Christians doubt whether it is literally true that the human race once existed in a prelapsarian state of moral innocence in a garden called Eden. But whether a Christian doubts this or takes the biblical portrait of humanity's original innocence more seriously, as I do, almost all Christians could agree that the present state of the human race (on which Russell based his dim judgment) is not the fullness of what God has planned and desires for us, much less the better human existence we desire for ourselves. A hallmark of Christian proclamation is that humanity falls short of the mark. At our worst, a nadir to which we descend all too often, not only are we unworthy of one's boasting, but we are something to lament and to judge (and to *be* judged). The image of God in which we were created is marred, smeared, and sometimes almost wholly eclipsed from sight. The full flowering of humanity and the noble heights we are capable of reaching will yet come, by God's grace, but only in the shalom of God's coming kingdom.

Russell, naturally, would not be much moved by such theological talk. But even if one squarely looks at humanity "warts and all," the finest things we humans have already achieved are stunning. The singularity, even if it once existed, knew neither itself nor anything else. Yet in the mystery of the cosmos, somehow this nonconscious energy has given way to conscious beings—a human race whose knowledge and awareness has expanded all the way back to the singularity that, even if it existed, was incapable of conscious thought or awareness. We are a race that has gone far beyond seeking mere survival (which, as we saw earlier, some evolutionary biologists claim is the principal driving force in the evolutionary progress of the universe). We are beings capable not only of studying and enjoying other creatures but also of attempting to ensure *their* survival, for no other reason than that we esteem their unique otherness. We are beings who have written poetry and music, literature and songs, for the sheer creative joy of it. We have looked into the fundamental units of our molecular structure and have managed to probe subatomic levels. The advent of an Einstein may be relatively rare in human history, but though he was a genius, Einstein's mental hardware was essentially the same as that possessed by all other human beings.

Hence, what is truly stunning is that the universe now contains beings able to investigate matters as fundamental as light and time (and in nearly one fell swoop, Einstein revolutionized our understanding of both). For all our faults—which Christian theology most certainly addresses in its central symbol of the cross—the human race Russell so flippantly dismissed as not much to marvel over is, as a matter of fact, quite marvelous indeed. In fact, some scientists claim that human complexity exceeds that of the universe itself. According to neurologists, every human brain contains trillions of neurons. As Ian Barbour points out, "the number of possible ways of connecting [those trillions of neurons] is greater than the number of atoms in the universe. A higher level of organization and a greater richness of experience occur in a [single] human being than in a thousand lifeless galaxies. It is human beings, after all, who reach out to understand that cosmic immensity."[13] Or as Barbara Brown Taylor has so eloquently written,

> Since science proceeds by proof, it cannot say where complexity comes from, but it is hard not to be charmed by this idea: that in us, the design has evolved creatures who are capable of discerning the design. Like chickens penetrating the mysteries of their own eggs, we have been given the ability to glimpse our own origins. Imagine your own eyeball pressed against the eyepiece of a microscope, looking down at the kind of light-sensitive cell from which it evolved. Now imagine that light-sensitive cell squinting back at you. How many millions of years are spanned in that glance? . . . How much more time does it take for quantum particles to mature to the point where they may compose hymns of praise? Whether your answer is seven days or fifteen billion years, it remains a miracle that we are here at all, and able to praise our maker. God may well prefer the sound of spring

peepers, but I have to believe there was joy in heaven when the first human being looked at the sky and said, "Thank you for this."[14]

Whether you believe that God created humanity in one special act without a hint of evolutionary development or by means of evolutionary development, the fact that humanity exists at all is the universe's single most arresting development of which we know. It is all the more astonishing when one considers how extremely unlikely it is that we exist at all. The so-called anthropic principle states that this universe had to be very finely tuned to yield biological life-forms and ultimately to yield the conscious life-form of human beings. On a purely physical level, the anthropic principle does no more than highlight the series of minute factors that had to go exactly right in the early universe for life to arise. This is sometimes called the weak anthropic principle in that it says little more than, yes, we are here because that is simply how things happened to work out. A more metaphysical or spiritual extension of this principle, sometimes called the strong anthropic principle, further claims that it is so inconceivably improbable that all of those factors would combine just right to produce a life-bearing universe instead of a universe barren of life that an excellent explanation is the existence of some kind of divine being who stacked the deck, so to speak, so that it would all work out in just this fashion. This explanation is, of course, by no means accepted by those who are willing to acknowledge only the weak anthropic principle.

In general, the origin of the anthropic principle, in both its physical and metaphysical forms, is the fact that the difference between this universe being life bearing or being devoid of life teetered on the razor's edge of a series of minute factors. In the very moments—literally a matter of seconds, not minutes—after the big bang, much had to go exactly right if life were ever to arise and survive in the universe. Ian Barbour has explained it well:

If the rate of expansion one second after the Big Bang had been smaller by even one part in a hundred thousand million, it would have re-collapsed before it reached its present size. On the other hand if it had been greater by one part in a million, the universe would have expanded too rapidly for stars and planets to form. . . . For every billion antiprotons in the early universe, there were one billion and one protons. The billion pairs annihilated each other to produce radiation with just one proton leftover. A greater or smaller number of survivors—or no survivors at all (if they had been evenly matched)—would have made our kind of material world impossible. If the laws of physics are symmetrical between particles and antiparticles, why was there a tiny asymmetry here? [As physicist Free-man Dyson has said,] "The more I examine the universe and the details of its architecture, the more evidence I find that the universe must have known we were coming."[15]

Or to employ the "Goldilocks and the Three Bears" analogy once used by Owen Gingerich, one bowl of cosmic porridge would have been too hot, another would have been too cold, but our universe is the bowl of cosmic soup that is *just right*.

The argument supporting the anthropic principle's notion that the universe was designed precisely and minutely to yield humanity is not airtight (what argument is?). The argument is, however, strong enough to unsettle those who resist the possibility of a Designer God who stacked the cosmic deck. At least some of the ways people like Richard Dawkins and others have sought to get out from under the weight of the strong anthropic principle have strained the limits of credulity. For instance, some propose that the way to explain how uncannily this universe seems to have been set up to get to this point of cosmic self-awareness is that there was an infinite series of alternative universes in the inaccessible reaches of the past. Maybe the singularity has exploded, expanded, collapsed, and exploded again untold numbers of times over gazillions of years, each time yielding slightly or even vastly different results.[16] In such a long series of galactic games of chance, eventually a universe that could yield life would surely be among the possibilities, and we are, of course, in the one where everything went just right. Still others claim that perhaps right now parallel universes exist to which we do not have empirical access because they exist in other dimensions of the space-time continuum. Perhaps all of the other parallel realities are barren of life, but we, again, just happen to be in the one that is fruitful and life filled. In short, eventually somewhere, sometime, a universe like ours just *had* to happen.

Such explanations, however, clearly smack more of science fiction than of science. These theories were developed out of thin air as a way to escape the force of the strong anthropic principle. Sometimes the line of argumentation used in these theories is called "cosmic promiscuity." Dawkins admits that the possibility of everything combining in just the right way to yield our level of human complexity really is exceedingly unlikely if left to chance alone. He also clearly recognizes that all of what we have become via our mind-bogglingly long chain of DNA could rather cogently be used to argue for the necessity of a Creator God purposively leading this otherwise unlikely process along.

Barbour quotes biologists Fred Hoyle and Chandra Wickramasinghe, who point out that left to chance alone, the existence of even the most basic protein chain is inconceivably improbable. "Suppose you were assembling amino acids to form a hundred link chain. There are twenty different amino acids from which to choose every time you add a link to the chain. If you assembled chains at random a billion times a second, it would take many times the history of the universe to run through all the possible combinations. . . . To hope for a particular set of interacting proteins to be produced by chance would be like hoping to make a complete airplane by stirring up a heap of metal parts in a junkyard."[17] As Barbour goes on to point out, however, this would be so only if the protein chain came into existence instantly. If, however, the production of a given protein chain took place through various stages over a longer period of time, certain combinations begin to look more likely. But ultimately a staggering number of possibilities remains; mere chance is an unlikely explanatory candidate for the final production of the complex protein chains that had to come together in precisely the way they did if life such as we possess were going to exist at all.

Again, atheistic thinkers often recognize this. Astronomer Owen Gingerich relates the discovery by Fred Hoyle and Willy Fowler that the difference between there being sufficient carbon to produce life in the universe and there being no carbon at all is a matter of the narrowest of margins. Had the situation in the early universe been different by as little as one-half of 1 percent, virtually no carbon would be in existence. Although an atheist, Hoyle has admitted that nothing ever shook his atheism quite like the discovery of how precisely everything had to come together just to yield carbon atoms: "Would you not say to yourself [in the light of this finding], 'Some supercalculating intellect must have designed the properties of the carbon atom, otherwise the chance of my finding such an atom through the blind forces of nature would be utterly minuscule.' Of course you would. . . . A common sense interpretation of the facts suggests that a superintellect has monkeyed with physics, as well as with chemistry and biology, and that there are no blind forces worth speaking about in nature. The numbers one calculates from the facts seem to me so overwhelming as to put this conclusion almost beyond question."[18]

Of course, not all nonreligious scientists are willing to make such an admission. So to get around the strong anthropic principle, some thinkers are willing to go to fairly wild extremes of speculation in an attempt to explain the sheer inexplicability of our existence. As just noted, Richard Dawkins promotes the theory of cosmic promiscuity, which claims that given infinite time, almost everything will eventually happen. Everything that could happen, every conceivable universe, would pop into existence at some point if given enough time, including this improbable universe that has led to humanity. But as Keith Ward points out, this theory is not only desperate but incoherent. The notion of cosmic promiscuity cannot be true because it is impossible that *every* conceivable universe would exist at some point. After all, Ward says, certain possible universes, were they ever to exist, would automatically exclude a lot of other possible universes. The most obvious case of this would be a universe designed by a loving, omnipotent, eternal God. If even *once* a universe made by an eternal God were to exist, that would necessarily rule out the possibility of there ever being a universe without God (since an eternal God would, by definition, exist in every possible world). Conversely, if Dawkins believes that this present universe exists without an eternal God watching over it, that means Dawkins is excluding the possible emergence in infinite time of a universe *with* an eternal God watching over it. In short, on this particular point Dawkins appears to defeat Dawkins.[19] So it is patently false to claim that given enough time everything that could exist eventually would.

Additionally, however, I find it curious that thinkers who so easily deride the supposedly "naive" way faith embraces things unseen can at the same time promote theories of unseen existences and even of whole universes, the belief in which requires a fairly significant leap of faith all its own. Christians at least claim that the content of our faith is revealed to us in ways that fully accord with our legitimate and multiple sources of reliable information about reality. We claim to have been *told* the things we believe by a loving God who both can and does convey information to us. Scientists who launch into theories of parallel dimensions or theories of an infinite series of universes cannot claim even that much. Instead, they pitch theories that are themselves less probable than the existence of a Creator who, by sheer dint of his universal design, answers the questions of how and why our extremely unlikely existence has nevertheless occurred. As John F. Haught has written, the development of this universe as we now know it (including of human beings, who alone have the power to study and to know the universe) stems from "a congenial blend of contingency, predictability, and duration. Explaining in an *ultimate* way why the universe has these generic features, and why it has them mingled in a way that allows for the evolution of life, is a legitimate function of theology."[20] Science, in other words, shows us what exists but not why. Science poses the question of why the cosmic deck looks as if it were stacked to yield life. Theology provides an answer.

Of course, still others, perhaps recognizing the freewheeling and wild nature of cosmic promiscuity and other similar theories, seek to take the wind out of the anthropic principle's sails by simply shrugging it all off. What's the sense, they claim, of wondering how we came to be here or how unlikely it may be? We *are* here, and that's that. That which exists is neither likely nor unlikely; if it happened, it must have been likely in some way we don't understand, and there's really not much more to say about it. But this cosmic shrug of the shoulders is what led Polkinghorne to point out that we would never settle for such a line of thinking in other, much more minor areas, so why put up with it on such a grand scale?

> Is it no more than a simple tautology, saying that this universe which contains ourselves must be compatible with our having appeared in history? For sure that must be so, but it is surprising—and many of us think significant—that this requirement places so tight a constraint on the physical fabric of our world. . . . John Leslie believes that it is no more rational to think that no explanation is required of fine anthropic coincidences than it would be to say that my fishing apparatus can accept a fish only exactly 23.2576 inches long and, on casting the rod into the lake, I find that immediately I have a catch, which is simply good luck—and that's all there is to say about it.[21]

Alvin Plantinga once made a similar observation regarding the work of Daniel Dennett and his claim that the universe just happened to spin out the way it did and so there's no sense in saying anything more about it. Plantinga wondered how using this kind of explanation would have played out in Dodge City in the Old West. Suppose you were the card dealer at a saloon poker game, and every time you dealt the cards you yourself got all four aces plus the wild card. In such a scenario a fellow player would likely not be much moved if—upon your noticing his increasingly suspicious glare—you were to say, as Plantinga puts it, "Waal, shore, Tex, I *know* it's a leetle mite suspicious that every time I deal I git four aces and a wild card, but have you considered the following? Possibly there is an infinite succession of universes, so that for any possible distribution of possible poker hands, there is a universe in which that possibility is realized; we just happen to find ourselves in one where someone like me always deals himself only aces and wild cards without ever cheating. So put up that shootin' arn and set down 'n shut yore yap, ya dumb galoot."[22]

The question of the origin of the universe could be framed this way: either we explain our unlikely existence by reference to an unseen but very real God who set up the universe and guided it along so that it would be life bearing and fruitful *or* we explain it by reference to an unseen series of alternative or parallel universes, of which ours is the lucky one that just happened to yield life. Christians clearly embrace the first option; scientists with a naturalistic perspective are willing to entertain the second option. But at least Christians can and do say more about how they receive the content of their faith in fully rational ways that accord with how we know many other true and valid things in our daily lives. Scientists who propose vast scenarios of cosmic promiscuity can make no such claims for the source of their ideas—at least I know of no such attempts to ground a multiple-universe theory epistemologically.

Quantum Beginnings

Twentieth-century scientific advances were not restricted to theories of the origins of the universe but also included the extremely complex development in physics of quantum theory. Beginning in 1905 when a clerk in the Swiss patent office published an article on the nature of light, our understanding of the nature of this cosmos has undergone what can only be described as a revolutionary revision. This clerk's name was Albert Einstein. Even a summary of Einstein's work quickly leads to areas of significant complexity, but a few of his salient insights (and the further insights they sparked in a series of subsequent thinkers worldwide) can be briefly stated. The following summary is presented here because of my contention that preachers would do well to understand at least the broad contours of the world in which we live and preach and to which we hope to forge meaningful connections for the sake of all who hear the gospel proclaimed from the pulpit each Sunday.

Prior to Einstein, it was assumed that the entire physical universe was filled with something called the "ether." This ether was some kind of gas through which light (and everything else) traveled in more or less straight lines and in fairly predictable ways. But the nature of that most fundamental reality, light, had long been a deep puzzle. What made up a beam of light? No one was sure, since it sometimes looked like a stream of particles and other times behaved like a wave. According to the classic physics of Sir Isaac Newton, the universe consists of fairly straightforward particles that move right along, sometimes bumping into one another but pretty much behaving themselves even then. In other words, at the most basic level of the atom, the universe was like a tableful of billiard balls. At any given moment you could observe the movement of any ball on the table, project its forward momentum, and see what would happen if it bounced off an edge of the table or smacked into another ball.

But as scientists explored the atomic and subatomic levels more closely, Newton's rather mechanical views began to fall apart. In short, it became apparent that the most fundamental particles of energy in the universe did not behave like little balls hurtling through space or billiard balls bouncing around on a pool table but were in fact much less predictable. As it turned out, electrons jumped around in a confusing way, acting at times like particles and at other times like waves. It even began to look like energy existed in little "packets," which Max Planck called quanta of energy. These quanta sometimes jumped around space in startling and unpredictable ways, appearing in one place and then, suddenly, appearing somewhere very far away. At times a particle could even act as though it were in two places at the same time. As Tom Stoppard put it in his play about the quantum universe, *Hapgood*, each electron is its own unique twin—each electron is its own alibi. It is not literally the case that the electron is ever in two places at the same instant, yet in retrospect it can *look* as though it had been.

What's more, Einstein completely shook the foundations of physics when he proposed first his theory of special relativity and later his grander theory of general relativity. In essence, Einstein dispensed with the notion of the universal ether, through which light and energy had been supposed to move in straight lines. Instead, Einstein showed that space is not a flat plane but is *curved* through the gravitational forces created by the presence of stars and planets and all other celestial bodies. Something as large as our sun possesses so much mass that it bends or curves the fabric of space around it in all directions and dimensions. So strong is this force of gravity that when even a light beam zooms past a mass such as our sun, it takes a lazy turn along the curve that the "weight" or mass of the sun creates. A partially accurate way to visualize this is to imagine a trampoline. If you were to place a heavy bowling ball in the center of the trampoline's tautly stretched fabric, the material would curve around the ball; the ball would sink in a little, thus making a round indentation on the trampoline. The heavier the ball, the more the trampoline would sag and the steeper the indentation around it would be. Were you to place a small marble at the edge of the trampoline, it would begin to roll toward the bowling ball, rolling faster if the indentation were deeper. Objects in space create a similar effect on the "fabric" of space, curving space around it in all directions. But as opposed to the single direction in which a bowling ball would sink into a trampoline, objects in space create a curving effect up and down and sideways in three dimensions.

As if this insight into gravity's effect on space were not enough, perhaps the most mind-boggling idea Einstein ever dealt with involved the nature of time. Throughout history it was assumed that time is constant as we move from the past, into the present, and directly into the immediate future. Everyone moves through time at the same, predictable pace. An hour sitting in the doctor's waiting room may seem like forever, whereas an hour spent over a special dinner with a loved one zips right by. Your watch, however, runs the same during both sixty-minute periods; it just seems longer when you're bored as opposed to when you are happily engaged in something enjoyable. This phenomenon, however, is just a mental trick that has nothing to do with the actual time as measured on your watch. Your watch does not tick slower in the doctor's office and faster while having dinner; only your own perceptions account for the differences between what feels like a "long hour" as opposed to "an hour that just flew by." (Although Einstein himself once humorously defined his theory of relativity this way: an hour spent with a loved one seems like a minute, whereas a minute sitting on a hot stove seems like an hour.)

But mental states aside, it was assumed that nothing could interfere with time's chronological passage. Einstein proved that notion wrong. Through precise calculations Einstein demonstrated that the speed of light is *always* the same, no matter where the observer of the light beam is or what direction he is moving relative to the direction the light beam is moving. At one time or another we have all experienced what science calls the Doppler effect of sound. When you are on a train zooming through a train crossing, you can hear the ding-ding-ding of the crossing bell that warns motorists of the train's approach. To the people sitting in their cars waiting for the train to cross, the ding-ding-ding of the bell has the same sound or pitch with each ring. But if you are traveling on the train, a high pitch is heard as you approach the location of the bell and a lower pitch as you move away from it. The reason for this, as Doppler showed, is that when you are traveling toward a bell, you get to the sound waves faster, which in effect scrunches them up and raises the pitch. But as you move away from the bell, the sound waves cannot get to you as quickly since you are speeding in the other direction, so the sound waves slowly get stretched out, which results in your hearing a lower pitch. The bell's sound itself never changes pitch; only your *hearing* of it changes, affected as it is by your motion toward and then away from the bell.

Now suppose you were on a train going fifty miles per hour. Suppose that two bolts of lightning struck the train tracks at the exact same moment, one bolt exactly twenty-five yards in front of the train and the other twenty-five yards behind it. To a person standing motionless next to the train tracks, it would be clear that these lightning bolts did indeed hit the track at the same moment. But if you were sitting in the middle of the speeding train, you would see the light from the bolt in front of the train before you saw the light from the one behind the train. So unlike your friend standing next to the train tracks, you would conclude that the two bolts of lightning did *not* hit the track at the same moment but that the one in front hit just a bit earlier than the one behind the train. It had always been assumed that this difference in perception could be explained in a way similar to our explanation about the changing pitch of the train-crossing bell: you simply encountered the beams of light from the forward bolt of lightning more quickly than the beams coming from behind since you were racing toward the front light even as the light from behind took a little longer to "catch up" with you. This idea might be clearer if you think of a car one mile away from you, traveling sixty miles per hour. If you are standing still, it will take one minute for the car to travel that mile and get to where you are. But if you are moving in the same direction at thirty miles per hour, the car will take a little longer to catch up with you since it has to travel not just the one mile in one minute but also the distance you have traveled during that same minute.

The conundrum discovered by Einstein, however, is that light doesn't work this way. It is impossible to get at a light source more quickly just by moving toward it. If you were at the midpoint of the train, the speed of the light coming at you from both bolts of lightning would be exactly the same, just as it would be for the person standing next to the tracks. Well then, how can you explain your seeing one bolt of lightning before the other one? Einstein's answer is that it is not your traveling toward the front bolt of lightning that explains this difference in temporal perception. Rather, *time itself* is relative to your location, speed, and motion. Time, it turns out, does *not* always tick away the same for everyone. Gravity, position, speed, and motion influence the very passage of time.[23] This was later demonstrated when two extremely sensitive nuclear clocks were synchronized before placing one clock at the top of a high tower and the other at the base of the tower on the ground. As it turned out, the clock at the top of the tower, which was farther away from the earth's center of gravity and therefore was traveling faster, measured time more slowly.

Needless to say, the universe got a whole lot more complicated and interesting in the wake of these discoveries. Space is curved, not flat and straight. Gravity is so powerful a force that it bends even light, and motion through space changes the passage of time relative to the observer. As twentieth-century science proceeded to follow Einstein's work, still more was discovered about the quantum level of energy and how it interacts. Scientists increasingly observed that elements within this universe appear to be more interconnected than had previously been thought yet also wildly unpredictable. By the mid-1920s scientist Werner Heisenberg came up with his now-famous uncertainty principle, which states that at very small levels of matter we can never be sure precisely what is going on. If you take any given particle of energy, you can say where it is or what it is doing, but you can never say both. This is true either because the quantum world is indeterminate and uncertain or because measuring such things requires us to intrude in ways that change the equation. Every time you shine a light on an electron to take its picture, you disturb it, bump it, and so change where it had been prior to your intrusion. No matter how dim the light beam is, even if it is the dimmest beam possible of just one photon, its presence changes the situation. In this sense, it may be rather like a father wondering what is going on behind closed doors while his daughter and her boyfriend are nestled on the living-room couch together watching a movie. Something more than mere movie watching may be going on in the living room, but once the father opens the door and pokes his head in to ask, "How's it going in there?" he may well change the situation by sheer virtue of his presence. So also in quantum physics: it is possible that by shining a light on some particle of energy, we intrude on that particle in ways that will alter its behavior. It is an open question, however, just how jumpy and indeterminate particles of energy are when we are not looking at them.

Other thinkers, however, believe that our inability to verify the exact what and where, much less the precise why, of energy at the quantum level is not because we alter energy particles by poking our head in to check on things but simply because at this microscopic level of existence the universe *is* chaotic and unpredictable, filled more with potential than actuality. After Heisenberg proposed his uncertainty principle, it wasn't long before he and many others began to assert that our inability to nail down the quantum universe with precision is not merely an intrusive measurement problem but is a reflection of the indeterminate, vaguely chaotic nature of energy at the quantum level.

Other oddities have also been discovered, the most amazing of which is the so-called EPR effect, named after its discoverers, Einstein, Podolsky, and Rosen. These scientists discovered that if two particles of energy have significant interaction with one another at any point, these two particles will continue to be linked even after they separate from one another, no matter how far apart they are. This so-called "quantum entanglement" says that if you keep one particle in a laboratory in Los Angeles and fling the other particle to the far side of the moon, the particle beyond the moon will change if you spin the particle in the L.A. lab. This defies Einstein's theory that nothing can travel faster than the speed of light, yet the linkage between these particles has been tested and proven. (Einstein had a very technical scientific term for this effect: he called it "spooky.")

It should be noted that such experiments show real changes in the particles, not just apparent changes (ontological, not just epistemological). John Polkinghorne uses this analogy: Suppose you place one black marble and one white marble into a bag. Then suppose that you and a friend each reach into the bag, grab one marble, and then pull your hand out in a fist so that neither of you can see who has which marble. Then suppose you each start walking in opposite directions. When you have each walked one mile, you then open your hand to see which marble you have. You might open your fist to discover that, as it turns out, you took the white marble. Instantly, even though you and your friend are now two miles apart, you know that your friend has the black marble. This does not represent any kind of a real change; you had the white marble all along. The only thing that changed when you opened your fist was that you then knew which marble you drew from the bag and which marble your friend drew. The EPR effect is more than just a change in perspective or knowledge. EPR says that if upon getting one mile away from your friend you split your marble in two, instantly the other marble will likewise split in two. On the quantum level of particles that have been significantly linked to one another at some point, when you change the configuration of one, the other will correspondingly change no matter how far away it has now traveled (which is spooky indeed!).

All of these indeterminacies and odd indications of a larger unity have contributed to the formation of chaos theory (which sounds like an oxymoron—how can one have a set theory about something that is, by definition, not set?). As Polkinghorne notes, in this case, "chaos" does not mean the world is completely out of control or unpredictable.

Clearly, we do not live in such a universe. But scientists have learned that the universe is made up of a series of interlocking and highly sensitive systems in which the smallest disturbance in one place can create wide effects in another place. Polkinghorne explains:

> In a phrase going back to Karl Popper, [particles of energy] are "clouds rather than clocks." A picturesque way to symbolize this situation is to refer to the butterfly effect: the Earth's weather systems are so sensitive to small disturbances that a butterfly stirring the air with its wings in the African jungle today, could have consequences that grew so rapidly that they would bring about storms over London or New York in about three week's time. The account of these hypersensitive systems has been given the name "chaos theory." The nomenclature is unfortunate . . . since although their character generates future behaviour that appears haphazard, it turns out that this is not totally so but the range of future possibilities is contained within the limits of what is called a "strange attractor." There is both order and disorder in the behaviour of a chaotic system.[24]

As Polkinghorne goes on to note, this effect could paradoxically be called "deterministic chaos." Although matter on the quantum level is ceaselessly in motion and therefore is unpredictable in many ways, oddly enough nature again and again settles into a fairly orderly set of patterns in any given system or set of systems. Why this is so is by no means clear, but it does point to a universe that is interconnected and interactive, not to mention sensitive, in ways more marvelous than the mechanical view of Newton (who never had the opportunity, of course, to observe anything much smaller than the clearly visible). When you get down to very small levels of existence, the universe fights your desire to treat matters atomistically. You simply cannot reduce everything to independently existing little parts that just happen to add up to a larger whole.

Why mention all of these facts and theories in a book such as this one? I have several reasons. One reason is simply because it is all so fascinating. God's world is truly marvelous, and if the biblical writers found cause to praise God for the wonders they could see and uncover in the physical world three thousand years ago, contemporary believers have even more reasons (an entire quantum universe of reasons) to praise God, from whom all blessings and wonders flow! The more science peels back the layers of the universe, the more layers it discovers. God's creation is a richly textured tapestry.

A second reason is to note from our faith perspective all of the ways the biblical God of creation can still be seen as being very much active in the newly discovered quantum universe. Far from having boxed God in or having chased God into a corner, much less having eliminated the need for God altogether, contemporary physics and cosmology have found many facts that may well require God, or at the very least the possibility of God's existence helps to make better sense of certain features of our world than does the absence of God. Certainly we've discussed a number of mysteries that, although they have been assigned some scientific-sounding name, are matters that science has most definitely not explained. But as I noted at the outset of this chapter, we are not merely looking for gaps or for fuzzy uncertainties in current cosmology or physics so that we can insert God into those nooks. The mystery of the singularity, the fine-tuned nature of the universe that has led to the anthropic principle, and the shadowy specter of the "strange attractor" may indeed be places where believers can claim to see God at work. But even if new scientific discoveries one day illuminate these matters and show them to be less mysterious and shadowy than they now seem, savvy believers will nevertheless see God at work (even as we ought to see God at work in the things science can already explain perfectly well). The Christian doctrine of creation has never claimed that God's work of creation "ended" at some past point. We believe that the sustaining, redemptive, providential presence of God has never ceased its operation and never will.

A third reason for mentioning specific aspects of contemporary science as I have done in this chapter (although I freely admit I've skimmed so lightly over much of this material that well-informed scientists can but cringe) is to engage in some thought experiments as to how, even with all the changes in our view of the universe that have only recently been introduced, faith and science can nicely mesh to help us understand the ways God may interact with this world to bring about his purposes, including the miraculous. As we saw earlier, many past arguments against God's being able to perform miracles may now be moot in the light of a hypersensitive universe. If a butterfly's wing can help generate a typhoon and if this is the "normal" way of things in a world of deterministic chaos, then the number of ways God could direct ordinary and miraculous events becomes greater, and the amount of divine influence required to bring about some very great effects may be much less than past critics of the miraculous could have guessed. Again, quantum theory, even if correct, does not mean that the *only* way God could cure a cancer, head off an accident, or answer a prayer is through subtle interactions with the hypersensitive quantum web. God, being

God, can work his will in nonquantum ways as well as in ways we may never know about. But it is titillating (and theologically "fun," if one may use such a term) to ponder the richly complex nature of God's ways with God's outrageously rich world. It is just such theological ponderings to which we turn in the next chapter.

5

Science's Story
in Theological Conversation

The Quantum Web and Providence

Let us now take several big steps back from the last chapter's summary
of specific features of the contemporary scientific view of the universe
in order to consider a few of the broader strokes the scientific community uses today in painting their view of the universe. We will then
attempt (based on my relationship model presented in chapter 3) to bring
these scientific insights into fruitful dialogue with some of the equally
broad strokes that biblically informed theologians have been using for
a long time to paint a view of the universe—a cosmos that Christians
believe belongs in its every detail to God alone. Questions relating to the
details of cosmic evolutionary development, not to mention the really
big questions relating to human evolutionary development, are myriad,
frequently complex, and routinely controversial. Taking a broader perspective, however, we can say that scientists are increasingly certain that
we live in a very ancient universe, somewhere in the neighborhood of
13 billion to 15 billion years old. It is increasingly clear that all that we
now know has developed over long eons of time.

While I was working on this book in Princeton, New Jersey, my wife
and I took our children to New York City's American Museum of Natural
History. Nearly every display in that massive museum contains tremen-

dous amounts of data, most of which points to a very old universe, a very ancient planet Earth, and the real existence (on the order of millions of years ago) of the very dinosaurs whose complete skeletons take up a large chunk of the display area. When you move on to the planetarium section of the museum, you are again confronted with massive amounts of evidence supporting the notion of a billions-year-old cosmos whose current size and complexity have been unfolding and continue to unfold through a very long and interesting process of development. The last century opened new doors of discovery, and we have come to glimpse for the first time a quantum universe of hypersensitive, interlocking systems that are marvelous in their complexity and almost "spooky" in their unity. Although we can clearly see and trace out patterns of broad development on a macro scale, the twentieth century's discoveries about the quantum world have rendered naive the idea that even big events are ever caused by simple definable mechanisms. If a butterfly's wings can whip up a thunderstorm, who is to say with any certainty just what contributes to what anymore?

Thus, if Christians once viewed God and his providential care of the universe as somehow like the image of an engineer sitting in front of a control panel with a few levers and switches on it, the image has now shifted to God as a puppeteer in whose hands are held untold myriads of strings. And we now think that the least little tug on any one of those quantum strings can lead to quite surprising and interesting events in faraway places. What's more, the indeterminacy of the quantum world and the development of chaos theory have led to an increasing awareness that chance and choice and randomness seem to play a significant role in the universe. This saws against the grain of the traditional belief that everything follows a set of divine decrees and is driven by the decisive hand of a God who is, by definition, the opposite of all things random. Many Christian believers resist or reject any theory that describes a world whose future is unfolding in random ways.

Can the quantum world described by physicists and cosmologists be brought into fruitful interaction with the theological belief in a loving Creator God who's "got the whole world in his hands"? Many Christian physicists, such as John Polkinghorne and Ian Barbour, believe so. Polkinghorne has even adapted the traditional theological argument of the freewill defense to argue for what he calls a "free-process defense." Philosophers and theologians have used the classic free-will defense when grappling with the existence of evil in this world. Throughout history many atheists have alleged that we cannot accept both a loving, all-good God and a world in which terrible things happen to innocent people. In defense of a belief in God, theologians and philosophers, in recent years, most notably Alvin Plantinga,[1] have cogently argued it is possible that in granting humanity true freedom, God allowed for the possibility of bad things happening. God does not cause a bank robber to shoot a hapless clerk, but perhaps God allowed the possibility for such bad things to happen instead of creating an entire universe of robots who were programmed to do only good things. God set up a world in which the possibility, though not the necessity, of bank robbers was present. If God had programmed the world so that bad things would not happen, maybe a lot of good things would have been ruled out as well. In a robotically programmed world, perhaps we would lose the opportunity to love God freely (or anyone for that matter) or to serve God willingly and joyfully. The goodness of true love as an action chosen by people with a free will was, the free-will argument suggests, perhaps sufficient reason to run the risk of a world in which bad things could also be chosen. Similarly, Polkinghorne has suggested that it is *possible* that the reason the world has the character it does (developing, evolving, and taking billions of years to do it) is because God so enjoys the larger creative process that he desires it to have all of these stages and all the abidingly creative quirks that this universe does in fact possess. God *wants* to let the universe be free to be and to become all that God intended in the beginning, and what's more, God takes divine delight in that entire creative process.

I wish to make it very clear that I firmly believe in the doctrine of God's providence. God really does have the whole world in his hands. However, it also seems to me that believing in God's care, providence, and guidance can be distinguished from a view of life that insists that God micromanages and programs my life or anyone's life right down to the tiniest choice, event, and detail. John Calvin is one of many theologians in history who struggled to prevent the view that God is in any way the cause of evil (evil in general as well as any given bad or sinful event). At the same time, Calvin insisted that for God to be sovereign, it would necessarily have to be the case that everything that happens must eventually be traceable to the will of God after all (or to what Calvin once called "the secret will of God"). But to say both that everything happens ultimately because God wills it to happen and that many things happen in this world that cannot possibly reflect God's desires seems inconsistent and untenable. It seems to me that the free-will defense suggests a better possible solution to the conundrum of there being both a genuinely good God and undeniably evil events.

Similarly, the free-process defense of Polkinghorne may credibly suggest a possible way to relate a good, providential God to a world that appears to be developing in curious ways. (This is, of course, *only* a possibility. What follows is just one suggestion for envisioning how God might deal with our universe.) By way of analogy, I would compare the idea of free process to a host arranging a dinner party. When you are the host of a party, you provide all of the raw materials for a nice evening—good food, wine, drinks, napkins, plates, and so on—and you do so because you have in mind the kind of evening you would like to see develop and you know that the food and libations you provide will help to ensure an evening of fellowship, chatter, serious conversations, and just plain old fun.

But you cannot foresee, much less plan for, certain aspects of how the evening will develop (and maybe it is better this way, because spontaneity is half the fun). Precisely how things will develop in the course of the evening is not known, even though you have laid out the broad contours of the event. It's possible, of course, that bad things could happen. Someone could choke on a piece of egg roll, say, or someone may quaff altogether too much of the libations you provide and become a rude drunk who provokes a fight. On the other hand, however, many good things may happen: stimulating conversations, new insights, uproarious laughter, and a good time that may well serve to cement bonds of friendship in the sharing of life's bounty. A fully planned, regimented evening over which the host exercised total control would perhaps rule out unhappy events, but it would likely restrict the good things, too. Who would enjoy an evening during which the host measured out every glass of wine, precut every cube of meat, and prescribed every single bit of the conversation? In such a controlled and constricted setting, surely most guests would rather flee into the night than be so confined. A humorous *New Yorker* cartoon once captured the oddness of such a situation: the cartoon shows some bewildered party guests being confronted by a hostess wearing a baseball cap. With a whistle around her neck and a clipboard in one hand, she is urgently pointing in a certain direction, obviously ordering her guests around. Her husband apologizes to the shocked guests, "You'll have to excuse my wife," he says. "She's a bit of a control freak." Although few go to such absurd extremes of hyperorganization, in a sense when planning an evening, a host both plans the dinner party and also plans for—or at least makes room for—the unplanned.

This is very similar to what Polkinghorne and others claim for the free-process defense. The free-process defense can, however, slip into the contours of process theology, replete with a God who is *only* a fellow traveler with us through the forward movement of time. In its extremes, process theology renders God nearly helpless to prevent pain or to shape the outcome of any event. Instead, comfort is drawn from the image of the God who weeps with you but who will not and possibly cannot do much to keep sad things from happening in the first place. As for God's ability to know the future, some process theologians speak as though God is every bit as ignorant about the exact shape of the future as we are. Some process theologians (though not just process theologians, but others as well) claim that God's omniscience means that God knows all that can be known at any given moment, but since the future does not yet exist, it is unknowable, even for God. Although I like the idea of giving free process its due as a legitimately possible way God operates (similar to the free-will defense), I also want to give *God* his due in terms of not limiting God's abilities even to know and shape the future.

Hence, I would suggest that although, like a good dinner-party host, God provides the raw materials and allows things to unfold on their own (and takes joy in the unfolding), God nevertheless has more power and knowledge than the average dinner-party host. He can step in here and there to set in motion conditions that will cause good and edifying things to take place, even as he also has the option of stepping in to quash evil or bad things. Whether or not God does so in any given situation, as well as why he does or does not do so, depends on a myriad of factors so vast as to burst our conceptual abilities and boundaries. But unlike process theologians, I believe we ought to grant God the divine prerogative of more actively shaping and guiding at least the overall trajectory of the cosmos (if not here and there the specifics of it) to yield the cosmic resurrection victory and restoration of shalom that he has promised in Christ through the gospel. For surely that kingdom is *one* hugely significant thing about the future that Christians most certainly believe God does already know (and that has, therefore, its own kind of knowable existence already).

William Schweiker once noted that most people live out their lives every day with the assumption that tomorrow and the future in general is neither predetermined nor full of any meaning or potential. Such an outlook considers the future to be devoid of content; it's an empty container waiting for us to pour something into it once we get there. Time is often perceived to be empty in another sense as well, namely, in the sense that we cannot really see or touch time. As Schweiker explains it, "'Time' is, we can say, a form for knowing anything that we in fact know. . . . Yet time itself is empty. This is important. It means that the most basic form in which people organize experience is without content."[2] Schweiker also traces the connections between the conception of time as empty and the way people sometimes think of human morality. According to Immanuel Kant, morality also is just a "form" that rational minds impose onto the world in day-to-day contact with other people. Like time, which has no objective existence but is merely the empty form by which we impose order on our experiences, so also morality is not to be discovered "out there" in the wider world but is something we create by common consent as we go along.

Schweiker goes on to point out that in the Christian worldview neither time nor morality are empty but are instead rich and full. The New Testament conception of the "new creation" could be called a future reality, yet it is already a reality now. "If we learned from modern moral cosmologies the need to explore 'forms' of experience, then we can reclaim, but transform, an insight from apocalyptic beliefs about 'full time.' This will lend a note of realism to cosmological inquiry avoiding the impression that 'new creation' is simply a matter of how we decide to interpret the world. What is at stake are beliefs about the ways things are."[3] Using this line of thought as a springboard, I would further point out that when Paul writes in 2 Corinthians 5:17, "Therefore, if anyone is in Christ, behold: new creation" (my translation), this may well be the apostle's way of saying that the future fullness of God's covenant renewal of humanity in God's coming kingdom impinges also on our present moment through the Holy Spirit and the renewal of hearts and lives now. If, as Pannenberg has suggested, the resurrection of Jesus is an eschatological event that has already happened in our past, perhaps the presence of new creation, which is available to believers through faith, now presents a similar paradoxical phenomenon: glimmers of God's future fullness are available now to renewed believers. As our lives are renewed, we begin to live into God's future. Thus, we become able to recognize the goodness of God in this creation, even as we can begin to see the greater glory of the new creation that is yet to come.

John Haught recently pondered what he calls "the power of the future," by which Haught means that far from being an empty, yet-to-be-determined phenomenon, the future is already so real that God may well draw all reality toward it. God is, according to Scripture and to the Christian tradition generally, the Alpha and the Omega. As Alpha, God is surely the one who created and began the entire cosmos and who provided for the future of that creation and all the vibrant life God desired for this cosmos in the beginning. But perhaps what drives the cosmos now is not God as Alpha, pushing the universe from behind, but instead God as Omega, drawing the universe forward toward Godself and the future glory he has forever planned for us all. Haught says, "We are not accustomed to envisaging the realm of power as that which lies up ahead rather than behind us or up above us. . . . And yet a metaphysics of the future should not be completely foreign to any of us who have been formed religiously by the traditions that have come down from Abraham, the exemplar of all who live out of the future."[4] Haught then goes on to note that even science is beginning to see that natural systems seem to have some kind of orientation toward the future. "In ways we do not yet understand fully, complex physical systems unfold in time almost as if they 'know' where they are going."[5]

Contrary to at least some strains of process theology, I would hold out for the claim that the future is not completely empty or devoid of knowable content—certainly not for God but not for believers, either. There may well be a God-granted dimension of process and development in this cosmos and, as just suggested, it may also be the case that God takes joy in the free unfolding of that cosmic process. This insight, however, need not mean that random process and development is the *only* way by which the cosmos unfolds or by which God superintends the universe and therefore need not rule out God's still having a larger, firm plan for what will be and what will happen ultimately (and perhaps here and there specifically) in the universe and in the course of human life.

Thus, I would suggest that as science uncovers the various processes of nature, both long-term cosmic processes by which stars are born and planets are formed as well as microprocesses that go on inside the cells of our bodies every day, Christians need not see either the fact or the specifics of these processes as any threat to the idea of God as Creator and Sustainer of all that exists. A God who set up the universe to have precisely such processes by which new and good things can unfold would surely take joy in the creative energy and synergy that these processes entail. Like a good host watching an evening develop through the use of the raw ingredients and materials he provided, so God may well take divine delight in watching the universe make use of the basics that he provided long ago and that he continues to refresh and provide today.

In recent years theologians and philosophers have increasingly been returning to the traditional theological tenet of the kenosis of Jesus and are now widening its scope. In the history of Christian doctrine there has long been a teaching about the kenosis of Jesus Christ. The word "kenosis" comes from the Greek verb *kenoō*, which means "to empty" or "to pour out." The key place where this word occurs in the New Testament is Philippians 2:7, where the apostle Paul claims that in order to save humanity from sin and death, God the Son "made himself nothing" or "emptied himself" of a great many divine privileges. Jesus left behind heaven's glories for the dirty streets of the earth; he held back on his divine power and knowledge and became a servant who ultimately allowed himself to be killed by the very creatures he had created in the beginning. The tenet of the kenosis of Jesus claims that God can, for the achievement of some higher good and purpose, restrain and limit his divine power and knowledge by leaving to one side or temporarily rendering inactive the characteristics God otherwise possesses naturally and to an extreme degree by virtue of God's divinity. Such self-limitation does not point to any inherent deficits or weaknesses in God but to the fact that out of abundant divine love God is sometimes willing to hold back his divine powers for the sake of creatures whom God loves very much.

Some theologians today are attempting to widen the scope of this tenet. Instead of saying that God the Son "emptied himself" of certain divine prerogatives only in the incarnation and life of Jesus, these theologians claim that perhaps the entire act of creation—and by extension the sustaining and superintending of that creation—required some kind of kenosis by God. God, being God, could have preprogrammed every human life and every cosmic event. God could have written a cosmic script that would always unfold word for word according to how God composed the story in the beginning. But, as already indicated, perhaps God resisted doing so for the sake of some larger good (like having creatures who could freely love God and each other instead of robots who would have no real choice over anything). If this kenotic view of the entire creation is correct, then God's having made room for free will and free process (and hence God's taking genuine joy in watching how life develops) would be a result not of some weakness in God but rather of a choice God made to hold back (as Jesus clearly did when on this earth) so that the creation would be free to develop. Again, I would still contend that even if this is true, God has the power to pull the whole cosmos along according to a larger goal, even as God has the power to intervene dramatically in this world, which Christians believe is preeminently seen in God's resurrection of Jesus from the dead. A larger divine script for how God intends things ultimately to go does not necessitate its being a detailed script that prescribes every single event, word, or happening down to the last and smallest item.

Some writers today believe there is even some good news in the fact that the universe seems somewhat indeterminate. Polkinghorne, for instance, sees our inability to predict exactly how everything will go in the future as an opportunity for genuine action. If we always knew everything in advance, we could not legitimately claim to be moral agents who can make a difference. But if everything is not predetermined—if the cosmic game is not "fixed" in every single way—then both God and God's creatures can make a genuine impact on the way life goes. God's providence need not mean that we are robotically programmed to follow a course of action in which it only *seems* as if we are having an influence but that in actuality is more like a computer's simply spewing out data based on a prewritten program. It is instead possible to see that God has provided the conditions in which we live and has now also provided in Christ the Holy Spirit to guide us along, without reducing us to mindless automata.

Human Consciousness and God

Picking up on our earlier summary of the anthropic principle, Christians can also see that chief among God's provisions for the cosmos is the development of humanity—the most creatively complex and complexly creative beings of which we know. As we have seen, many contemporary scientists believe that the entire universe, including humanity, can be explained in naturalistic terms based solely on biology and evolutionary development via coincidence and happenstance and the genetically driven desire to survive. Such reductionist thinkers may well be missing, however, an important insight articulated by many thinkers, including Polkinghorne and van Huyssteen. Regardless of *how* God created self-aware fully conscious creatures such as human beings, and regardless of *how* (to invoke the traditional language of theology) God created humanity in God's own image, the fact is that once human consciousness came onto the scene of this planet, its presence introduced a new, shaping factor that goes beyond mere biology. With the emergence of human consciousness, a new, nonbiological set of variables came onto the scene that disallows reducing the whole of galactic history (much less terrestrial, human history) to a purely physical portrait.

Even if one were to accept the notion that human consciousness and our ability to know anything at all—and to know that we know—is in some way a result of how humanity has evolved biologically, it is difficult to miss seeing that once the conditions for conscious existence, creative thought, and self-awareness arrived, that very consciousness now forces us to include into the mix of our assessment of life on this planet factors that are *not* merely physical. Of course we *are* physical beings, and God never intended us to be otherwise. Christianity believes that this physi-

cal aspect of humanity is important; physicality is the vital core of who
we are in God's good creation design. Christian theology has traditionally taught that human beings are properly embodied, not temporarily
embodied, much less accidentally or tragically embodied.

Traditionally many Christians have believed that it may be possible for
the essence of each person (the soul) to survive the death of the body in
some kind of conscious state "with the Lord" between death and the final
resurrection, in what is often called "the intermediate state." But only
strains of the Christian tradition that were eventually labeled heretical
ever claimed that this temporary state was a good thing or that these
disembodied souls would remain forever free of all physicality and that
this likewise would be a good thing since the physical side of humanity is the ugly problem from which we need to be delivered in the first
place. The orthodox Christian tradition has affirmed that we belong in
our bodies; the ultimate vision for life in "heaven" with God includes
an embodied existence through the resurrection of the dead, of which
Christ Jesus is seen as the first cosmic example of our future. Thus,
those in the neurosciences today who suggest that human consciousness is, in some still mysterious way, a by-product of our astonishingly
complex brains and their never-ending interconnections are not saying
anything too terribly surprising for biblically informed Christians. In
the beginning God did not create vapory souls to float freely through
the ether of pure thought. God created persons with bodies, and God
seems to like us this way so much that in order to save us, body and
soul, God the Son became a person with a real body and was then raised
from the dead with a real body. Christianity is, after all, the religion of
the incarnation.

So Christians can happily affirm that of course there is a connection
between the structure of our brains as a biological phenomenon and our
consciousness as a spiritual phenomenon. Christians would, however,
claim that consciousness is not merely physical; it lifts us into a new,
higher realm. As van Huyssteen says, biology may satisfy the necessary
conditions for us to be self-aware beings, but it does not provide us with
everything we need to know in order to understand humanity as it now
exists in the multivalent dimensions of spirituality, faith, imagination,
and creativity.[6]

If God desired beings with whom he could have meaningful fellowship
in a freely chosen loving relationship, it only makes sense that he would
of course create the physical conditions for conscious existence to come
into being. He would provide the physical and biological materials, as
well as the divine guidance over the development of those materials,

necessary to the creation of humanity in God's own image. The result would be that God could then convey information to these beings even as he would receive fellowship, communication, and praise from them. If God exists, God would surely want this and would therefore provide for it. Once the biological conditions for consciousness to arise were met, however, God would then begin to convey information, via revelation and the Holy Spirit, that would bring into human consciousness ideas, insights, and knowledge that, though made possible by the physiobiological conditions God brought about, would go well beyond the merely physical and introduce the realm of the spiritual and the divine (realms to which those who study only the physical world will not necessarily have access).

Curiously, however, even some thinkers today who do not claim that information from God would change history in nonbiological ways nevertheless see nongenetic, nonphysical factors as being integral to explanations of humanity. Paul Ehrlich of Stanford University stresses the need to factor in "cultural evolution" when assessing human nature. Ehrlich asks fellow scientists to recognize that once human thought, creativity, and culture entered the scene, these features of human existence exercised their own, third-party influence over the development of the human mind and consciousness. These features cannot easily be slid under a microscope, but they are real shapers of mind, destiny, and human nature. In an interview with the *New York Times*, Ehrlich stated emphatically, "You can never remove culture from the mix. . . . Cultural information can change much more rapidly than genetic information. It's not constrained by the human generation time, which is about 20 years, and it's not constrained in the direction in which it flows or in the number of people who can acquire that information. My grandchildren may not be able to give me genes, but they can, and do, teach me things that to an extent restructures my brain."[7]

Recently there has been a great deal of discussion on the relationship between brain and mind. Those who are in various reductionist camps claim that human beings and their sense of conscious awareness are nothing but the result of physical neurological activity in the brain. There is no separate entity called a "soul," no need to posit the proverbial "ghost in the machine." Human beings are biological machines, nothing more, nothing less. Everything in humanity as it presently exists, as well as everything in the whole of human history that has led up to this point, is fully explainable from a physical, biological point of view. There is nothing "extra" to humanity now, nor has there ever been a spiritual "extra" in the past. Nonreductionists attempt to hold on to human uniqueness in various ways, ranging from those who still posit a spiritual soul—a soul uniquely created by God and then attached to the physical body or brain—to those who like Nancey Murphy and her coauthors in *Whatever Happened to the Soul?* hold out for what is called "nonreductive physical-ism." This position claims that though the physical makeup of the human brain is the necessary condition for human consciousness to arise, it is not sufficient to give a full accounting of that consciousness once it arises. In the course of advancing this argument Warren S. Brown deals with the vital aspect of human language. Along the way Brown takes note of studies that have demonstrated that it is possible to teach monkeys and apes a kind of protolanguage that in certain sustained efforts has enabled chimpanzees to attain a level of linguistic comprehension quite similar to that of a two-year-old human child.[8]

But although this finding may say much about a monkey's ability to learn if given the right kind of instruction by human beings, it in no way diminishes the abiding uniqueness of humanity's linguistic abilities. Humans are born with an innate sense for grammar and grammatical constructions, and to acquire a language, they need only to be placed in an environment where they can hear that language being utilized. Like most parents, I have been astonished not only at the ability of my children to learn words and expressions sheerly by hearing and imitating them but even more at their ability to learn entire grammatical patterns and rules despite the fact that no one ever pointed out these patterns to them, much less expressed any grammatical rules. Why should a child grasp the idea that there even *are* larger rules and patterns? After all, few parents ever sit a two-year-old down to explain that the way to form the plural of most any noun in English is by adding an *s* to the end of the word, nor does the average mother or father lecture their children about how the past tense of most verbs can be achieved by adding the suffix *-ed*. Yet children pick up on these larger patterns of the language, as can be immediately detected when they make verbal goofs with the exceptions to the rules. Following the rules a child has internalized, he might say, "Yesterday we see'd three mooses." Now, of course, the "see'd" should be "saw" and the "mooses" should be "moose," but what you realize upon hearing this kind of mistake is that the exceptions to the rules trip a child up precisely because, without any overt instruction, he has already comprehended that there are, as a matter of fact, larger rules that apply to almost any noun or verb.

So the fact that long and patient instruction can help an ape to achieve a two-year-old's ability to comprehend spoken language, and in some sense to reply, albeit in mostly nonverbal symbols, is interesting but not terribly impressive in comparison to what the average, well-functioning two-year-old human child can do sheerly by dint of what she was born with. But I mention all of this to make two points: First, once human language emerged on the scene—replete with the ability it gives us not only to communicate information but also to organize thoughts in creative, imaginative ways—the very presence of language changed the face of this world and its history in ways that go beyond that which can be explained in purely biological terms. Second, and even more important, the example of people teaching apes to understand rudimentary language illustrates a larger truth, namely, that not everything should be reduced to physical explanations. Given the right conditions, apes can learn some form of language. But without human beings, there would be no language to learn in the first place. Furthermore, there is no evidence that without the presence of human beings to teach the apes, the average ape would ever learn on its own the kind of language we can teach it.

With human presence and help, however, something new can emerge for a well-trained monkey, which has something to do with the monkey's mental hardware but has far more to do with the outside influence of human teachers and all that they provide. When a creature already possesses a fair degree of sophistication and complexity, the introduction of an outside, third party can change things significantly, which is exactly the point I am making here. The physical complexity of the human brain is the necessary condition for our kind of creative, self-aware consciousness to arise. Once that consciousness does arise, however, making possible the emergence of new thoughts and ideas (not to mention that, as Christians claim, this consciousness makes it possible for us to receive revelations from God), factors are introduced that will shape and change the human condition in ways that go beyond the bedrock biology of it all. A biological foundation may well have started the process, but it is transcended by the results of the process it began.

As Polkinghorne and others have suggested, the human ability to think consciously, to speak, and to create introduced something entirely new to the human sphere and cannot be reduced to mere physical sources or explanations. Albert Einstein became *Time* magazine's Person of the Century largely because of the new thoughts he had. Einstein's insight that led to the formula $E = mc^2$ cannot be explained simply in terms of the positions of the electrons and the firing of the neurons within his brain at the moments before, during, and after he arrived at this formula. No amount of biological investigation of Einstein's brain prior to the moment of this profound insight (or after his death, as has actually been done) would have predicted that he would have *any* kind of an insight into quantum physics, much less this *specific* insight.

Perhaps, as a recent study of Einstein's pickled gray matter has revealed, a study of his brain prior to 1905, when he constructed his relativity theory, would have revealed that the larger than normal development in certain sections of his brain indicated at least the potential for genius. But even had such a study been possible back then, there would have been no guarantee that Einstein would indeed be a genius (he could have squandered his life on drink, for instance), much less a guarantee that he would come up with such significant theories. Each human brain, barring disease or damage, has the potential for a great many thoughts and ideas. But are the thoughts, emotions, and experiences of any given person ultimately predictable based on only the physical hardware of that person's brain? Clearly not. Once it arose, human consciousness changed the shape of the universe, not least because, as a faith-informed perspective would claim, the presence of this consciousness opens the door for communion with God.

The outrageous complexity of human consciousness and the long stream of new ideas, theories, art forms, religion, and spirituality to which this consciousness has led are so stunning that they all but force one to reckon with the reality both of God and of that God's having created this universe to yield beings like us—beings who can appreciate God and his handiwork in the cosmos. Writers like Keith Ward have argued forcefully that the existence of God is not just likely but is indeed *necessary*. I will not attempt to duplicate Ward's arguments here since I am already operating on the model of faith seeking understanding. Still, even if you did not believe in God but were able to recognize, as most scientists do, the uniqueness of human thought, consciousness, and creativity, how could one avoid pondering the following scenario: If God did not exist—if, à la Carl Sagan, the universe is "all that there is, all that there ever was, and all that will ever be"—then we humans who are conscious and aware of the universe could quite possibly be seen as the greatest beings in existence. We who know not just ourselves but so much beyond ourselves, and we also know that we know, would be more stunningly wondrous than all the vastness that is unconscious, more wondrous than even the infinitely dense singularity of energy that exploded the universe into being in the first place but that knew neither itself nor any other.

If there were no God (who by definition would know all that is knowable past, present, and future, including us and the full range of cosmic possibilities), a single human individual who could conceive of even *some* possibilities outside of him- or herself would be greater than all the vastness of space that is unaware and unconscious. But if there is a God, who by definition of divinity as well as by virtue of being the one who made humanity's rise to consciousness possible, surely this divine being would be the greatest of all reality. Humanity's conscious existence, though stunning, would be seen in its proper light as but an echo or a reflection of the vastly superior divine consciousness and being in whose image humanity was fashioned.

Conclusion

We live in a universe that has only recently been discovered to be a place of vast subtlety, suppleness, and wonder. Humanity has come to understand that despite all of what we now know about some of the most fundamental structures of life and matter—a staggering amount of which has come to light comparatively recently in just the past one hundred years out of the many billions of years of cosmic history—there is still a large amount that we simply cannot comprehend. It is no surprise that even some of the physicists whose work helped to form the recently emerging picture of the quantum universe were uncomfortable and unsatisfied with their own results; they were uncomfortable with the uncertainty and unpredictability they uncovered at the universe's tiniest levels of reality. Einstein is said to have lamented the apparent disorderliness of the quantum world and, as is now well known, declared that God does not play dice with the universe—in other words, there simply *must* be a larger order and sense to life that has thus far eluded science. A less well-known saying of Einstein (now engraved above a fireplace in Princeton University's mathematics department) is, "God is subtle, but malicious he is not."[9] Einstein and others dearly desired to maintain a sense of larger purpose in the face of the mind-boggling discoveries of recent decades. The sense that orderliness was slipping away from science is perhaps what prompted physicist Erwin Schrödinger to wish he'd never had anything to do with the development of quantum theory.[10]

Our cosmic home is a grand display of awe-inspiring complexity. Those in the scientific community who desire less mystery and more fact may be discomfited by hard-to-explain features of our world and perhaps cannot rest content in not having figured everything out. But the truth stubbornly remains: we don't know and understand everything, and maybe we never will. Christians, however, are perhaps less unsettled by this, because the fact that we know anything at all (even if we know only how much we *don't* know!) is a startling development in the cosmos. Whether or not the subatomic universe of electrons and quarks really is "awake," as Tom Stoppard put it in *Hapgood*, we human beings most certainly are awake, aware, and curious.

Christians believe they know why this is so: because we were created in the image of a God who wants us to be conscious, awake, and curious so that we cannot only seek knowledge about the world God made but ultimately receive knowledge about and from God himself. Having received such knowledge through faith, Christians rest secure in knowing that whether or not scientists, believers, or anyone else can now or ever will understand the way everything works in this universe, the fact that will never change is that the God who is the wellspring of all life and creativity is also a God of grace who loves his creatures enough to have created this universe in the first place. This God still loves his creation enough to draw the universe onward in Christ toward that day when the new creation will burst into full view, dawning on the cosmic horizon as the fulfillment of every fond hope that ever stirred in the hearts of all God's creatures. In Job 38:7 God answers Job from out of the whirlwind, saying among other things that on the day when God first laid the foundations of this universe, the morning stars sang together for joy. Faith reminds us that those stars are still reflections of the glory of the God who made them, and one day they, and all God's creatures, will sing for joy forever.

Does it seem strange to conclude this section on a note of doxology? It shouldn't. To the faith-filled heart and mind, every pondering of God's handiwork is an act of praise. That is why I now turn to specific ideas on how preachers can help congregations join their voices in this chorus of doxology.

Part 2

6

The Gospel's Content in a Cosmic Context

Connecting Content with Context

The story is told that one day at lunch a five-year-old named Callum earnestly asked his mother, "Mommy, is God everywhere?"

"Yes, dear, God is always with us no matter where we are," was the mother's devout reply.

"Is God in our house?" the boy pressed.

"Yes, Callum, God is in our house, too."

"Well, is God here in the kitchen?" The mother was getting a little less sure of her theology now but nevertheless replied, "Yes."

"Is God in my milk cup?" By now the mother was clearly uncomfortable. "Er, yes, I suppose if God is everywhere, then he is in your cup." At that point young Callum quickly slapped his hand over the cup and declared, "Got 'em!"

Whether or not this story is true, it reflects a temptation with which people of faith, young and old alike, struggle. Christians, of course, recognize and proclaim that they worship the God of all might and glory—a triune God whose grandeur bursts conceptual boundaries and transcends all time and space. But nevertheless, too often we come to worship with the quiet assumption that within the enclosed space of the sanctuary and through the regular and predictable rhythms of the weekly liturgy, we have, in a sense, captured God. We close the back doors of the sanctuary, open the bulletin to follow the service, and suddenly we have the vague feeling that when it comes to God, for at least the next hour or so, we just possibly have "Got 'em!"

Faith, of course, proclaims that God truly is present to the church when it gathers for worship services. Worship is a living encounter with the living God. It may be wrong to believe that within a given worship service we have "got" God, but it is surely correct in some sense to believe that in worship God has got us. God encounters people of faith through liturgy, sacrament, prayer, and preaching. Such living encounters may sometimes be deeply soothing and comforting, but if God is to be God, surely there will be times in every believer's life of worship when the encounter is unsettling, startling, and challenging.

In a now widely quoted comment, writer Annie Dillard once observed how foolish it is to enter a worship encounter with the living God as though it meant no more than grabbing a cup of coffee with a coworker. We dress up in our Sunday best, drive to church, and casually slide into our favorite pew as though we know exactly what we're doing and what will happen during the next hour or so. But what we ought to wear to church, Dillard claims, is not just our nicely pressed suits and skirts but also hard hats! We ought to maintain a wide-eyed expectation that something quite surprising could happen through our meeting with God, and so we'd best slouch a little less and keep an eye out a little more. Like construction workers building a skyscraper, we ought to recall that if we are not watchful, we could get clunked on the head with the spiritual equivalent of an I-beam or lose our footing on the holy scaffold. All in all, worshipful vigilance is prudent.

Dillard's image is similar to a comment once made by a teenager in a Bible study group. The young people, under the leadership of the pastor, were studying the story of Jesus' baptism from Mark 1. The pastor pointed out that when the story talks about heaven's being opened as soon as Jesus emerged from the Jordan River, the Greek word there means "to rip or to tear"; it is the same word used at the end of Mark when Jesus dies on the cross and the curtain in the temple is said to rip from top to bottom. The heavens were ripped open, and God's Spirit, in the form of a dove, descended on Jesus. The pastor told the young people that what this shows is that the barriers between God and us have now been removed; we once again have gracious access to God. But one young man in the group saw it in a slightly different way. "That's not what it means, pastor. What it means is that God can now get at *us!* God is on the loose, and now nobody's safe!"

Both Dillard's hard-hat image and the young man's commentary on Mark 1 are a bit extreme; for believers, God is not a dangerous presence. But most Christians would admit that they really do not wish to act as though they had God stowed away in some safe little box. We are, however, more comfortable with the predictable and the reassuring. Encountering the difficult or grappling with complex facets of a complicated world is not something we necessarily expect in a worship service (it may, as a matter of fact, be something we would just as soon *avoid* in such a setting). The German writer Goethe was once quoted as saying that when he came to church he did not want to hear about the preacher's doubts; he wanted to hear about the things the preacher was sure of. We've all got enough doubts of our own, Goethe said. We don't need to add the preacher's uncertainties to our own list of doubts.

Perhaps some people operate with a similar opinion when it comes to new theological ideas or information from the wider world that may be unsettling: preachers should keep such matters to themselves and present only what is tried and true, neat and tidy, traditional and familiar. There is new material galore in society: new ideas, new fashions, new technologies, new patterns of morality and immorality. Ours is a world where the slogan "new and improved" is constantly getting slapped on all manner of products, social movements, and technological innovations. Yesterday's cutting-edge cellular phone is tomorrow's piece of outdated junk. The superfast computer you bought last spring is easily eclipsed by the autumn release of an even faster system. So in a time when society hungers for the novel and becomes quickly impatient with anything that seems old, perhaps Sundays should be the one day of the week when Christians resist the new by insisting on what is old. Sermons should not be about what is "new and improved" but should proudly proclaim all that is tried and true.

In a sense, this line of thought is wholly appropriate for the preaching enterprise. Preaching is, after all, rooted in an ancient text. Scripture is a living Word, as it is animated by the same Holy Spirit who first inspired its words so many millennia ago, but the historical (that is, *old*) nature of Scripture stubbornly remains. I have already argued in this book against those who seek to promote contemporary ways of thinking by demoting the biblical viewpoint. Scripture must not be reduced to a mere conversation partner with whom we may politely disagree and then ignore. The inner testimony of the Holy Spirit assures believers not just that God's Word is true but that it represents life itself. It is God's grand story of creation and redemption; if we wish to know who we are and how we fit into the larger scheme of the universe, it is God's Word that will provide this information.

Christians are therefore correct to hope that in worship and preaching they will be secured yet again to things very ancient. Scripture provides the fundamental content of Christian proclamation; it does not, however, provide the *context* in which the content of Scripture must be heard and understood. Indeed, it could be argued that the reason the church needs preachers at all is largely to bring scriptural content and cultural context together. In order for Scripture to be the living voice of faith, it needs to speak within the context of the actual lives of Christians in any and every given time and place. Christianity has never claimed that to hear and understand God's Word a person must first be transported to some other realm.

As a matter of historical fact, the Christian church has regularly condemned as heretics those who have claimed that the secret to Christian living is to escape the physical world in order to achieve some misty spiritual knowledge. Nowhere in the New Testament can you find Jesus (or anyone else) giving advice on how to meditate in the Eastern sense of emptying one's mind of all thought through reciting a mantra or entering some kind of hypnotic state. Some religions do, of course, commend a form of meditation that seeks to cut a person off from the present world (hence the term "transcendental meditation," wherein the goal is to *transcend* the mundane details of ordinary life). The goal of many forms of meditation is to lift a person up into a transcendent realm of pure thought, where the desires of the flesh melt away and the world itself likewise grows dim and vapory. In the light of the divine radiance, this life is made to look shabby, maybe even counterfeit.

Christianity, however, proclaims that the transcendent God condescends to us in all our physicality and historical specificity. To invoke the famous image used by John Calvin, God "lisps" to us so as to be understood. Through incarnation and through inscripturation, God brings himself and his revelation into relationship with this very real physical world and the very real, very specific lives of people in this world in every time and place. The transcendent is to be found right here and now. Furthermore, applying God's Word (in Jesus through the Holy Spirit and in the Bible through the Holy Spirit) is likewise to be seen in patterns of daily living in the real-life situations of any given time and place. Encountering the Christian God in worship, sacrament, and preaching does not cut people off from the wider world but rather helps them interact with that wider world and brings their day-to-day lives into the light of God's presence.

Preachers, therefore, do not only present the content of God's Word but place it in the context of a given time and place. Proclaiming the content of God's Word in a sermon is, naturally, the primary aim of all preaching. But it could nevertheless be alleged that presenting only the content of Scripture as though it did not need to be understood and applied in a very specific context would be a homiletical failure and that a preacher who did this would be doing only a half job in the pulpit. But I suspect this matter may be more radical than merely proportions of content and context. It seems to me that content shorn of context is like trying to make bread with only half the ingredients (flour and water), leaving out the other half (yeast and salt). The result of such a culinary effort would yield something no one would call "half bread"; it would instead yield something very unlike real bread that would likely be inedible.

Thomas Long has written that he at one time greatly admired the sermons of a certain Scottish preacher. The sermons did a fine job in presenting theological basics and carefully explaining the biblical texts in language that was both fresh and clear. But one day Long realized with a shock that all of these sermons he so admired had been delivered in the throes of World War II to congregations in Britain, whose future was at best an open and precarious question at various points during the war. Yet the sermons made no mention of that larger context. They were "timeless" in the worst sense of the word; these sermons could have been delivered in any time and in any place. But because of this, they were not well fitted to the specific time and place in which they were delivered. The desperate concerns, burdens, and fears that this preacher's congregation must have carried into the sanctuary each Sunday during that perilous time were politely bracketed.

The challenge of preaching is to construct bridges between God's content and his people's context. If listeners are not allowed to carry their real lives into the sanctuary, it is unlikely they will carry much of the sermon back out with them, either. If people have to hang up their deepest concerns in the narthex along with their coats, how can the sermon ultimately avoid the appearance of being no more than a diversion or a respite *from* the world instead of being what it ought to be, namely, a presentation of a better way to see and to understand the world so that listeners may better live in that world once the church service is finished? As Herbert O'Driscoll has said, good sermons create the impression that the Bible, through the Holy Spirit, strikes a "bargain" with worshipers each week. The Bible says, in effect, "If you will come with me into my past, I promise to return back with you to your present."[1] But if the truths of Scripture speak only about the ancient past (or conversely, if they speak only about some wispy future "heaven" that will come to us by and by), what should Christians do, think, or believe come Monday morning?

O'Driscoll insists that a connection of our past, present, and future should be made each week and in every sermon. Referring to Christ's birth, death, and resurrection as the "big bang" of gospel hope, O'Driscoll asserts that preachers need to talk not just about what was the case long ago but also about how the gospel events shape what is true now and what will yet be true as we continue to move into the future. Picking up on O'Driscoll's cosmological metaphor (apropos of a book about preaching and science), I would extend this image a bit. In 1948 scientists theorized that if the universe really did begin in an ultra-hot big-bang-like explosion, background radiation should still be scattered throughout the cosmos—a kind of radioactive "echo" that would still be detectable today. Nearly twenty years later, in 1965, scientists Arno Penzias and Robert Wilson, armed with better and more sensitive equipment than had previously been available, were able to detect this universal background radiation. Just as hearing the echo of fireworks from across a canyon would let you know that somewhere across the canyon fireworks really had been launched, so the discovery of this cosmic background radiation seemed to confirm that the universe started with a very hot bang—a blast so powerful that the echo has still not died off, all these eons later.

This is what O'Driscoll refers to in his analogy: the life, the death, and the resurrection of Jesus were events so singularly stunning and cosmically vital that their explosive effects are still detectable and real today, and they always will be. Jesus affects us now. Good preaching not only declares that these events happened once upon a time but, through the Holy Spirit, also provides people with the necessary spiritual equipment so that they, too, can detect the spiritual background radiation that continues to reverberate throughout the universe. Moreover, good preaching makes the work of Jesus a living reality that engulfs believers and changes them in every way.

If the Word of God (which presents us with the larger story that has led to the advent of God's Christ) is to be a real and vital and living Word for people of faith, that Word must speak to believers in the context of real life. Hence, if people are living through a world war, God's Word must have something to say about that great cataclysm. If people are living in the midst of a land filled with superstition and native religions based on animism and taboos, God's Word needs to address these phenomena. And, as has been my point all along in this book, if God's Word is proclaimed in a world increasingly shaped and informed by science, this scientific world is likewise a context in which that Word needs to be heard, understood, and applied.

Approaches

Doing this well will not be an easy task for preachers. Particularly in congregations where science tends to be viewed with anxiety and suspicion, attempting to reflect a more positive appreciation for science in sermons may require a certain amount of subtlety and nuance as well as careful advance thought on the part of the preacher. The suggestions and illustrations that I will offer in the balance of this book are intended to foster this kind of thoughtfulness and nuance. The subtlety and thoughtfulness of this approach is important in that it is not my intention to suggest that science should be brought into the preaching life of the church in any heavy-handed or artificial way. Nor do I wish to convey the idea that congregations need to be hit over the head with science or scolded for past or present fears about what science teaches. Instead, I suggest that the goal of helping congregations better appreciate science can be reached through a series of strategies that include:

1. An overall emphasis on the biblical and theological importance of the physical creation;
2. Pastoral modeling of a positive attitude toward the sciences;
3. Occasional sermons that introduce specific examples of scientific discoveries in an affirming and positive manner.

These strategies aim less to educate a congregation in scientific matters and more to frame both preaching and science in a larger context. Science becomes just one more feature on the cultural landscape that is encompassed by a larger theological world-and-life view. As such, Christians can think about science theologically, critically, and appreciatively, in ways similar to how they already reflect on any number of other aspects of the larger world (politics, literature, mass media, and so forth). Occasions arise in preaching when a specific Scripture passage or a certain theological topic overlaps quite naturally with certain scientific investigations and what scientists have to say about those investigations. These are the occasions when some kind of acknowledgment of and dialogue with science only makes sense.

Similarly, when addressing the topic of sexuality, most preachers recognize that the wider culture has much to say about sex—viewpoints that are sometimes close to what the church proclaims, sometimes vastly different from what the church proclaims, and at other times somewhere in between. Recognizing this, a pastor may present the Christian vision for the gift of sexuality against the backdrop of these ideas from contemporary culture—notions about sexuality that many in the congregation, including many young people, are familiar with and that therefore need to be addressed with a certain degree of directness. A good preacher will want to help people understand their faith in the face of the larger social context of their lives.

Similar comments can be made in the area of economics and finances. On Thanksgiving Day a preacher may talk about the proper gratitude that people of faith have for all that they possess. But this same preacher will also recognize that greed and covetousness can creep into people's hearts where possessions are concerned; gratitude and greed are cousins who often work the same side of the street. So in the light of the materialism so rampant in our society, preachers will quite naturally speak about thankfulness with reference to, and perhaps in contrast to, the attitudes prevalent in the larger society, again referring to facts of contemporary life that members of the congregation are familiar with and that therefore ought to be acknowledged and addressed from the pulpit.

So also with scientific matters: the wider culture has much to say about creation, human nature, and other such topics. Preachers who are aware of what the culture has to say on these topics will, as in the sexuality and materialism analogies just given, mention these viewpoints to articulate Christian hope more clearly. But this is not likely to happen if pastors themselves ignore the topic of science, much less if they fear it. If preachers ignore science, obviously they will have no resources to draw on even if they do happen to see an area of theological and scientific overlap, and quite possibly they may not even see such overlaps to begin with. If science is feared or viewed as a perennial opponent, then even if areas of theological and scientific overlap are recognized, science will be mentioned in a negative light or as a way of thinking that theologically informed Christians can and must defeat by wielding the sword of God's Word.

Yet it is the Word of God that helps Christians to appreciate the physical reality of the cosmos as God's gift to us. Hence, a first step for helping both preachers and laypeople to see areas of natural overlap between theology and science is to focus on the importance of the physical creation of God. Christians are *not* uninterested in the world science explores! So sermons should help listeners to celebrate creation's beauties and to find cause for astonishment and awe over the handiwork of God. The time in which we live makes a recovery of the Bible's presentation and celebration of the physical creation a good and even necessary focus. The heightened awareness we now have about ecological concerns and the ongoing leaps in our scientific understanding of human life and the cosmos provide a context in which we can quite naturally notice the fact that the Bible is likewise interested in the physical universe.

The Bible, of course, has not changed. The words in the books of Scripture are the same now as they have been for nearly two millennia. But *when* you read the Bible can influence *how* you read it, at least in terms of what leaps out at you from the page. There is, for instance, a reason why you can read a Reformation document like the Heidelberg Catechism and find very little—indeed, almost nothing—about the physical creation: the chief concern of people like Martin Luther and John Calvin was not whether or how God created the heavens and the earth but how Jesus saved people. If there is a fire in your kitchen, you don't throw water into an upstairs bedroom on the other side of the house. The location of the fire determines the focus of your attention. In the sixteenth century the "fire" was centered on questions about grace versus works. At that time there was little, if any, concern about ecology, species extinction, or industrial pollution in the form of carbon emissions and overdevelopment of sensitive wetlands. Nor was there any kind of Darwin-like threat to the notion that God, through his power and out of the goodness of the divine heart, created all that exists. Naturally, therefore, issues related to the physical creation received very little attention in most of the catechisms and confessions of faith that came out of the Reformation era. It is not that people like Calvin were unaware of the Bible's teachings about the physical creation—indeed, Calvin writes quite a bit about creation and providence in his commentaries and in his *Institutes of the Christian Religion*—but it clearly was not the burning issue of that time.

But were we to write a catechism or a summary confession of the faith in these early years of the twenty-first century, we would need to pay special attention to what the Bible has to say about the physical creation, for the same reason we would likely want to address sexism, racism, abortion, and pornography: these are key issues that uniquely define our time. Unlike Christians in the past who did not need to worry about things like ecological threats, we now need to pay attention to these issues and must read the Bible accordingly to discern God's guid-

ance on such issues. Again, the Bible has not changed, but the issues that
we need God's Word to address have changed. So we are going to notice,
think about, and preach about parts of God's Word that may have made
less of an impression on believers four hundred years ago. Lifting up the
parts of Scripture that help to set the stage for a contemporary Christian
appreciation for what science has to offer does not mean that we are
adding to the Bible or retrofitting God's Word in spiritually illicit ways.
Instead, such a reading of Scripture highlights yet again the wonder of
God's Word: it has endured through the centuries and will continue to
endure precisely because through the Holy Spirit it addresses the real
lives of God's people.

Preachers today, therefore, would do well to display those parts of
God's Word that will enhance people's awareness of and appreciation
for God's physical creation. If this is done well and often, preachers can
further help people to see that at its best science can be a good partner in
helping Christians to explore and comprehend the creation better—the
very same creation that the Bible claims God has given to humanity to
tend, nurture, keep, and enjoy. It seems that all too often, however, this
is not a common emphasis, at least not in many evangelical and fundamentalist congregations. Our first order of business in what follows,
therefore, will be to consider not just *how* matters related to the physical
creation can get more airtime in worship services and in sermons but
also *why* it is too often the case in the church today that earthly matters
do not assume a very high profile. Why haven't we thought more about
the creation's importance in the past, and what can we do to change
this situation?

Emphasizing the creation's importance and fostering a generally positive attitude toward science may, however, be as much about pastoral
modeling as it is about direct statements made from the pulpit. Even
as a joyful, friendly pastor may influence a congregation to be similarly
joyful and friendly, a pastor who has a relaxed and positive attitude
toward science may over time help a congregation adopt a similarly
relaxed and appreciative perspective. Even as a studious pastor who
cares about careful use of language in her sermons may influence a
congregation to be similarly articulate about their faith, so a pastor
who models a thoughtful and appreciative perspective on science may
encourage others to do the same in their own thinking.

A pastor may find many occasions to mention science in a sermon. A
specific scientific discovery or theory may be used as a sermon illustration, or an ethical dilemma that has resulted from a new development
in medicine may be specifically addressed. These would be obvious

and direct references to the realm of science. But often a preacher's references to science and the way he tries to instill a more positive appreciation for science in his congregation may be more subtle than this. It is analogous to how authors of textbooks and children's books have attempted in recent decades to influence the minds of young people simply by using the personal pronoun "she" to refer to a doctor or a lawyer instead of "he," as was long the standard practice. Preachers in recent times have sometimes used a similar tactic to encourage gender inclusiveness in the church by saying things like, "One week the preacher of a small congregation was struggling mightily with *her* sermon preparation."

In this scenario the preacher is not overtly telling the congregation, "Women may be preachers, too, you know!" but is instead merely *reflecting* that viewpoint through the simple use of a feminine pronoun. Similarly when authors of school textbooks and children's books began weaving in feminine pronouns to refer to people in what were once seen as exclusively male professions, these authors nowhere wrote in bold print, "Get it through your heads, kids: women can be surgeons and attorneys!" Instead, the authors wove this idea into the text subtly, thus making a more gender-inclusive perspective seem very natural. People who are exposed to gender-inclusive language may find that over time their viewpoints are shaped and molded by that language.

Of course, it may well have been a bit startling the first time a congregation heard a sermon in which a pastor was referred to as "she." But if it became clear over time that preachers would regularly be referred to as either "she" or "he," the shock would wear off; it would be a normal and expected pattern. I am aware, however, that for someone who ardently believes that women may never serve as ordained clergy, the shock value would remain, and each new reference to ministers via feminine pronouns would be yet another occasion for irritation and maybe anger. But in the absence of such a belief, the subtle use of feminine pronouns may indeed broaden a person's perspective over time.

But is this recommendation of subtle pastoral modeling actually *too* subtle, too simple? Is it really true that if a pastor exudes a more positive appreciation for science, the congregation will eventually adopt a similar viewpoint? As just stated, someone ardently opposed to women serving as pastors would almost certainly bristle every time he or she heard a reference to a female pastor. Would something similar happen with Christians who fear or despise contemporary science? Would even subtle positive references to the fruits of science, to say nothing of overt comments on this subject, raise red flags in people's minds and ultimately be destructive instead of constructive? It may well be that now and again this will be the case with at least some people. That, however, is all the more reason to weave references to science into the larger warp and woof of both Scripture and the doctrine of creation generally. If positive references to science appeared suddenly and overwhelmingly in a preacher's sermons, such references would appear forced, artificial, maybe even suspiciously out of place. That is why I suggest that people need to perceive science within the context of a larger world-and-life view that is principally informed by Scripture and the theological tradition of the church. As long as the scientific enterprise is kept in a completely separate compartment from theology and spirituality and the Bible, any sermonic references to science may strike the congregation as an intrusion from the outside. But if science can be viewed within the larger context of Scripture's consistent love and celebration of the physical handiwork of God in creation, the natural overlap of science's realm and theology's realm will be that much easier to see.

For at least some people in the church, however, it may not be enough to emphasize that Scripture, like science, is interested in the physical creation. If science is seen as a foe to the faith, a preacher's positive reference to something scientific would not only seem like an intrusion from an outside realm but may even strike such hearers as outrageous—perhaps on a par with making a positive reference to pornography! Bad things should be shunned and critiqued in sermons, not embraced. But this is why we spent so much time earlier trying to separate the chaff of scientific naturalism from the kernel of what science can teach us about physical reality. Preachers need to be able to do this kind of thoughtful separating not only for their own sakes but also so that the congregation can sense that careful thinking has taken place in advance of a sermon. To put it in terms of our analogy, over time people may come to realize that science is not like pornography but more like the broader field of photography. Photographers, both amateur and professional, capture many glorious and moving images on film. No one would deny the importance of family photo albums to most people; indeed, if a house burns down, few losses are as grievous to most people as the irreplaceable loss of family pictures. Yet the same technology that makes a family photo album possible also makes *Hustler* magazine possible. This fact does not, however, prevent an appreciation for the positive uses of photography. No one would suggest, for instance, that just because some people use cameras to take dirty pictures a Christian church has no business printing a photographic directory of the congregation!

Of course, in this analogy the distinction between good photography and bad photography is obvious; when it comes to science, the distinctions that need to be made are significantly more complex, as we have seen. But if a congregation senses that its pastor is working to make such distinctions, that is, if they know their pastor is not some naive person who has simply swallowed contemporary science hook, line, and sinker, people may be more willing to listen when that pastor refers to science in a positive manner.

Working to make such distinctions takes time and patience. The suggestions in the next chapter are longer term strategies by which congregations (particularly those whose current attitude toward science is hostile or suspicious) can become more open to learning from and, when necessary, critically analyzing contemporary science in ways that will help connect Sunday's worship and preaching to Monday's world of science and technology. The more preachers emphasize the spiritual significance of the physical creation, the more congregations should want to learn about that physical creation. And the more science can be seen as a tool or partner in learning about God's creation, the more positive sermonic references to science will seem not only natural but downright biblical.

The plan for the balance of this book is to present a number of broad ways by which preachers can begin to focus more on the physical creation in their preaching and thus help listeners begin to sense those areas where theology and science intersect and overlap quite naturally. Contemplating the physical creation sets the stage for pondering science and its own way of investigating that creation. But not all scientific discoveries dovetail neatly with theological claims, so we will also need to reflect not just on how to talk about science in church but how to talk about science *in a theological way* based on the model that I presented in chapter 3—preachers and other people of faith do not need to talk like scientists in order to make a legitimate use of science in a biblically informed context. People of faith must not, of course, use science as an excuse to compromise the gospel or the hope that the gospel presents, but if believers are going to articulate their faith in ways that can be understood in our contemporary scientific context, they would do well to reflect on that context and hear what it has to say.

As many roadside billboards proclaim, Jesus is the answer, but what are the questions he answers? What are the problems he solves? In the two-thousand-year history of the Christian church, Jesus has provided "the answer" for many different kinds of people in vastly different circumstances. But who the people were and what the times were like shaped the questions people asked. The nature of the question needs to be taken into account before we respond, because only then can we show how Jesus can answer the question. The apostle Paul provides the church's earliest model for this, as can be seen in the Book of Acts. When Paul is among Jews, he explains how Jesus, though not inconsistent with the works of the law, nevertheless saves above and beyond anything we are able to do or observe by our own efforts. When Paul is among previously pagan Gentiles, he explains the wonder of how God's grace saves them despite the lives they once led—they don't have to make up for their past sins because Jesus has done it all for them already. And when Paul is in Athens, he explains the gospel by making use of Greek philosophical tactics and by quoting a well-known Greek poem. Jesus was indeed the "answer" for all these people in all these different stations of life and cultural circumstances. But how Paul presented the answer was determined largely by the people in front of him and the precise way they phrased life's toughest questions.

So also in our present context: the hope of the gospel is the same now as it ever was, but it needs to be articulated for people who live in a time when science has revealed a universe headed for annihilation in some kind of cataclysmic ending. Who we are as creatures created in the image of God has not changed, but evolution and the neurosciences provide a new setting in which Christians need to explain our fundamental human nature. The truth of God's providence is still a source of great comfort and assurance for believers, but even as the existence of evil in this world has long presented a great challenge to Christians who believe in an all-powerful and all-good God, so today the exceedingly long history of this physical universe, its development over billions of years, and its present state need to be taken into account when we claim and sing that God has "the whole world in his hands."

So what follows is meant to be the merest beginning in helping preachers wrestle with these issues so that their congregations can in turn do the same. Since this is a book about sermons, after the next chapter I will conclude with a few sermons I have preached, sermons in which I attempted to do the very things I have suggested in this book. These sermons are included not as the best examples of what I have recommended but simply as examples of one preacher's efforts to accomplish the goals toward which we have been heading all along.

7

As It Was in the Beginning . . .

What Jesus Saves

"In the beginning God created the heavens and the earth."

"Where were you when I laid the earth's foundation? . . . On what were its footings set, or who laid its cornerstone—while the morning stars sang together and all the angels shouted for joy?"

"You are worthy, our Lord and God, to receive glory and honor and power, for you created all things, and by your will they were created and have their being."

"Then I saw a new heaven and a new earth. . . ."

Christians familiar with the Bible will recognize that the verses above come from Genesis, Job, and Revelation. In other words, these reflections on the creation are from the very beginning, the middle, and the very end of the canonical order of the books in Scripture. Creation is where God's story begins and ends. Between the first creation of Genesis 1 and the new creation of Revelation 22, the Bible regularly pays a great deal of attention to the physical universe in which humanity finds itself. Physical phenomena such as clouds, mountains, and winds are frequently used by God to convey his presence to Israel. The Psalms praise God for the moon and stars, for whales and birds, and for many other natural wonders as well. Indeed, the poetic sections of Scripture frequently say not just that God is worthy of praise because of the natural wonders he has created; these ancient Hebrew poems say something more interesting and radical: they claim that the trees of the fields, the birds of the air, and the whales in the oceans *themselves* render praise to God. To the divine ear the sounds of creation are like hymns!

Similarly, the Book of Job, as seen in the verses quoted above, concludes when God paradoxically answers Job's queries about why bad things happen to good people by crooning a long song in which God takes great delight in singing about storks and deer, hippos and eagles. This is hardly the kind of answer Job expected! Yet the sheer magnitude of God's creative power on display in the physical world is clearly important to God; ultimately it appears that this creative magnificence has something to tell us about many other things in the cosmos as well, including (in Job's case at least) questions we might have as to why things in life go the way they sometimes do. Neither Job nor his friends (nor we readers of Job) anticipated God's presentation of the physical creation at the end of a book dedicated almost exclusively to what could be termed more weighty "theological" concerns about good and evil. Given all of the theological wranglings, harangues, and speculations that fill the Book of Job almost to the very end, one might anticipate that God would answer in kind with some manner of explanation about the theological ins and outs of suffering. But God's turning everyone's thoughts in the direction of the physical creation, though surprising, reveals that the physical order of creation looms perhaps larger in the divine mind than it typically does in ours. There is doubtless a lesson for the contemporary church in that fact alone.

In the Old Testament, from the time of Abraham forward, the promise of land is what makes the people of Israel dream of a better day to come. What God offers as the sweetest of all hopes is something very earthy: God's promise is to provide a tillable land plentiful with good fruit, running with milk and honey, dotted with vineyards on a thousand hillsides producing the finest of wines. As Larry Rasmussen once noted, sometimes in the Bible, especially in the Old Testament, it is difficult to distinguish salvation from good highlands agriculture!

Similarly, the imagery of prophets like Isaiah is full of promises of verdant valleys, soaring mountains, bubbling streams, and a peaceable kingdom where all God's creatures will dwell together in safety and shalom. Even in the New Testament we find Jesus invoking the creation in numerous parables and other teachings. Consider how many of Jesus' parables and sayings deal directly with the physical creation or with the agricultural cultivation of the earth: the mustard seed, the sower, the weeds, the yeast in dough, the lost sheep, the vineyard, the growing seed, the sheep and the goats. Jesus' rhetoric was laced with references to bread and wine, to great banquets and feasts, to vines and branches, to birds of the air and flowers of the field.

Yet such words on the lips of our Lord ought not to be too surprising. Not only did Jesus live in a largely agrarian, rural period of history; he is also (as the Gospel of John makes preeminently clear) the Word of God who created all things in the beginning. The Son of God can never forget the physical wonders he made! Thoughts about the physical creation are never far from Jesus' mind (even as such thoughts were apparently not far from God's mind when countenancing the hard questions that fill the Book of Job). Perhaps that is why when the apostle Paul later interpreted Jesus' saving work, Paul made it clear that the scope of that holy work most certainly includes the whole creation. "The creation itself will be liberated from its bondage to decay and brought into the glorious freedom of the children of God" (Rom. 8:21). "For by [Christ Jesus] all things were created . . . ; all things were created by him and for him. He is before all things and in him all things hold together" (Col. 1:16–17). Peter added his voice to this line of thought. Near the end of a letter Peter seems to have known would be his last, he wrote, "But in keeping with [God's] promise, we are looking forward to a new heaven and a new earth, the home of righteousness" (2 Peter 3:13).

By the time New Testament readers arrive at the Book of Revelation, it is therefore no surprise to discover that even *before* the apostle John hears the heavenly choirs praising Jesus for saving humanity by his shed blood (the famous song in Revelation 5), John *first* hears the lines quoted above from Revelation 4, which state that Jesus' role in creation renders him worthy of receiving all the honor and power and glory the angels can muster. Finally, at the Bible's climax in Revelation 21–22, what John sees as the culmination of all history is not the transportation of humanity to some ethereal realm of vapors and wispy clouds but is instead a new heaven and a new earth that comes *down* to where we already live in this very creation. The dwelling of God comes to us, not the other way around. Once that happens, the first order of divine business is the Great King's declaration, "I am making everything new!" (Rev. 21:5; and notice: in the Greek of this verse God declares he is making *ta panta* new—*everything*, not just *everyone* in the sense of a renewal of only humankind).

Beginnings often exert a big influence on all that follows. Perhaps that is why a favorite saying of one of my seminary professors was that where you begin in theology determines where you end up. Theological studies, therefore, have traditionally begun with what is called Prologomena, or "first things." Among the first items on the theological agenda is usually the doctrine of revelation and inspiration. The first thing that needs to be nailed down decisively is that in Scripture God has already provided all that we need to know about his nature, work, and salvation. We take our cues from God alone. If that is established up front, it will determine the shape of subsequent theological reflection on creation, sin, salvation, the nature of Christ, and eschatology. Where you begin determines where you end up.

By way of extension I would note that where the Bible itself begins— namely, with a focus on the physical creation—is a very telling fact as to what the Bible (and the God who inspired that Bible) will be interested in from that point forward. So if readers of the Bible understand that Genesis 1 and 2 are sounding the keynotes for all that follows, these readers will listen for the melody and notes of creation that are repeatedly sounded throughout the Bible. If readers do this, then when they arrive at the Book of Revelation, some sixty-six books and thousands of verses later, they will not be at all surprised to discover that the Bible comes full circle in the end and presents a new order of creation that is pressed right onto this current physical order.

In Scripture, creation matters. *All* of creation matters, not only that part of creation that has to do with human beings. (Though as the very image-bearers of God, who alone are able to receive and comprehend God's revelation, humanity quite naturally assumes a very high profile in the Bible. There is a difference, however, between assuming a high profile and being the only thing the whole story is about from first to last.) The God who had the delightful creativity to paint butterfly wings and fish scales, the God who made a giraffe whose neck is impossibly long and a hippopotamus who seems to have no neck at all, the God who hurled comets through outer space and who spun electrons in inner space, the God who takes note when sparrows fall and who knits garments of daffodils to clothe the fields—this same God does not desire to lose any creature he has made. Indeed, Anthony Hoekema once wrote that when talking about the kind of existence that Christians can expect in "heaven," it would be wrong to envision that realm as anything *other* than a place of meadows, brooks, mountain lions, and apple trees. If such features of the physical creation are *not* a part of the landscape of heaven, Hoekema asserted, such a vision would essentially concede defeat to the devil. From the biblical beginning, Satan has seemed intent on sullying the works of God. If humanity one day gets placed into a world devoid of the very creatures and things we see around us in this present order, we would have to conclude that the devil won after all—even the Creator God had no choice but to chuck this entire cosmos in favor of something very different. But since we do not wish to grant the devil that kind of victory, we do well to follow the Bible's own lead and do as the apostle Peter did: look forward to a new heaven and earth all landscaped with righteousness (as Eugene Peterson once paraphrased 2 Peter 3:13).

As the church has been proclaiming for so long now, "Jesus saves!" But *what* Jesus saves is consistent with what Jesus first made when, as the Son of the living God, he originated the cosmic process with the words, "Let there be light!" Jesus is the Alpha and the Omega, as Christians well know and believe. But who Jesus is as Omega will not be very different from who he was as Alpha. As both Alpha and Omega, the Lord Christ Jesus is the divine Lover of all that exists. There can be no joy at the Omega point of history unless everything created by the Alpha of cosmic history is still present and still vibrant, liberated from its bondage to death and decay but nevertheless undeniably and definitely *there*.

Putting Scripture into Practice

But if all of this is biblically true (and I would contend, biblically obvious), why is it so often the case that matters related to the physical cosmos do not assume a very high profile in our churches? Generally speaking, the church failed to take the lead in working for ecological and environmental preservation in the twentieth century; as a matter of fact, the church was even quite slow in catching up to the environmentalist movement once it was started by people outside the church. Indeed, it seems that the more theologically conservative a given church or denomination is, the less inclined it is to get involved in ecological concerns. Not surprisingly, therefore, there have been some voices in the secular environmental movement that have accused the church of actually having *caused* the kinds of global ecological crises we have only lately begun to recognize and regret.

For one thing, critics allege, the church has long taught some version of the cultural mandate from Genesis 1–2, whereby God handed humanity the whole creation on a silver platter to do with as we please. The world is humanity's playground to develop, use, even use *up* if we so choose, as if exercising our various consumerist prerogatives is something God himself has authorized. Additionally, such critics continue, Christians often proclaim that since we are all headed for a better world in heaven by and by, the destruction of this world may well be an inevitable, if not necessary, precursor to God's bringing us home to himself in the eternal kingdom "above."

Of course, there is much that could (and probably should) be said in response to such critiques, but perhaps we should first admit that at least some Christians past and present have exhibited and still exhibit some of the attitudes that have been seized on by critics of the church. Some Christians appear to give the degradation or diminishment of the physical creation no more than a shrug. This world is not our home anyway, some claim. It's got to get worse before it will get better. And anyway, more "spiritual" matters related to God's heaven are a better focus for a Christian's mind than earthly concerns. So why would Christians want to devote undue amounts of time and energy working to shore up a world that God's own Word has revealed to be merely transitory and temporary, destined for the fires of judgment?

Near the conclusion of the movie *Titanic* there is a scene that shows the great ship's architect, a Mr. Thomas Andrews, standing before a fireplace in one of *Titanic's* grand dining rooms. Apparently this was the last place anyone ever saw Andrews before the ship went down, taking him with it. In this scene from the movie, the *Titanic* is already well on its way to sinking, and yet Mr. Andrews, apparently in shock that his fine and "unsinkable" vessel would soon be at the bottom of the north Atlantic, is staring at a fancy clock on the mantle. The last thing viewers see him doing is comparing the time on that clock with his pocket watch, finally adjusting the hands on the mantle clock to make it more accurate. It's a sad and tragic scene, but it is also somewhat ludicrous: only a deluded person (or in this case, a deeply shocked person) would bother to adjust a clock on a sinking ship!

Unfortunately, however, some Christians seem to take a similar attitude toward the physical creation: It's on its way into an abyss of sinful destruction and divine judgment anyway. Taking much interest in the physical features of this planet, much less trying to preserve these features, is like fiddling with a clock on a sinking ship: it just doesn't make sense. Hence, some in the church today regard an undue focus on ecology and the preservation of the environment as a lost cause, or at very least as a cause that should be ranked pretty close to the bottom of the church's collective "to-do" list. Some worry that paying too much attention to the earth may lead to some form of New Age pantheism, while others may think that ecological concern on the part of Christians is the result of a liberal theology that takes its cues less from God's Word and more from the contemporary cultural landscape.

But even if a given congregation does not have any overt hostility or suspicion toward the celebration and preservation of the environment, the physical cosmos does not typically receive much routine or extended consideration in the course of the average worship service or sermon. For many years a religion professor of my acquaintance made a wager with his religion classes each fall: the professor said he would pay twenty dollars to any student who could find a televangelist preaching on the Minor Prophets and particularly on those prophets' repeated cries for social justice. When recently I met up with this now-retired professor, he claimed he never once had to part with a twenty-dollar bill as a result of this wager! A similar wager could be made regarding the environment of God's physical creation: I would bet that even if someone were to spend several months sampling the sermons of the preachers who regularly appear on various cable TV channels, this viewer would be hard-pressed to find sermons that focused in any extended way on the wonders of the physical, nonhuman creation or on the need for Christians today to adopt environmental preservation and ecological interest as a proper act of discipleship. (Vastly less likely, I would further wager, would be finding any sermons that utilize science in a positive way as one fruitful avenue to pursue in the attempt to become better acquainted with the creation.)

Again, however, this is the case not just with TV preachers and worship services but with any number of preachers and congregations, particularly within the evangelical and fundamentalist wings of the larger church world. If where one begins in theology determines where one ends up, it is clear that the starting point in the practical theology of many congregations is not the creation but the cross. The Son of God who was incarnate as Jesus of Nazareth indeed created all things in the beginning, but this is not the first thing many Christians emphasize. Instead, their emphasis begins (and therefore often ends) not with creation but with redemption (and with the redemption of *humans* above all else).

The cross of Jesus Christ is properly the focus for the Christian faith. Few things have bothered me more in recent decades than the fact that some contemporary church sanctuaries are devoid of the symbol of the cross. Some years ago I was informed of a church in Texas that, upon hearing that some baby-boomer seekers found the cross to be a bit offensive, actually removed the cross from the front of its chancel! But to remove the cross is to remove from our sight a chief locus of our faith and hope as Christians. The cross blazes forth from the center of the Christian story as a paradoxical beacon of hope: from an instrument of raw, bloody execution we somehow manage to see the radiance of God's victory over death and sin and hell. The cross reminds us of the cost of our salvation, it instills humility in our hearts when we recognize the sheer grace of Jesus' death on our behalf, and it provides hope for life beyond death even in the midst of a world that seems mostly hell-bent on viewing death as the final word on everything.

Christians are, of course, right to emphasize the cross. They are not right, however, to make the cross the beginning of the entire divine story as Scripture presents it. The story begins and ends with creation: the original creation as lovingly made by God, and the new creation as lovingly redeemed and renewed by that same God in Christ. When on the cross Jesus uttered his famous cry, "It is finished," he did not mean that he or his life was "finished" in the sense of being a failure. Instead, the Greek word translated as "finished" stems from the root verb *teleiō*, which means "finished" in the sense of being brought to completion. Richard Lischer once pointed out that in England you may well hear the word "finished" used in more than one context and hence with more than one meaning.[1] If you ask the waitress in a restaurant for another slice of kidney pie, she may reply, "Ah, sorry, luv, but the kidney pie is *finished*," thus letting you know that there is no more. It's gone, consumed. On the other hand, a craftsman may hand you a wooden sculpture after putting one last buff on the varnish and declare, "There! Now it's *finished!*" In this case, however, he means not that it's ruined but that it's complete, perfect, just the way the craftsman always wanted it to be. Similarly, someone observing a presidential election in the United States may see the electoral vote tally tilt decisively toward one particular candidate, causing a television news pundit to declare that the other candidate is "finished": he cannot win anymore. And then again, there was a time when girls were sent to "finishing schools," not so that they could get defeated or wiped out but so that they could become polished in the social graces.

When Jesus declared from the cross "It is finished," he seems to have meant that the whole story of creation—the entire universe and cosmos that Jesus as Son of God created in the beginning—was now achieving its completion in his death. Through his death, Jesus set all wrongs to right, defeated death, and flooded the universe once more with hope: the hope that all life would continue, that shalom among all creatures would be restored, and that the entire cosmos would once again have a very bright future indeed. Like a master craftsman, Jesus as God's own Son had labored long on his masterpiece of creation. Midway through the creative process, though, it seemed his fondest wishes for the universe would not be realized, as sin and evil and death roared onto the scene, sullying the world's beauty and threatening its every creature. Not to be outdone, however, God found a way to salvage the creation after all, though it would require a great sacrifice. Through the death of the Son, the Creator was finally able to remove the last threats to his work. As all Christians know and believe, in his death Jesus was neither a failure nor done in. He was not "finished" in that sense of the word, nor was the creation for which he died. Instead, it was "finished" in the sense of being brought to completion, achieving the *telos* or goal toward which it had been headed all along.

The cross, in other words, is indeed the focal point of faith. But as such, the cross needs to be the place where the *whole* of Scripture comes together. Although the cross and the death of God's only begotten Son are shocking developments in Scripture, there was and is a very long history leading up to Golgotha—a history that alone helps us understand and make sense of Jesus' death. The cross signals the undoing of all that threatens the works of God, but that same cross does not therefore diminish or wipe away those works! Jesus' life, ministry, death, and resurrection aim to preserve all that is good in God's universe. The cross shines a light forward and backward in history, not only providing a beacon of hope to show the way into the future of God's kingdom but also illuminating the past to reveal all of the created wonders of God—creatures and creations that were and are so supremely valuable as to warrant a death as hellish as the one suffered by God's Son to salvage it all.

From Cross to New Creation

The light that blazes from the cross helps us better to see and appreciate what God holds dear. Yet there is a constant struggle within the Christian community to remember this. Few heresies are older or more perennial than Gnosticism, which tries to wrench our attention away from all things physical and earthly in favor of focusing only on realms of pure thought and spiritual insights. Although Gnosticism was condemned as heretical centuries ago, traces of a gnostic mind-set continue to crop up. Contemporary Christian songs sometimes invite us to "turn our eyes upon Jesus," promising that once we do, "the things of earth will grow strangely dim." Despite being the religion of the incarnation, Christianity too often shunts fleshly matters and concerns aside in favor of thinking about only the salvation of our souls. In the most famous of all Christian creeds, the Apostles' Creed, the last stated belief is in "the life everlasting." But that article of faith is preceded by a belief in "the resurrection of the body." Clearly, the nature of "the life everlasting" needs to be understood in a physical way, not merely in some spiritual-ized way, since the promise of a restored bodily existence sets the stage for Christian reflection on life everlasting—life in what we often wispily refer to as "heaven."

Of course, it is one thing for people outside the church to depict the afterlife as consisting of clouds, vapors, and people who have turned into angels replete with wings and halos (such as can frequently be seen in the images used in advertising or in the pictures on greeting cards). Non-Christians should not be expected to recognize that life everlasting will *begin* with "the resurrection of the body." Christians, however, have no such excuse if they likewise envision eternal life with God as being fundamentally different from an embodied existence in a physically real, tangible creation.

Christians should know better. Christians should have much to say to the cynics and critics of the faith who claim that by holding out the promise of a better life in "heaven" believers thereby show a contempt for life on earth now. This critical viewpoint is promulgated by Brit-ish author Phillip Pullman, who has written a trilogy of fantasy novels that, by Pullman's own admission, provide a direct counterpoint to C. S. Lewis's well-known Chronicles of Narnia. The problem with the Narnia tales, Pullman once told the *New York Times,* is that they are "so anti-life, so cruel, so unjust. The view that the Narnia books have for the material world is one of almost undisguised contempt."[2] But although it is true that the Chronicles of Narnia reach their climax in the new Narnia (a clear analogy to the new creation, or "heaven" as it is commonly called by Christians), that new realm, far from showing contempt for the old Narnia, instead deepens that prior reality. The children and animals of Lewis's novels do not find themselves transported to a nonphysical realm in which they forget all about their prior life on "earth," nor do they end up regarding that prior existence with disgust. Instead, they discover a new world that bears striking resemblance to the old Narnia, except that the new creation is deeper and richer in every way.

Lewis once directly sketched the thinking that lies behind his fanci-ful Narnia tales in a sermon titled "Transposition." When Lewis first delivered this message in London in 1944, he was so overcome with emotion at one point that he had to stop and leave the pulpit for a time to compose himself before finishing the presentation.[3] Clearly, these thoughts were very close to the heart of the man who wrote the Narnia tales. We discover in this sermon that Lewis most certainly did not possess any kind of contempt for all things earthy and physical, as Pullman has alleged.

In "Transposition" Lewis claims that the connection between our future life with God in "heaven" and our present life on earth could perhaps be compared to a symphony that is transposed for the piano alone or a three-dimensional landscape that is transposed into the two-dimensional medium of a pencil drawing or a painting. When a symphony written for a full orchestra is transposed into a piece of music that can be played by a single pianist, the full richness of how the piece sounds when violins, flutes, and timpani all play together gets "lost" in the translation. Yet when the music is played on a piano alone, there is no mistaking the tune, which nevertheless remains very beautiful.

Thus, anyone familiar with Beethoven's Fifth Symphony would recognize a pianist's rendition of the work as readily as a symphonic performance of it by the Berlin Philharmonic. It is, after all, the same music, the same composition, whether played on a piano or performed by a full orchestra. Even though the piano rendition lacks the full power Beethoven had in mind when he wrote the symphony for a full orchestra, this rendition would still be moving, would still convey great power, and would even display at least some hint of the larger drama that comes through when a full orchestra plays it.

Similarly, Lewis claimed, the wonder of truly skilled artists is that they know how to skew lines and convey depth so that a two-dimensional sketch or painting not only looks a lot like the actual landscape that the artwork depicts but even creates the illusion of depth where no true depth is present. The richer reality can be rendered in a poorer medium. But, of course, the reason a drawing of a mountain conveys such things to us is because we have seen actual mountains and are familiar with three-dimensional reality. To appreciate the imitation, one needs to know something of the real thing. Recall the Flatland analogy used earlier in this book, a version of which Lewis also employed in his "Transposition" sermon: a being incapable of sensing a third dimension would not believe anyone who claimed that the two-dimensional drawing is but an imitation of a three-dimensional reality. If someone lacked the ability to perceive a third dimension, talk of a reality beyond the two-dimensional sketch would seem like nonsense.

But suppose that a given person *is* able to experience the world in three dimensions but has been locked away in a windowless cell for his whole life. If someone tried to show him what the world looked like by drawing pictures of mountains and streams and valleys, he would be hard-pressed to imagine what the reality behind the art must really be like since he had never seen or experienced the wider world. Of course, if this person ever got out of his cell to see the real thing, he would recognize it immediately, based on the artistic renderings he had seen, but this recognition would be accompanied by a shocked sense of how much richer and better the three-dimensional reality is than the transposed versions he'd seen in the drawings.

This idea could also be rephrased in the terms of the music analogy: if you had never heard a symphony orchestra or if the only instrument you had *ever* heard was a piano, hearing Beethoven's Fifth on the piano would be a different experience for you than it would be for anyone who knew what the full-blown orchestra version sounds like. It's even possible that you would be less moved by the piano rendition of Beethoven's Fifth than a person who had previously heard the full-orchestra rendition, because that person's memory of the Berlin Philharmonic playing Beethoven's music would color even the much simpler piano rendition. When you have a sense of the richer, fuller reality, you are better able to understand the transposed version, appreciating it for what it is yet also sensing its relative poverty compared to the genuine article.

Or think of the frustration you may have experienced at one time or another after returning from a vacation in some majestic landscape: you wish your vacation pictures of a mountain could convey to others the same sense of awe you felt when you stood before the mountain and snapped the photo. But it usually does not work that way. Unless a person has been to that same place, the mere photograph, though perfectly accurate in showing what the mountain looks like, cannot duplicate the experience of being there. Some pretty significant things get lost in the translation, and so we may often find ourselves saying things like, "Well, you just had to be there." Indeed.

In all such examples of transposing a richer reality into a poorer medium, Lewis's analogy to this life on earth and its relationship to life in heaven is clear: when one day we experience the full richness of God's new creation, we may come to see that this life was the transposed version of the richer reality. But far from rendering our current physical existence tawdry, contemptible, or disgusting, Lewis's point of view on this subject shows the beauty and importance of our current life. Beethoven's Fifth transposed for the piano is, after all, *still* Beethoven's Fifth. You'd recognize that tune anywhere, and even if some day you graduated from hearing the piece played on only the piano to experiencing the full orchestra version, you would still know exactly what you were hearing. It would be very familiar, albeit richer and with a few surprises (like the blare of a cymbal or the sudden lilt of a flute). But the point is that the orchestra version of the symphony would *continue* and further the notes heard on the piano, not replace them altogether, much less render the piano version disgusting.

So also with the new creation that Christians believe has been made possible through Jesus' death and resurrection: it will be *more* substantial, more earthy, more physical than this current realm, not less so. As Lewis put it, "If flesh and blood cannot inherit the Kingdom, that is not because they are too solid, too gross, too distinct, too 'illustrious with being.' They are too flimsy, too transitory, too phantasmal."[4] This is very far from an antiphysical, anticreation perspective! The person who believes that mountain lakes have a niche in God's coming kingdom is much more likely to appreciate, celebrate, and even preserve mountain lakes today than the one who sees no future whatsoever for the physical things of this earth. If God will eventually destroy everything in favor of replacing the whole universe with some new realm that bears no resemblance to this current order, why should we today take much interest in such things as lakes, trout, and butterflies? But if we understand that this present life is a simpler rendition of the symphony that will forever and ever play to God's glory in the new creation, our interest in getting to know this music is enhanced. We want to recognize the tune when we hear it in God's kingdom. Not a single note will be lost, even though these same notes may well be played better and more richly in the new order God will inaugurate.

Weaving It Together

The point of all this is to bolster my contention that proclaiming the wonder of the physical creation of God needs to assume a much higher profile in the preaching life of the church than it typically does in some congregations. It is further my belief that if and when this happens, the stage is then set for a more positive acknowledgment in sermons of what is good about science and the many ways it can further our appreciation for a universe that our God in Christ clearly holds very, very dear. But how might a more positive acknowledgment of science be accomplished? In addition to the sample sermons provided in the next chapter, the following material should provide general guidance as to how this could be carried out in sermons.

As stated earlier, the overarching idea behind "science on Sunday" is not simply that specific sermons or sermon series should consider at great length the physical creation or science (though, of course, an extended consideration of the physical creation will at times result from sermons based on certain Bible passages). Instead, I suggest that themes related to the creation and to the sciences that explore that creation become motifs that weave quite naturally in and out of many sermons over a longer period of time. In this connection Elizabeth Achtemeier once helpfully suggested that contemporary preachers would do well to do what Jesus and the biblical writers regularly did, namely, use the physical creation as a resource for illustrations and analogies in preaching and teaching.

When writing sermons, most preachers regularly reach for analogies or illustrations to help them apply God's Word to the lives and situations of the congregation. Whether it is an opening illustration to arrest the congregation's attention, an analogy midway through a sermon to make a difficult point easier to understand, or a concluding story that tries to cinch the entire sermon firmly into place in people's minds, preachers look for images or anecdotes that fit the occasion. Preachers mostly draw on what they already know: novels they have read, movies they have seen, stories in the newspaper from the week gone by, or their own personal experience. One can, of course, buy and use prefabricated collections of sermon illustrations, but many preachers keep their own collection of such potential sermonic helps in the form of an index file categorized by subject headings, such as "first commandment," "compassion," "resurrection," and the like.

In any event, the analogies or illustrations a preacher uses say much about what he or she finds interesting. Visit almost any congregation that has been listening to the same pastor for a couple of years, and most regular churchgoers could in all likelihood tell you what their pastor's hobbies are. "He often mentions snorkeling," or "I can't tell you how many times she has brought stories about tennis into her sermons!" More substantively, however, it could likewise be alleged that the topics a pastor brings up in sermons will over time allow a congregation to detect the kinds of things their pastor deems theologically and spiritually important. Some years ago when I came to a new congregation, I had preached only a handful of sermons when a woman came up to me after a service one Sunday and declared, "You're a reader! I can tell you read lots of different things." She based her assumption on the illustrations I had been using in my sermons. These illustrations had come from novels and biographies I had read and from which I had drawn various quotes for my index file of potential sermon helps and illustrations.

Congregations may also be able to tell if their pastor is a movie buff, a nature enthusiast, a bird-watcher, or a gourmet cook, all based on the stories that get woven into his or her sermons. Of course, to some pastors' chagrin, a great many other things may be detectable as well. Over time the congregation may begin to make some pretty good guesses about the pastor's political orientation or about her opinion on some of the hot social issues of the day. A pastor who brings up the subject of abortion two or three times each month in sermons and prayers may be perceived as being enthusiastic about the pro-life agenda, even as a pastor who fails to mention abortion even in a sermon where it could have been mentioned rather naturally (perhaps in favor of including some other issues she deems to be very important) may be perceived as being less enthusiastic about the pro-life movement. Yet all such information about the way a pastor thinks—everything ranging from hobbies to sociotheological stances—may be, and frequently is, conveyed without the pastor ever making any direct statements on these topics. These are things that are "caught not taught."

Preachers, like most people, tend to talk about what they know, tend to focus on issues they perceive to be important, and tend to draw on their personal experience, reading, and travel. Obviously, if pastors do not often think about the physical creation and if they do not read about ecological or environmental issues and concerns, they will be less likely to mention such matters in their preaching. Even if they did at some point decide to mention these things, they would have very little to draw on for ideas, images, or resources.

Elizabeth Achtemeier is surely correct in asserting that preaching that is biblical, both in its content and in its attempt to imitate the Bible's own way of communicating with us, ought regularly to include language and images drawn from the physical creation of our God. If a congregation can sense that its pastor is concerned about and interested in the creation, the people may be similarly motivated to reflect on the creation. Over time they may catch on to the idea that the life of discipleship properly includes reflection on, celebration of, and stewardship of the "natural world," better known in Christian parlance as God's beloved "creation." Obviously, I am suggesting this same approach as the first step in opening the door to helping people come to a more positive appreciation of and consideration of the scientific disciplines that open up the wonders of God's world for us.

The more preachers know about the physical world, the more likely they will be to weave aspects of that world into their preaching. The more preachers know about the science that explores the fabric of the universe, the more likely they will be to mention science in natural, useful, and positive ways. But clearly a pastor who never reads novels will never be able to bring fiction into her preaching. A pastor who knows nothing about cooking is unlikely to use culinary images in his sermons. And a pastor who thinks or reads very little about the physical creation or about science will likewise find it difficult to heed Achtemeier's advice about regularly invoking nature in sermons, much less follow my advice about modeling a thoughtful and appreciative approach to science.

An obvious solution, therefore, is for pastors to find ways to begin stocking the homiletical larder (as well as their imaginations) with information and images related to physical aspects of creation. But what are some specific strategies that could be pursued toward that end? The following ideas are only a beginning in a long list of ideas that could help answer this question and address this need.

Resources and Ideas

Perhaps the first and most immediate step preachers can take to connect more meaningfully with the creation is to make a regular and concerted effort to get out into that creation. Whether such excursions into the physical creation are part of a vacation or a Saturday afternoon hike, pastors can begin to heighten their awareness of the importance of creation simply by making routine efforts to explore that creation. This is particularly important for pastors who live in urban or suburban areas, but it applies equally to all ministers regardless of their geographical location. All Christians—starting with Christian leaders—should have a curiosity about what's "out there" in the wider world. Often, particularly for the many people of the modern world who live life at a frantic pace, time spent at a lakeside cottage or hiking in the mountains is viewed as "time off" or "time away" from the normal patterns of life. Preachers whose lives are likewise often a flurry of meetings, counseling sessions, lesson plans, and sermon preparations may similarly regard a vacation in a national park as a respite from all things religious instead of as an *extension* of religion and the life of discipleship. But viewed the right way, time spent exploring, reveling in, and learning about God's physical creation are holy activities that tie in with rather than distract from the larger work to which pastors are called in providing leadership for God's people.

Along these same lines, it might benefit pastors to find at least one particular aspect of the physical creation they enjoy and to turn this into a hobby (an *avocation* that is properly part of the larger *vocation* of ministry). God's creation is vast, and no one person could ever learn about everything that is in the world. But one has to start somewhere, and narrowing down the field of one's focus to a specific aspect of creation may be a good way to begin expanding one's thoughts in the contemplation of the creation. Each person is different, of course. Bird-watching will not appeal to everyone any more than gardening or mountain climbing will. Not everyone has the same interests, abilities, or tastes.

Yet I suggest that pastors find at least one particular area of interest (bird-watching, astronomy, geology, scuba diving or snorkeling, gardening, hiking) and work to learn more and more about that aspect of the physical world. Certainly, most adults can remember the things that most piqued their curiosities when they were children. Return to such interests! Recover the ability that most four-year-olds seem to possess rather naturally, namely, the ability to spend long periods of time watching the scamperings of a fuzzy squirrel or the busyness of ants on an anthill.

As various writers have noted in recent decades, for many people in the modern world the physical creation has become strange and foreign, a kind of *terra incognita*. We're simply not very aware of all that exists outside the office, outside the city, or beyond the suburban neighborhoods that many of us now call home. We live too much of our lives fundamentally disconnected from trees and fields, birds and beavers, flowers and fish. Increasingly the workaday world of many people, including pastors, has far more to do with computer screens, e-mail, faxes, and clogged traffic on the highways than with anything remotely related to the nonhuman creation. We eat steaks at fancy restaurants but seldom think about the sound of a cow's moo. We quaff good wine but cannot remember the last time we took the opportunity to survey the beauty of a vineyard on a hillside. We take vacations but opt for the artificially constructed environment of Disney World or a Las Vegas casino instead of immersing ourselves in the wonders of tide pools along the Maine coast or the flutter of warbler wings in a forest somewhere.

Of course, the news is not all bad. The national parks of the United States have become altogether *too* popular in recent years, making it difficult even to get into some of the more popular parks at peak times of the year. Additionally, the advent of cable television and its flurry of channels has made available specialty networks that deal exclusively with wildlife and other natural environments around the world. The rise of so-called ecotourism has also made it possible (and popular) to travel to rain forests in Costa Rica and other similar natural wonders around the world. The primary goal behind ecotourism is to teach people more about these places and raise an awareness of how vital it is to preserve these sensitive ecosystems.

There is much to explore in this world, starting with one's own backyard. As Sallie McFague has often pointed out, a person need not wait for a major excursion to an exotic setting to connect more meaningfully with the physical creation. Gardening in your backyard or keeping a pair of binoculars handy to zoom in on the birds that pass through your property can be a good way to keep thoughts about creation near the front of your mind. Additionally, small parks (sometimes called "pocket parks") can provide a chance to be in the natural world. The smaller a park or nature reserve is, the less biodiversity it will have, of course. Still, it may well be the case that over time something significant may happen to one's soul and mind by making a conscious, concerted effort regularly to look at, think about, and mingle with the nonhuman physical creation of God.

All such efforts to learn more about specific parts of the world, as well as to be out and about in the creation regularly, are necessary first steps for preachers if they are going to achieve the goal of weaving creation imagery, illustrations, and language into their preaching. We all tend to talk about what we know best. Whether in conversation around the dinner table or in messages spoken from the pulpit, we tend to revert to subjects we think about the most or subjects about which we feel the most passion. One reason too few sermons lift up the physical creation is because too few preachers think much about that subject.

But in the context of this book's primary goal, homiletical celebrations of and reflections on the creation are only the first steps preachers can take in helping Christians to appreciate and learn from science as a result of what they hear in Sunday sermons. It may well be true that a positive application of science will never occur in sermons if the physical creation is seldom mentioned. But even if a preacher tries to raise the profile of the physical creation in the course of sermons week in and week out, he or she still may not bring science into the sermonic picture. Elevating the importance of the physical creation, therefore, is a first but insufficient step toward the larger goal of weaving the scientific picture of the world into sermons. Something more is needed if preachers are going to help bridge the gap between theology and science.

Given the line of thought we have been pursuing in this chapter, it will come as no surprise that the first item I suggest in attaining that "something more" has to do with education. In an earlier chapter, I mentioned Barbara Brown Taylor's thought that prior to pursuing an education in seminary with the goal of becoming a minister, she had a fair amount of interest in scientific matters. But no sooner had she turned in the direction of a theological education than science dropped off her mental radar screen. Most clergy could tell a similar story. Near the end of my freshman year at Calvin College, I announced my intention of pursuing a preseminary education track in my undergraduate years. Immediately my science core curriculum requirements were reduced to almost nothing. Indeed, in four years of education at Calvin College as a pre-sem student, I was required to take exactly one science-related course: Biology 111, which was an exceedingly basic, one-semester over-view of the same basic biology I had already learned in high school. One or two other courses were required in the fields of sociology and psychology, but the physical sciences were all but bracketed for me. Instead, my education docket became loaded with history, philosophy, classics, and language studies in Greek and Latin.

The result of this trend is that by the time most students reach sem-inary, they may know quite a bit *less* about the physical sciences than their fellow college students pursuing other career paths whose science requirements may well have been more substantial. Needless to say, the typical seminary curriculum does not include many science courses, either. The results are obvious: if you are an ordained minister reading this book, the odds are good that you are "on your own" in terms of learning some science. In chapter 4, I tried to address this gap in the scientific knowledge of clergy by summarizing a few of the things I learned in the course of researching this book, but what I presented in that chapter is the merest of summaries. Additional and regular immer-sion into scientific knowledge—or at least a few occasional dips into the scientific swimming pool—will be required if the average preacher is going to have any scientific illustrations or awareness to draw on when writing sermons.

Before going much further, however, it would be good to throw in some caveats. Obviously, science is an ever-expanding, highly complex field. In this book I have revealed something of my own interests, in that I have tended to focus on physics and astronomy, with some attention being paid also to neurology and human biology. But very few people (certainly very few scientists) would ever conclude that I fully under-stand even *some* of the scientific facts I tried to summarize, much less the vast tracts of knowledge not even broached here. As I worked on this book during December 2000, an article in the science pages of the *New York Times* focused on the one hundredth anniversary of Max Planck's discovery that atoms emit their energy not in a steady stream or wave but in packets released in spurts: packets that Planck called quanta of energy, thus beginning quantum physics. By the time Einstein, Bohr, Heisenberg, Schrödinger, and others were finished with their work in midcentury, the entire structure of the universe as previously understood had fallen away in tatters. But one of the things that the author of the article made clear is that despite the fact that the basic truths of quantum theory now underlie everything from CD players to MRI medical scans of the body, physicists do not yet really understand the quantum world! Some key elements of quantum mechanics do not make sense to even the brightest minds in the world today.

Needless to say, such a fact is hardly encouraging for any scientific layperson interested in learning more about science! If the Einsteins of the world are a bit mystified by their own science, what hope is there for the average person to even begin to fathom the subject? Wouldn't it be better simply to forget about even trying? And since science—be it quantum physics or the intricacies of human biology and neurology—has become extremely specialized and hence difficult to grasp, would it not be prohibitive for people like preachers to attempt to learn more about it all? Life is short. Even keeping up on theological journals and books is an impossible task. So isn't my suggestion that preachers learn a little more about science as unhelpful as it may well prove to be unmanageable? This may seem like the *last* thing most preachers need!

Perhaps it would be good to admit that there is some validity to such sentiments. Still, even preachers who find it difficult to keep up on their theological reading often find time to read novels and see movies. Even given the time constraints of any given day, most preachers manage to read the newspaper, follow the latest political developments, and catch up on which restaurants are getting the best reviews. Preachers, of course, are not literary critics or English scholars by virtue of these activities. They do not become political pundits by following the politics of the day, nor does an interest in good food make one a candidate to become a gourmet chef or the local paper's food critic. But by exposing themselves to diverse areas of interest in the wider culture, pastors do put themselves in a position to draw on such matters in the course of preaching and teaching.

My suggestion is not that preachers become scientific experts but rather that they simply need to pay more attention to the scientific resources around them, because such resources do exist; the problem is that we tend to set them aside. Think of a Sunday newspaper: in most cities this is the single largest edition of the paper all week. Few people ever read the entire Sunday paper, and so most of us, upon lugging that large roll of newsprint off the front stoop, do a quick sifting of the sections, with one pile destined for the recycle bin and the other for the den, where we will eventually begin working our way through those sections that hold some interest for us. I tend to toss the advertising circulars, sports pages, fashion section, and business reports onto the recycle pile. Perhaps your own choices are different, but the idea is the same: we stick with what interests us and skip the rest.

But what about the science section? Many major newspapers now print a science section either on Sunday or on a particular day each week. Most weekly magazines also have a few pages devoted to science and technology. Since these are popular venues, as opposed to a jargon-laden specialty magazine or a paper aimed at experts in a given field, most of the articles pertaining to science are accessible and understandable. Perhaps preachers would do well to stop tossing such material onto the "don't read" pile and to begin including it in the "must read" stack.

Another good resource now available to many is the Internet. In the Psalm 29 sermon below, the material presented about thunderstorms and lightning (research on which was prompted by that psalm's image of a storm rolling in across the sea) turned up when I did a web search on thunder and lightning. As with newspaper and magazine articles, information on science and on specific scientific subjects is readily available on the Internet. But the availability of information will not help preachers or their sermons unless they regularly keep in mind the possibility of accessing this information in the course of their homiletical research and work.

A more concentrated and focused way to gain information on science is of course to read books specifically devoted to scientific matters. In the course of this book, readers have no doubt taken note of various authors whose books have been very helpful to me in this regard. The following volumes offer good and accessible summaries of contemporary science as well as thoughtful theological commentary on the relationship between theology and science: from John Polkinghorne I would recommend *Science and Theology: An Introduction* (Fortress, 1998), *Belief in God in an Age of Science* (Yale, 1998), and *The Faith of a Physicist* (Fortress, 1996). Ian Barbour probes the relationship between faith and science in volumes such as *When Science Meets Religion: Enemies, Strangers, or Partners?* (HarperSan Francisco, 2000) and *Religion in an Age of Science* (SCM Press, 1990). J. Wentzel van Huyssteen's book *Duet or Duel? Theology and Science in a Postmodern World* (Trinity Press International, 1998) provides a thorough examination of theology and science. Keith Ward has written two significant books: *God, Chance, and Necessity* (One World Publications, 1996) and *God, Faith, and the*

New Millennium: Christian Belief in an Age of Science (One World Publications, 1998). Another volume to which I have referred is Elizabeth
Achtemeier's *Nature, God, and Pulpit* (Eerdmans, 1992), in which she
directly addresses not just theology and science (as these other volumes
do) but *preaching* and science, as I am attempting to do here. Theologian
Alister E. McGrath is currently composing a three-volume systematic
theology series titled "A Scientific Theology" (volume one, *Nature*, is
available from Eerdmans, 2001). Though this series provides a longer
and more thorough treatment of theology and science than most of the
above-mentioned books, preachers who wish to delve more deeply into
these matters would do well to read McGrath's trenchant analysis.

These are just a few examples of contemporary Christian writers
whose formal training in science (or avid interest in science) has helped
them to write significant volumes from which lay readers can glean a fair
amount of scientific knowledge and insight in summary form; indeed,
just reading two or three such good books on science could conceiv-
ably stock a preacher's mind and index file with images and facts that
could be used bit by bit over a very long period of time in preaching to
a given congregation.

Other things that have helped to stock my index file of illustrations,
specific examples of which come up in the sermons that follow, are
those "fact-a-day" tear-off calendars that present a brief vignette about
a creature each day. Sometimes these calendars are about birds or fish
specifically; at other times they range more broadly to take in any number of stunning, startling, and curious facts about the universe in which
we live. Some of the facts I have learned from these calendars were so
startling that those particular tear-offs went directly into the "Creation
Wonders" heading in my preaching index file.

Still other sources of such information are the many scientific journals
to which one can subscribe. *Creation Care*, a quarterly publication of the
Evangelical Environmental Network, presents columns, articles, and
book reviews that focus both on an overall celebration and preservation
of creation (such as I have been advocating), as well as scientific information. Certainly the scientific standard bearer, *National Geographic*,
presents more than just good-looking photos that children can snip
out for school projects. Additionally, the *National Geographic* television
series on PBS and the Discovery Channel likewise can introduce us to
areas of the creation to which we do not otherwise have access.

Ideas such as the ones presented above are just a beginning; many
readers could probably add a few other resources to the list of opportunities that pastors could exploit in an effort to round out their scientific

knowledge. But if, as I hope was accomplished in the first section of this book, preachers can come to see science in positive and affirming ways, then a desire to learn more about science may likewise increase. Further, if it is true that the pulpit is a good place to address issues related to theology and science (and to do so in positive ways that will bolster a congregation's ability to connect faith with the whole of life in this world), then the desire to find scientific resources on which to draw in writing sermons may become as routine in a preacher's life as is delving into other pools of information in culture, literature, history, and the arts.

Sample Sermons

How Majestic!

PSALM 8

This message on Psalm 8 serves as an example of an entire sermon specifically focused on the celebration of the physical creation. As stated earlier, being able to refer to science in the course of preaching and being able to discern the places where science and Scripture quite naturally intersect is more likely to happen and will occur more naturally if the topic of the creation is a regular component of the worship life of the church. Sermons on themes similar to the ones reflected here may help to set the stage for science on Sunday.

The poet of Psalm 8 stared into the night sky and was properly dazzled at what he saw. But to put it mildly, what he did *not* see was a lot! Had this psalmist been able to spend a scant ten minutes looking through a telescope, he would doubtless have fainted in wonderment. Ancient astronomers were quite skilled at mapping out the night sky, even to the point of being able to predict star movements. What puzzled these early scientists, however, was a handful of stars that refused to behave.

There were about a half dozen stars that did not march in lockstep with the others but instead meandered all over the place. The Greeks finally called these mystery stars "wanderers," believing them to be errant or rebellious stars that had somehow lost their way in the universe. The Greek word for "wandering" is *planao*, from which we derive the English word "planet." For we now know that the reason those wandering stars behave so funny is that they are not stars at all but other worlds all their own.

We've now seen close-up pictures of Venus and Jupiter, of Saturn and Mars, and their beauty is stunning. But the poet of Psalm 8 didn't know any of that. He saw pinpricks of light twinkling in the night sky and was overjoyed. How much more cause for joy we have! Recently the Hubble space telescope actually recorded the birth of a new star. The photo shows a cloud of gas 170,000 light-years away from here. That means that if you could travel at the speed of light (which is around 186,000 miles per second, or 6 trillion miles per year) it would take you 170,000 years to arrive at this cloud. In other words a journey of 102,000,000,000,000,000,000 (102 quintillion) miles! That's 102 followed by eighteen zeroes! The cloud itself is 150 light-years wide and is the nursery for stars ten times bigger than our own sun.

It is estimated that there are at least 10 billion galaxies in the universe, with each galaxy containing perhaps 100 billion stars. In other words, not only are the stars we see in the night sky far away, but they are a mere fraction of what's really out there. Now you can take all of that mind-numbing data and do with it what you will. Recently *Time* magazine published some of the Hubble telescope's magnificent photos of luminous, gorgeous, enormous pillars of clouds and gas. A few weeks later someone wrote a letter to the editor stating that these photos should finally put an end to the religious idea that humanity amounts to something. Not only are we clearly not the center of the universe, this person wrote, we don't even register.

Even Psalm 8 admits that the wonders of the universe are humbling. Of course, you don't need to go into space to see such wonders. Scoop up a teaspoonful of topsoil from the forest floor, and with the help of a microscope you could probably find upward of fourteen hundred beetles and springtails, not to mention about 2 billion fungi, algae, and protozoa. Or look at the birds of the air. Arctic terns fly a ten-thousand-mile round trip each year from their winter home in the Antarctic to their summer home in Asia. Meanwhile, the northern fulmar spends its whole life out on the ocean, having a wondrous ability to drink seawater. The fulmar has an entire desalinization factory in its beak, removing the salt from the water, excreting it through a tube on the top of its beak, and then drinking the now fresh water!

The universe abounds with wonder. On both the macro- and micro-levels, in both human and nonhuman creatures, the cosmos teems with life, with complexity, with music, and with movement. It is all every bit as humbling as Psalm 8 claims.

But Psalm 8 is not designed to make us feel like nothing. Instead, in a remarkably brief compass of only seventy Hebrew words, Psalm 8 directs us how to think about God, creation, and their relation. In other words, this psalm could be properly seen as the touchstone for human life in the cosmos. We do well to pay attention to it.

Psalm 8 is the first psalm of praise in the Book of Psalms. It is also the only one of the 150 psalms that is a direct address to God throughout the entire poem. So how very curious and instructive it is that the first psalm of praise in the Bible is about creation. As recently as fifty to seventy years ago, biblical scholars were convinced that the ancient Israelites did not much care about creation. Many scholars thought that Israel was far more interested in redemption—the covenant with Abraham, the exodus from Egypt, and the like.

Psalm 8 is one of a bevy of texts that prove those sentiments wrong. Creation mattered enormously to the Israelites. The cosmos is the handiwork of God and is the target of redemption, so much so that the Israelites could not even conceive of salvation apart from the promise of a good land flowing with milk and honey. Throughout the Old Testament, as Larry Rasmussen once pointed out, it's difficult to distinguish salvation from good highlands agriculture. God's plans, purposes, and promises are again and again tied together with things like soil and fruit, flocks and meadows, wine and wheat. Indeed, as Rasmussen said, perhaps the ultimate reason we will one day beat swords into plowshares—or maybe today we would have to say "convert armored Howitzer tanks into John Deere tractors"—is not only so that warfare will cease but also so that we can return to our proper vocation of earthkeeping, of tending and tilling the garden of God's good creation.

Creation matters because, as Psalm 8 makes clear, God himself loves it. These days many Christians are fearful of New Age pantheism, which declares the earth to be a divine goddess. Unhappily, however, our desire to put daylight between such heresies and ourselves has caused us also to steer clear of biblical ways by which to describe the cosmos.

In Psalm 8 the psalmist has no problem saying that the physical world is the glory of God. The stars, sun, moon, flocks, beasts, birds, and the rest declare the glory of God. This psalm begins and ends with a declaration that God's name is visible in all the earth. What that means is that it is proper to point to a star and say, "I see God there!" It is by no means pantheistic to see a field of wildflowers and connect it to God. When an art expert comes across a painting and declares, "That's Picasso!" he does not mean that the artist and that oil-streaked canvas are the same thing. Instead, he means that the artist's handiwork is so clearly on display that you can see the artist in his or her work.

So also with Psalm 8: God's presence in the cosmos runs the gamut from the gossamer threads of a moth's wings to globular clusters of stars in space. God made it all, remains active in its preservation, remains vitally interested in its flourishing. Psalm 8 authorizes us to look for and to find God in the beauties of the galaxy. Whether you're peering into a telescope or a microscope, watching a white-tailed deer leap through a meadow, or noticing the wondrous design of your own foot, what you're seeing is nothing less than the glory of God.

All of that, however, is just half of Psalm 8's larger purpose. The other half addresses what is sometimes called "the humanity question." Who are we? How do we fit? Again, without even knowing how vast space really is, the psalmist saw the moon and stars and felt like nothing by comparison. We have still more cause to feel that way today, and many thinkers do now proclaim that humanity is nothing—or at least nothing special.

Two factors have converged to bring about a certain demotion of the human race. One is our sense for how vast the cosmos is. The other factor is how badly we've treated this earth. We really have caused the extinction of untold species. We have razed and wantonly burned large patches of this planet. We have spilled oil that killed creatures of the sea. We have belched sulfurous fumes that cause birds to drop from the sky and people to develop lung cancer. In only the last forty years the world has awakened to the unsavory side of the Industrial Revolution, and what we're seeing is not pretty.

Thus, many writers, including some Christian theologians, have been scrambling to find ways to clean up the world. As I'll explain in a minute, that is a wholly proper goal, even given what Psalm 8 tells us. However, not a few folks have concluded that the real problem in all of this is precisely something else Psalm 8 proclaims, namely, the idea that human beings are special. For too long now, some say, we've lived with the delusion that humanity is distinct.

Well, no more! It's time, many say, to knock humanity off its high pedestal so that we can look at our fellow creatures at eye level. Human beings are part of the web of life on a par with amoebas and jaguars. Or as theologian Sallie McFague says, we need to promote "ecological egalitarianism." We must recognize that we are but the ashes of dead stars, close cousins to elephants and angelfish, and so we care for them because they're family. The left-wing extreme of all this is Deep Ecology. Deep Ecologists sometimes put up display booths at conventions. In the center of the display is a full-length mirror. When you step in front of this mirror, you see not just your own reflection but you also read on the mirror the words, "You are now looking at the worst piece of pollution on the planet!" Like all pollution, the Deep Ecologists say, humanity needs to be cleaned up, eradicated like DDT. Once the human race becomes extinct, the planet will at long last be able to flourish without our intrusive presence.

The Bible disagrees rather heartily. If there is anything more marvelous than the sheer scale and splendor of the universe, it is the revelation that, in all of that vastness, we really do matter. We have been endowed with the image of God, or as Psalm 8 puts it, with a crown of glory and honor. Because of this gift so graciously doled out by God, we are put in charge of this cosmos to tend and keep and rule it on God's behalf.

It goes without saying that non-Christians don't buy that, the same way they don't buy much else that is in the Bible. Still, if you pay attention, you can detect evidence of this divine image. After all, it is precisely our Godlikeness that allows us to feel small in the first place. We have an ability that, so far as we can tell, no other critter on the planet has, namely, the ability to note, study, appreciate, catalog, photograph, record, and celebrate otherness.

The midnight parrot fish that swim around coral reefs don't do that. When my wife and I snorkel, we are attentive to details and keep careful track of all the many different fish we see. Upon returning to the shore, we consult our Caribbean Reef Fish Identification book and carefully check off what we've seen on our life list of fish species. But the fish don't do that. They don't keep track of one another, nor upon seeing us visiting them on the reef do they check us off on a list somewhere. Fish don't say to themselves, "Oh, there's a blonde Caucasian human female. Great! So far I've only seen brunettes!" No, only human beings seem capable of noticing and enjoying the variety of God's creation.

Sometime back the folks at Coca-Cola made a TV commercial showing polar bears sitting around oohing and aahing over a display of the northern lights. But, of course, real polar bears don't pause to observe that colorful spectacle. They just lumber along the tundra way up north while that incredible spectacle blazes over their heads. They don't stop to watch. We do. When once in a while we can see the northern lights from here, we pile out of our houses to watch and gasp.

Curiously, some people take the fruits of our observations and use them as the occasion to claim that we are the same as polar bears and parrot fish. The Deep Ecologists are so enamored by the creatures they have studied that they fail to celebrate their own unique ability to make such studies in the first place!

As Simone Weil once noted, as curious as anything else in the Bible's account of creation is the revelation that God is not God-centered. God has the ability to transcend himself. If, as we Christians believe, God is himself glory defined, if God has within the resources of his own self inestimable power as he dwells in the splendor of light inaccessible, then isn't it particularly marvelous to know that even with all the glory he has within his own self, God is still able to get out of himself in order to gaze at and enjoy the spouting of whales? God gets out of himself to get into others. Our ability to do that is God's gift; it's a major part of the glory and honor with which God has crowned us.

But it's not the only part. Another application of our Godlikeness, as Psalm 8 makes clear, is that we are to take care of and rule over this planet on behalf of God. Psalm 8 may tell us that God has put everything under our feet, but that hardly means we're allowed to trample those things with our feet. Because, as verse 6 makes clear, what God has placed under our feet is the work of his hands. You don't want to smash God's fingers with your feet!

Throughout the Bible we are given tasks and commands by God. But in every case the expectation is that we will carry out those mandates in a Godlike way. When in the Old Testament God demands that his people pay attention to widows and orphans, when in the New Testament Jesus charges the disciples to pay attention to the poor, it is a given that we are to carry out those tasks in ways that glorify God. Only a fool would think that paying attention to widows means exploiting them. Only a fool would think that Jesus' command to be with the poor means no more than keeping track of their poverty in some well-kept ledger without ever lifting a finger to help change their situation.

So also anyone who thinks God's mandate that we rule this planet means ripping it to shreds or doing whatever we want is a moral fool. If a famous artist gifted you with one of his sculptures, you would not put it in a precarious place where the kids might knock it over, and you surely would not let them color on it with their crayons. Nor would you place it in a closet somewhere and never look at it again. No, you would tend it, keep it, display it, appreciate it, show it off to guests, and protect it from harm.

So also with God's world: we rule it because God has given us the authority to do so. But we thus tend it in a way reminiscent of God so that we can protect, celebrate, display, appreciate, and love the gorgeous work of the Creator. If through either a gradual decimation or through a sudden atomic holocaust the day were ever to come when no one would be able to look up at the night sky or look down at the ocean depths and say, "O LORD, our Lord, how majestic is your name in all the earth," if such a day comes, then it will be God whose glory will be diminished.

None of this means that we are not allowed to enjoy the fruits of creation. None of it means we may not use trees for wood or oil for cars or water for boating and fishing. But all of it does mean that as we do those things we always keep God in mind, thanking him for the bounties we can consume but also giving careful thought to how we can simultaneously keep alive the works of God's creative fingers. In a fallen world, that kind of balancing act is precarious and often difficult.

Yet the Bible everywhere assumes that it is possible. It is possible to tend, keep, till, and consume the fruits of Eden while still keeping it Eden. It is possible to care for this cosmos in a way that will keep the majesty of the Creator on display for all to see. It may not be easy, considering how all-encompassing this task is. But we can do it. Remember: we've been crowned with glory and honor by no less than the Creator himself! O LORD, our Lord, how majestic is your name in all the earth! In that holy name, Amen.

Every Creature

COLOSSIANS 1:15–23

Earlier in this book I stated my contention that too often the practical, everyday theology of many Christians today begins and ends with the redemption that Jesus wrought for us on the cross. Redemption not only tends to edge out creation as a biblical theme in the minds of many believers but indeed redemption often eclipses creation. This message takes Paul's soaring and cosmic rhetoric in Colossians 1 as an opportunity to reconnect the Bible's twin themes of creation and redemption. Additionally, like the Psalm 8 sermon, this message can serve as yet another sermon in which thoughts related to the physical creation become a regular feature in the life of the worshiping community and the sermons that the congregation regularly ponders.

Like many of you when on vacation, so also my family and I recently had a nice summertime opportunity to enjoy the outdoor world of God's creation on our recent trip to northern Michigan. We climbed the Sleeping Bear Dunes and marveled afresh at what a colossal pile of sand the winds have heaped up there over the centuries, even as we watched a hawk soar along the thermals emanating from the warm sand. A hike through the forest revealed gorgeous wildflowers as well as a red fox bounding through a meadow. Bike and car rides were made the more fun by the sight of white-tailed deer with fawns, wild turkeys with chicks, and even a coyote carting off some prey for a midday feast.

These are the kinds of natural sights that we look for when on vacation. But how often do we ponder foxes and deer, wildflowers and hawks when we gather at the Lord's Table? The answer is probably "Not very often."

The truth is we have enough difficulty seeing in our mind's eye even the other people with whom we gather at this table. When we eat the body of our Lord, we thicken our union with Nigerian Christians in Idachi who have already worshiped earlier on this Sunday. We are one with the Navajo and Zuni Indians in Rehoboth. We are one with Chinese Christians who broke the bread and spilled the wine in some house church, tucked away from the watchful eyes of the government. When we gather at this table, we sit among a vast congregation of people from all over the world.

That's hard enough to remember on just the human level. So it seems unlikely that we would associate this sacrament with foxes and trout! And anyway, these days there are some who label "New Age" any association of Christian spirituality with the nonhuman creation. At a worship service a couple of years ago we used the classic "Canticle of the Sun" by Saint Francis of Assisi. Francis typically called the moon, sun, and wind his brothers and sisters. But no one in the thirteenth century or since condemned Francis as a heretic. Yet when his words are used today, such sentiments are labeled New Age or pantheistic, as indeed a few well-meaning folks did after that service some while back!

That kind of sentiment need not lead to some New Age way of thinking, of course, but on the other hand, given the recent rise in Mother Earth goddess worship, some hedging is needed. The Bible everywhere forbids any blurring of the line between Creator and creation. We worship God alone and though we give thanks to God for what he has made, we do not worship those things instead of God or along with God, nor do we worship God through those other creatures.

Those are the up-front matters we need to keep in mind. However, with all of that in mind, there is a sense in which Paul's words in Colossians 1 tell us that it is proper to sit at God's Table and envision the good news that the bread and wine also contain for foxes, fish, coyotes, and flowers. Let me explain why that is so and why it is even necessary.

Colossians 1 is a most remarkable passage. For one thing, Paul here goes on a verbal tear the likes of which you seldom see. In most contemporary translations you will find close to eleven or so English sentences between verses 9 and 23. Near as we can tell, however, in the original Greek Paul wrote exactly two sentences in those fifteen verses! The first whopper of a sentence has 218 words in it, running from verses 9–20. Verses 21–23 are one more sentence.

Paul is all but tripping over his own words, piling on one subordinating clause after the next. Even as his thoughts spiral higher and higher, so does his rhetoric. He is like an excited child who cannot get the words out fast enough to describe a day at the amusement park. "And then we rode the Ferris wheel and then we got some cotton candy, and, and, and then I think the next thing we did was go to the fun house, which was really spooky but I didn't get too scared because I knew it wasn't real, even though once I kind of screamed, but after that we walked right over to the roller coaster and, and, and, . . ." and so forth!

Paul's quill cannot keep up with the places to which his heart is racing as he realizes anew the truth of Jesus. And what a truth it is! Keep in mind that Paul is talking about Jesus of Nazareth here. Keep in mind that Paul wrote this letter probably sometime between the years 55 A.D. and 63 A.D., a scant thirty or fewer years after Jesus died. Any non-Christian in Paul's day who read Colossians would surely find his words absurd. This Jesus was someone who had died a quarter century earlier! What's more, even before he died he was just a carpenter's son, a peasant, a nobody from the redneck backwaters of the empire. But now Paul says this Jesus is the creator of every blessed thing that exists, he rules it all now, and is finally the one in whom and through whom all of reality hangs together!

That's outrageous! This is one of those places where you sense the poignancy of that comment C. S. Lewis once made about Jesus: either accept him as who he said he was (the Son of God) or consign him and the New Testament to the realm of mental illness. Because Colossians 1 does not allow you to accept Jesus as no more than an inspirational role model who, though just an ordinary human being, still has much to teach us. No, the New Testament insists that he is the One, God's One and Only, who created everything in the beginning and who more recently redeemed it all, too.

Yes, Jesus lived at a definite time on a piece of Middle Eastern real estate. But he was also the one who, when the big bang flashed, blew out the match with which he had lit the fire. He's the one who, as the galactic soup expanded, cooled, and slowly gelled into stars and planets, was cruising over that spectacle, shaping and molding it according to his and his Father's and his Holy Spirit's designs. So although he was born one night and laid in a manger, he is also the one who, a few billion or so years before that night, had created the atoms that made up the wood of that manger. Now through his resurrection he is preserving every creature in whose creation he took delight at the dawn of history.

He's the One. He's the Only One. If he is who Paul says he is, then Jesus is the key to reality: it all makes sense in him. If the universe has a future beyond the limits of time and space, it is because of him. If you have a future beyond that moment when the doctor looks at your heart monitor and declares, "A systole. That's it," it is because of Jesus. That's who we believe Jesus is. That's what we proclaim in the bread and wine of communion.

And that's why our thoughts at this table simply must range so broadly. Paul's thoughts clearly did so. Four times between verses 15 and 23 Paul uses some form of the Greek word *ktises,* which is the word for "creation." And though Paul is clearly including humans in what he has to say about the scope of Jesus' work, it is equally clear that he is wrapping his mind around all other creatures, too. In fact, at the end of verse 16 Paul caps off his list of creatures by throwing in the catchall Greek words *ta panta,* which literally means "all things" but that colloquially could be rendered "the whole kit 'n' kaboodle!"

Paul does not want to leave anyone or anything out. Just in case we still have not gotten the point by the time we reach verse 23, Paul goes so far as to say that the gospel has been proclaimed "to every creature under heaven." Clearly, this is an example of hyperbole. Paul is exaggerating. Even in 55 A.D. it was not the case that every person had heard the gospel, much less every creature. If that was true then, it is much more the case now, when the world has about 5 billion more people in it than it did during Paul's lifetime. So it is still not literally true that even every person has heard the gospel, much less the trillions of other creatures on the planet.

But it is literally true that the gospel has something to do with every creature, and that is Paul's point. Paul is willing to exaggerate a bit if that's what it takes to convey the message that Jesus has scooped up all things and every thing. Paul makes a similar move in Romans 8 when he says that even the nonhuman creation bears within it somehow the seed of gospel hope. So strong is this hope in the breast of chickadees and in the seeds of a sunflower that Paul imaginatively declares in Romans 8 that the whole creation is groaning for Jesus' return, craning its neck like a child at a parade eager to see the next spectacle coming down the street. The whole creation is waiting on tippy-toes, Paul says, because the whole creation is exactly the scope of what Jesus made and is even now in the process of salvaging.

One of the oldest heresies that beset the Christian church is Gnosticism. There is evidence that Gnosticism was present as early as the first century. Alas, there is evidence that the gnostic view still rears its head today, too. A key feature of this heresy is the notion that salvation is mostly a matter of what you know—indeed, the word "Gnosticism" comes from the Greek word for "knowledge." In Gnosticism, salvation is about receiving knowledge from God. Once that knowledge is in your heart, your interest in the natural world begins to fade away as a prelude to life in heaven, when God whisks you out of this gross physical world of flesh and blood, dirt and feathers, into a vapory heaven of only cloud and light.

Recently Harold Bloom wrote that in his opinion Gnosticism is the quintessential American religion. American Christians tend to focus much on having a "personal relationship with Jesus" even as they eagerly await Jesus to rapture them out of this world. So there has been suspicion in recent years toward those who celebrate the environment. Some dismiss concerns about the physical cosmos by hanging the tag of pantheism onto such matters, even as others ignore issues related to the earth because there seems to be no future in such things. We're going to heaven "and this earth ain't our home!"

The apostle who wrote Colossians 1 thinks otherwise! True, in verses 21–22 Paul talks to believers about their reconciled relationship to God through Christ. We've been given the gift of faith and we need to persevere in that faith, Paul says. In other words, the basic idea behind the "personal relationship with Jesus" line of thought is here. But Paul sets that into a huge context! Faith brings our hearts out into the wide-open spaces of Jesus' galactic project of salvation. Colossians 1:15–23 begins by talking about the entire creation and concludes with a reference to "every creature." Nestled into the middle of that is each believer's salvation by faith. But what that means is that faith, far from disconnecting us from our fellow creatures, actually serves to connect us in the common hope we all have.

All of which brings us back to how I opened this sermon today. When we come to our Lord's Table, we are right to give thanks to God for saving us, for granting us the gift of faith, and for securing for us a firm hope for an eternal future. But at our Lord's Table, we would also do well to give thanks to God in Christ for the gorgeous physical world he has made, even as we gratefully note that it, too, has a bright future. We do well to connect the joys of our vacations in God's creation with what we celebrate in the bread and wine.

This world's birds, fish, and fauna are craning their necks in anticipation of seeing what we will become when Christ Jesus is revealed. These other critters with whom we share the universe are eager for that day because then they will know that their long, sad history of hurt, decay, and travail will also be finished. We have plenty of hurts and woes in our lives, too, of course. That's why, like most of you, when I savor the bread and wine of communion, I look forward to an eternal life of rest, joy, and peace. But as we eat the bread and drink the cup, we should also remember that at least part of what will make that eternal kingdom a joy for both God and us is the fact that we'll share it with all creatures of our God and King. Amen.

Right at the Door

MATTHEW 24:1–35

This sermon, designed for the first Sunday in Advent, serves as an example of using science not as a mere illustration in a sermon but as a constitutive component of the message in that the scientific ideas discussed are made to parallel Jesus' own apocalyptic rhetoric in the Olivet Discourse. My aim in this sermon was to find a way to locate our eschatological hope as Christians within the real world, to find a way to make the faith and hope we talk about on Sunday remain relevant in the Monday-to-Saturday world as it is increasingly now described in scientific terms.

Advent, we often think, gets us ready to see again that shining star that led the Magi to Bethlehem. Yet Matthew 24 shows us terrifying images of the stars falling from their orbits. Advent, we often think, is about a very pregnant virgin beautifully giving birth to the Savior. Yet Matthew 24 takes pity on pregnant women as they flee into the hills, pursued by thugs with swords. Advent, we often think, is about shepherds worshiping the Child. Yet Matthew 24 shows the persecution and martyrdom of those who worship that same Child.

Welcome to Advent, Matthew style! Matthew devotes all of one verse in his first chapter to reporting the birth of Jesus. But at the end of his gospel he gives us several whole chapters dealing with themes related not to the first advent of Jesus as a baby in Bethlehem but to his second advent as the King of kings at the end of what we now know as history. Clearly, to Matthew's mind knowing about Jesus' beginning in life is important, but knowing how to follow and stick with this same Jesus through the tribulations and upheavals of history is what really occupies his mind.

And understandably so. Some commentators believe that Matthew may well have written his Gospel sometime shortly after the year 70 A.D. That was the year when the city of Jerusalem was laid waste by the Romans, following a Jewish revolt. So see in your mind's eye the evangelist Matthew, sitting somewhere outside of the desolated holy city, writing this Gospel. The pungent smell of gore from the decaying bodies in Jerusalem now and again filled his nostrils as he put down the holy words we now regard as the inspired Gospel according to Saint Matthew. How could Matthew's mind not be filled with apocalyptic thoughts? How could he not want to include at some length the apocalyptic things Jesus said shortly before he died? Death and the ending of all things familiar loomed large on Matthew's mental horizon. The Jesus whose gospel of Good News Matthew wanted to bring to the wider world simply had to speak to the reality of death, persecution, slaughters, and just generally to that chaos that we call human history.

We need to hear these words, too. Because many of us are aware of the sometimes grim things science tells us about our universe. We saw what the fragments of the comet Shoemaker-Levy did to a giant planet like Jupiter a few years ago. Jupiter is vastly more massive than Earth. Even so the twenty-one comet fragments or meteors that hit Jupiter a few years ago ripped astonishingly huge holes into Jupiter's atmosphere; in fact, some of the holes were larger than the entire planet Earth! If even one such meteor were to impact our planet, the likelihood of global catastrophe and loss of life in the billions would be very high.

Alas, scientists tell us that there are lots of meteors out there. All my life I've enjoyed watching the annual meteor showers that our planet experiences. Mostly all you see if you actually go to the bother of getting up around four o'clock in the morning so as to gaze into the night sky are little pencil-line streaks of light that last less than a second. The meteors that cause those little flashes are typically no bigger than a grain of sand. But recently I, like some of you probably, saw a meteorite that took my breath away. It lasted a good fifteen seconds in a fireball of significant width and startling brightness; you could even see visible sparks spraying through the sky. That meteorite was probably the size of a small pebble. It was beautiful to see, but if one day a much bigger chunk of rock strikes our atmosphere at over 100,000 miles per hour, the planet will experience the equivalent of a multimegaton nuclear blast.

And there are, of course, other indicators of entropy, decay, and possible destruction of the physical cosmos. The sun has only so much fuel and will one day burn out. Granted, it's got about 5 billion years of life left to it, but it is finite! But so, they now say, is the entire universe. It will either keep on expanding until it flattens out into a vast disc that can no longer support life or, like a rubber band, it will snap back and collapse in on itself into an infinitely dense wad of matter. And if all of this seems far away and unreal, we are altogether too aware that the only self-conscious, highly intelligent creatures of which we know, namely, we human beings, have found a way to develop weapons that could destroy all life on this planet many times over.

Do I have your attention yet? There is a fine line between being realists and being pessimists, but the simple fact of the matter is that there is a sense in which that one line from the hymn "Abide with Me" is accurate: "Death and decay in all around I see." Like Matthew sniffing the acrid smells of smoke and decaying flesh from the sack of Jerusalem, we can easily find things to look at, read, reflect on, or think about that fill the nostrils of our minds with the odor of entropy and decay.

So like the disciples on that long-ago day as reported in Matthew 24, maybe we want to come up to Jesus and say, "Master, what is all of this going to be like and how will we know when the end is near?" What prompted the disciples' question was Jesus' comment about the upcoming destruction of Jerusalem's grand temple. Jesus and company were in Jerusalem for the Passover, and the disciples were like typical tourists, craning their necks to see the big buildings, walls, ramparts, and other sites. If they had had cameras, they probably would have had a group picture taken in front of Herod's temple.

But Jesus does not seem much impressed. His thoughts appear to be elsewhere. So the disciples excitedly point to the temple and say, "Look at this, Lord Jesus! Isn't it something!?" "Not really," Jesus sadly replies. "Soon it will all be a ruin, with no stone still cemented to another." That proved to be something of a conversation stopper! So the disciples numbly follow Jesus back out of the city up onto the Mount of Olives. When no one else is around, the disciples ask the question that has been burning in their minds ever since Jesus made his grim prediction. "When is this going to happen? How will we know when it's getting close to the end?"

The long, rambling answer Jesus gives is confusing, intriguing, and ultimately very enlightening. Part of the confusion in this passage stems from the fact that, like almost all biblical prophecies, Matthew 24 points to more than one horizon of fulfillment. In one sense Jesus is talking about events that will soon happen in the first century: the persecution of the original disciples, the upcoming destruction of Jerusalem and the temple, the blasphemy of the Romans referred to in verse 15. In the same breath, however, Jesus points to a bigger picture of things that will be true throughout history as well as to things that will happen at the very end of history just before Jesus returns again to judge the nations and make all things new.

It's all rather jumbled together, and no one sermon has the time to disentangle all of the various threads. But perhaps it will be enough to follow the main lines of this passage and apply them in this Advent season of our lives. So let's investigate both what Jesus says and, perhaps just as significant, what he does not say. In verse 3 the disciples inquire about both the what and the when of the end. The very first thing that Jesus says in reply to this question is, "Be careful!" This entire subject area is going to become an area of great errors, calculated deceptions, and just generally a lot of zany sensationalism. As commentator Dale Bruner points out, it is instructive and also distressing to see how often Jesus uses the word "many" in these verses. Verse 5 says that many will come speaking on Jesus' behalf, that many will be deceived, and then later in verse 24 Jesus says that these many people will do many strong signs and miracles to lead people astray.

What does all of that mean? That the numbers of people who will blow smoke and tell false stories will be great. Worse, by all outward signs of success, they will appear to be serious folks to whom one ought to listen. They'll attract large crowds, sell lots of books, and a few of them will even perform miracles that will surely make it look as if God is on their side and that they are speaking Jesus' own truth. But they won't be, Jesus warns.

As important as anything else in Matthew 24 is the fact that in answering the disciples' question about when the end would be, Jesus replies that a vital thing to keep in mind is to stay away from the people who tell you they know when it will be! Don't buy their books, don't believe them when they tell you Jesus told them thus-and-so, because he didn't. Don't get scared by their lectures or sermons or be seduced by their success, by their tricks, or by their ostensible miracles. They won't know what they are talking about because Jesus basically tells us to not talk about it at all.

And anyway, as Jesus says in verse 27, when the real end is near, you'll know. You'll know with the same certainty of seeing a bolt of lightning flash from east to west across the sky. There will be no mistaking the real end. But if that is so, what are we to make of all the specific things Jesus mentions about wars, earthquakes, persecutions, famines, and heavenly disasters? Some of that material surely looks like a road map by which to figure out how and when it will all end, so why isn't it?

The answer seems to be that what Jesus is tracing out here is the normal—or perhaps better said, the subnormal—flow of historical events in a fallen creation. Even as many of the things Jesus talks about happened already in the first century, so they would continue to repeat themselves. In verse 15 Jesus refers to Daniel's prophecy of some blasphemous abomination standing in a holy place. Daniel's words referred most immediately to Babylon. Jesus' reprise of that prophecy applied it to what the Romans were about to do in his century. And there have no doubt been numerous other similar events that have happened since and that may yet happen again, too.

But all these things, as Jesus says in verse 8, are just the beginnings of the cosmic labor pains that will lead to a new birth of shalom. History repeats itself, as the old saying goes, and Matthew 24 is Jesus' way of saying the same thing. But when the real end comes, there will be no doubting it, denying it, or missing it. Jesus will return in great glory and power, and this is our hope. These are all birth pangs, Jesus claims, not death throes. Above all, however, is the beauty of verse 33: it is no one less than our loving Lord and Savior Jesus Christ who stands right at the door, waiting to come in and make all things new, just as he promised!

As theologian and physicist John Polkinghorne says, when we look squarely at the things science shows us about our decaying universe or ponder unstintingly the specter of nuclear nightmares, the vital question theology must answer is, "In the end, will all be well? Will I, my children, my future descendants be okay?"

Science really has no answer to that, or at best it can give only grim answers. It is faith that sees a doorway, on the other side of which stands Jesus. It is faith that sees a cosmos that is in pain but that interprets that pain as leading to a new birth, not a cosmic crunch that will make death the last, gasping word. It is faith that sees the life-bearing nature of the universe as intentional, not accidental. The universe has brought us and so much else to life because of a loving Designer, not as the quirky happenstance of a process that might very well have gone wrong. It is faith that sees the reality beneath the reality, a providence of God that holds all things together in heaven and on earth in hope.

But to hold this faith realistically, as Jesus himself clearly intended, means that we cannot deny death or its pervasive presence. People who march under a cross cannot and should not deny that death is here, that it is scary, that it looks final, and that we wish it were not here at all.

But then, everyone believes in death—personal death, cultural death, political death, ecological death, ultimately cosmic death. Christians, however, believe also in resurrection! We believe that this new life will come solely as the gift of God; it's not something that will result from some natural consequence of this physical universe. Resurrection is God's gift, and this belief allows us to endow life on this planet with splendid meaning despite the scary stuff we see around us.

In Matthew 24 Jesus is not trying to create starry-eyed disciples who keep scanning the horizon for clues. He is training some long-distance runners to stick with him over the long haul. He's creating disciples who will not let their love freeze up or grow cold but who will accept for now the reality of death but who will nevertheless see hope and meaning and beauty everywhere.

Why begin the Advent season this way? Because there's precious little sense, beyond Hallmark sentimentality, to do much if any celebrating in the next four weeks if the birth of that little one in Bethlehem cannot somehow take account of the "death and decay in all around we see." Even as Jesus telescoped together current events with ultimate cosmic events, so we must telescope together, see in the same glance, the little town of Bethlehem's event and the ultimate cosmic events that Mary's boy-child alone has the power to overcome and also transform into a force for new life, not final death.

As we wish one another the season's good cheer and say our "Merry Christmas" greetings, we do so knowing that somebody's right at the door. Even if the worst happens—and let's be honest that we all hope it won't and so we work for peace to keep it from happening—but even if the worst happens and heaven and earth pass away, the Word of the One who is right at the door will never pass away, and his Word is resurrection life! Believe that message and you will have more than sufficient cause to celebrate Christmas, the Advent of the Christ, with great joy, childlike hope, and lasting peace. Amen.

Holy Time

Exodus 20:8–11; Deuteronomy 5:12–15

Like the previous message, this reflection on the meaning of the Sabbath attempts to weave some new scientific threads into the old and familiar cloth of the Christian biblical and theological tradition. This sermon is also an example of attempting, in fairly short compass and in an admittedly watered-down way, to describe fairly difficult scientific concepts within the context of a sermon, albeit at an accessible, popular level. Whether or not this works is something readers and listeners will have to decide for themselves.

A couple of years ago *Time* magazine named Albert Einstein its Person of the Century. Curiously, the name of the magazine points you to the subject about which Einstein had his greatest insight: time. Before Einstein came along, people assumed that whatever time is, it is constant. "Time marches on," the old saying goes, and before Einstein we assumed that time always marches at the same pace. It does not matter who you are or where you are or what you are doing; you cannot affect time. If your battery is running out, your watch may run slow, but the actual time that passes around you can never slow down or speed up.

But Einstein realized that time is a truly existing dimension. Time is as real as the wood of this pulpit. And it is not constant. Time is affected by motion and position. It is relative. Einstein's classic illustration has to do with a train. Picture yourself riding on a train. Picture another person sitting on a bench alongside the train tracks, watching the train go by. Now imagine that two bolts of lighting strike the train tracks, one just behind the moving train and one just ahead of the train. To the person sitting on the bench it is clear that these two bolts of lightning struck the tracks at the exact same instant. They were simultaneous. But the person riding sixty miles per hour on the train would not perceive it that way.

If you were riding on the train, you would see the bolt of lightning ahead of the train before the one behind the train. At one time it was thought that this could be explained the same way you can deal with sound waves. If you are in your car waiting for a train to pass, you hear the crossing bell go ding-ding-ding-ding, always the same tone. But people on the train don't hear it that way. As you move toward the bell and then away from it, the pitch changes: first it sounds higher and then, as you speed past the bell, the pitch sounds lower. So perhaps the same thing happens with the lightning: you just get to the light waves of the one bolt more quickly since you're moving toward it (and away from the other one).

But it doesn't work that way. The phenomenal insight of Einstein was that you cannot explain this difference in perception by fiddling with the speed of the light, because the speed of light is constant. Light always goes the same speed; you cannot get light to come at you faster. So Einstein realized that what accounts for the person on the train seeing the lightning bolts differently than the person on the bench is that time is different for the person on the train. Time is relative. It can be affected by motion. Scientists have even discovered that if you take two very sensitive nuclear clocks, synchronize the time on both, and then place one at the top of a skyscraper and one at the bottom and let them tick away for a few days, it turns out the clock on the bottom runs slower because it is closer to the earth's center of gravity than the one at the top!

Well, it took an Einstein to figure that all out, but there is a sense in which the importance and impact of time is something Jews and Christians have known all along. The Bible itself lets us know that time can affect us but also that we can affect the time around us. That's why there is such a thing as Sabbath. God took care to weave Sabbath rest right into the richly embroidered tapestry of his creation. As such, Sabbath is not just a human technique for stress reduction; it is a way to take hold of time and make it serve the cosmic purpose of glorifying God by paying attention to the rhythms God instituted.

That's why the fourth commandment as spelled out in the Old Testament takes care to mention that Sabbath is not just for the well-off who can afford to take a break—for that matter, it's not just for people. The commandment says that your donkey and your ox need a Sabbath, too, and so do your servants, your staff, your employees, and even the out-of-town guest who happens to be with you at any given time. Sabbath is for you and your children, for your friends and animals, for the stranger who is within your gates. Every seventh year the Israelites were even supposed to give the soil a sabbatical year off!

Of course, the very fact that God had to make this into a law shows how foolish we are. In the Garden of Eden God did not command Adam and Eve to take a Sabbath rest. Adam and Eve were smart enough to recognize a divine gift when they saw one. But we're not so wise anymore. Now God needs to command us to take a Sabbath! When you think about it, that's about as ridiculous as giving a child a chocolate ice-cream cone and then needing to make it a rule that the kid start licking it! Yet for the likes of us God needs to put Sabbath in commandment form. Worse, even with this commandment firmly in place most of us do a pretty sorry job at taking the concept of Sabbath very seriously.

We've even come to view Sabbath in therapeutic and utilitarian terms. We run ourselves ragged every week, arriving each Friday or Saturday at the brink of exhaustion. The weekend then becomes a time to catch up on all the errands we didn't have time to get to in the throes of our busy workweek. If we're lucky, maybe we'll also have a chance to recharge our batteries just enough to reenter the rat race come Monday morning.

We've even allowed the biblical concept of Sabbath to be conquered by the comparatively recent secular invention of the two-day weekend. No one used to talk about a weekend, but now it's an institution. Sunday is just one-half of the larger weekend unit—it's just a sequel to Saturday. But to use Sunday as a day to catch up and calm down just long enough to prepare for another week of work, work, work is wrong.

As Eugene Peterson has often pointed out, Sabbath is not a "day off" to catch your breath, it's about completely reorienting your thinking. Sabbath means entering into God's grace and God's story and God's rhythms in ways that will not prepare you to reenter the rat race but that will make you exit the rat race for good. Truly to recognize Sabbath for what God intended is to change your life every day. To use the Sabbath as a launching pad for the same old destructive routines of busyness is to profane the Sabbath. The secular "weekend" is for recharging your batteries; the Sabbath is for transforming your mind.

You can sense some of this just by noting the different ways by which Sabbath gets grounded in the Bible. As we read both Exodus 20 and Deuteronomy 5, you should have noticed something, namely, the fourth commandment is different in those two passages. In Exodus 20 God commands Sabbath rest based on creation. "For in six days the LORD

made the heavens and the earth . . . but he rested on the seventh day."
Creation has something to do with Sabbath. But in Deuteronomy the
reason is different: "Remember that you were slaves in Egypt and that
the LORD your God brought you out of there." This time it is redemption
that reminds us of Sabbath rest.

Creation and redemption are the two big themes of the Bible. Strik-
ingly, both have something to do with Sabbath. The way we were made
by God and the way we've been saved by God aim us in the direction of
Sabbath. But if, as I just said, Sabbath is far more than just a day off,
then what is it? What lies at the core of this and how could it affect our
lives if we really both understood and practiced Sabbath?

We can begin by tying back into creation and redemption. Creation
tells us that in the end as in the beginning (and so at every point in
between) God alone is the Creator. God has taken care to create a fitting
world and home for us. Far from being some remote deity who set the
universe to spinning but then left it alone, we believe that God is still
vitally close to his creation. He takes care of us. Because God alone is
the sovereign maker and caretaker of everything, all that we can do is
enter into a work God already has under control.

Of course, it's important that we have jobs and tasks and that we do
them faithfully and diligently. There is such a thing as the deadly sin of
sloth, after all! But the creation perspective on Sabbath reminds us that
we can never do it all and that we don't need to, either. If we really are
faithful workers who carry out our God-given vocations as best we can
during the week, then with relative ease we ought to be able just to leave
that work for a while, too. Since we are merely participating in God's
larger creative work, we can be assured that when we leave off for a bit,
we are not abandoning our work to mere idleness, but we're leaving it
in God's hands, where our work is all the time anyway!

But suppose you are thinking right now, "That's all very fine, but if I
leave my desk and don't take any work home on my laptop, the fact of
the matter is that God is not going to fill out the unfinished month-end
statements that need to be done by Monday!" True enough. Yet I am
going to be bold enough to suggest that if any of us have jobs that are
so all-consuming we can never leave them and nestle into God's abiding
providence, then something is wrong. Sabbath tells us to fix it. That may
take time, patience, and creativity, but Sabbath tells us not to just put
up with as "normal" seventy-hour workweeks of high stress.

A similar point can be made about the Sabbath connection to redemption. To save us, God crucified us with Christ Jesus. We were dead. We
could not do a thing but could only have something done to us. The gift

God gave was resurrection. Grace sets the tone. Grace means we can stop running, stop performing, and know that we still are fully loved and accepted. Grace tells us that who we are in Christ is more important than what we do in life.

We forget that in our competitive society. Look at how we greet people when first meeting them. "Hi, Floyd, nice to meet you. I'm Scott. So, what do you do?" And if Floyd answers that he's an accountant or a plumber, we think that we already know a lot about him. But we don't know a thing yet. Were you ever to develop a true friendship with Floyd, his vocation would not figure terribly prominently in your interactions. Who wants to talk about work all the time? How we feel on the inside, what brings joy and what brings pain—these are the things that make individuals unique and precious. Maybe a Sabbath reveling in the prior grace of God will help us appreciate people for what they are, not just for what they do.

Few twentieth-century writers thought more about the Sabbath than Abraham Heschel. Among his famous phrases is that "the Sabbath has kept the Jews more than the Jews have kept the Sabbath." Heschel saw Sabbath as a kind of cathedral in time that keeps alive our sacred identity. Stopping, resting, leaving matters in God's hands because we know they are always in God's hands anyway; pausing, pondering grace, just doing things that much of our world might chalk up as "wasting time"—these need to be the bright center of our lives.

Yes, Sabbath may "recharge your batteries," but not in the sense of giving you more juice to burn off on the professional treadmill everyone else is on. Instead, Sabbath recharges your batteries in the sense of mentally taking you out of that system that says work controls everything. In the film *The American President* we see workaholic presidential assistants living life every day going six hundred miles per hour, furiously flitting around the president in a nonstop treadmill of busyness. At one point one of these aides says to another, "Well, maybe we should knock off for a few to celebrate Christmas." The other aide replies, "It's Christmas?" to which the first man says, "Yeah, didn't you get the memo?" Work is not everything. Sabbath ties us back into creation and redemption by reminding us of our proper place in God's world.

God gave this cosmos the gift of Sabbath as a source of delight. But we've fallen so far from what God teaches in creation and redemption that we sometimes chalk up Sabbath rhythms to laziness. As Christians, created in the image of God and now in Christ redeemed fully to bear that image once again, it's time to return to Sabbath as a wonderful gift.

Einstein told us that movement can affect the passage of time. It was a shocking revelation to the world that this is so. The Bible tells us that sometimes a lack of movement can affect time, too. The Sabbath full stop makes the times of our lives sweeter, richer, fuller. It is not empty time but full—full of grace and truth, full of creation revelry and redeeming joy, full of God and so also of shalom. People of God, remember the Sabbath day to keep it holy. If you do, the Sabbath of God's grace will keep you holy, too. Amen.

The Storm's Glory

PSALM 29

This sermon is included to serve as an example of how science can rather naturally be used to illustrate and spice up a sermon, if only preachers are looking for opportunities to utilize science in the first place. When I began working on this sermon, my commentary pointed out that the opening verses of Psalm 29 describe a thunderstorm. An Internet search for further information on thunder and lightning quickly yielded a glut of very interesting information (as web searches tend to do today). The resources for acquiring this kind of information are most certainly "out there" and readily available for preachers. The key is to want to tap into them. Underlying even that desire is having a homiletical mind that is open to bringing in the fruits of science when natural and appropriate. The natural phenomenon celebrated in Psalm 29 as a demonstration of God's power is surely another example of how contemporary scientific research can bring Scripture alive, even as such illustrative material may enliven a sermon.

There are perhaps as many as two thousand going on right now. Each day on this planet an average of forty-five thousand occur. They are among the most powerful forces we know. I refer to thunderstorms. In the simplest but also perhaps most boring sense a thunderstorm is little more than an atmosphere stabilizer. Acting like a giant heat machine, a thunderstorm forms when there is a lot of cold air sitting on top of a lot of warm air. In order to rebalance the atmosphere, a thunderstorm pumps the warm air upward and the cold air downward until the atmosphere evens out. Once that happens, the thunderstorm has achieved its stabilizing purpose and it dies out. In that sense thunderstorms exist only to destroy themselves.

But along the way these storms can and do produce some of this planet's most stunning marvels, because that shifting around of cold and warm air can produce incredible winds. Here and there an outflow produces a microburst that can puff down toward the ground at one hundred miles per hour; we've all seen those grim pictures of what such wind shear can do to airplanes. In addition to wind, thunderstorms also produce rain and even ice. The storm's strong currents can supercool water particles to well below freezing, and if enough of this ice builds up, it falls to the ground as hail; though usually no larger than pebbles, some strong storms have produced so much ice that it falls in chunks as large as a grapefruit. But there's more: the forces within thunderstorm clouds are so great that particles of energy smash into one another with enough wallop to exchange electrical charges. So some particles get stripped of electrons while others add electrons, thus producing both positively charged particles and negatively charged particles. Typically the positive particles zoom to the top of the cloud and the negative ones sink to the bottom, creating a high-voltage chasm that equalizes itself through a fiery flash of lightning. Lasting only 30 microseconds, a bolt of lightning peaks out at 1,000,000,000,000 watts (1 trillion) with a surface temperature of 20,000 degrees centigrade. That, my friends, is three times hotter than the surface of the sun! (You may all gasp now!)

Psalm 29 is an ode to a thunderstorm. But this poem is not just that. In truth, the real aim of this psalm is not to wow the reader with the kinds of facts and figures I just gave you. No, the primary aim here is to move through the storm to the Lord of the storm, the King of Creation, the one, only true, sovereign God: Yahweh. As such, Psalm 29, for all its lyrical and poetic beauty, is actually a fairly feisty piece of polemic or argumentation.

This psalm throws down the gauntlet of challenge to some of the other religions of the ancient Near East—religions that claimed that the forces of nature are gods and goddesses in their own right. Psalm 29 reveals the falseness of those idolatrous claims by saying that the God of Israel is the one who creates all those wonders. More, he's the one who is greater than them all. So in a way you could read this psalm as a rebuke to those who worshiped the creation instead of the Creator.

As such, Psalm 29 walks a fine line. This is the only Old Testament text that so extensively identifies God directly with what people today might call "natural phenomena." The thunder simply *is* the voice of God, the lightning *is* the strike of God's voice, the wind *is* the effective speech of God that is so stunning it twists even the mightiest of oaks the way a child might mold Play-Doh. This is indeed the treading of a fine line as the Bible, including the Psalms, is always very careful to distinguish God the Creator from the handiwork of God in the creation.

But despite its close identification of God with the manifestations of a thunderstorm, Psalm 29 never crosses or blurs the boundary line between Creator and creation. Yahweh can be seen in, through, and by the thunderstorm, but he's never just the same as the storm. The thunder, lightning, wind, and the very power of the storm are the effective presence of Yahweh in the same way that my voice through the loudspeakers here this morning reveals my presence among you. But I am not just the same thing as the sound from the speaker. So also God is manifest in the storm without being the same thing as the storm.

Because in the end Yahweh is seen as seated in glory on his throne above it all. Though something of his glory and strength can be seen in the storm, all of that is at best but the faintest of hints as to his true grandeur. It is almost as though the psalmist points to the magnificence of the storm and then says, "If you think that's something, you ought to consider the God who doesn't even break a sweat in producing such wonders!"

To help keep the ultimate focus on God alone, this psalm begins and ends with pairs of verses that direct us to think first of all about Yahweh. Verses 1 and 2 open the psalm with a call to render Yahweh alone glory. Then, in conclusion, verses 10 and 11 redirect us to the heavenly court of Yahweh, where he rules as the supreme King.

The middle portion of this psalm, verses 3–9, serves as a kind of illustration. Verse 2 ends with a call to worship Yahweh "in the splendor of his holiness." That sounds kind of abstract. What exactly is "the splendor of holiness"? Holiness seems to be an invisible quality. You can no more see holiness than you can see kindness. You can't see kindness the same way that you can see blonde hair or a tree. Kindness needs to be embodied by someone for you to see it.

So if I tell you to praise Leanne for the splendor of her kindness, you may respond, "What do you mean? What kindness?" And true enough, just looking at a picture of Leanne won't reveal kindness to you. So perhaps I would then say, "Well, look over there, for instance. Do you see how Leanne plays so tenderly with those homeless children? That's just one example of what she's like all the time. She's got kindness all sewn up and so deserves to be respected for the splendor of her kindness."

So also in Psalm 29: the psalmist says that an example of God's splen-did holiness is a thunderstorm. It's not the only example, but it is one example that can be seen and appreciated. It's a window through which to glimpse the one true, almighty God of Israel. So the psalmist takes us to the edge of the ocean as a storm approaches. Many of us know this kind of experience. Sound travels exceedingly well and far over open bodies of water. And so even on a clear day at a Lake Michigan beach, you may suddenly hear a distant rumble. Soon it gets closer, and as you look out from Michigan toward Wisconsin, the horizon gets dark.

Often it is astonishing how quickly the conditions can change. A chill wind kicks up as the thunderstorm begins its pumping effort to move the warm surface air up and the colder air down, flashes of lightning become visible, the thunder louder. The waves kick up and start to wash over the pier. Hail begins to bounce off the beach like popcorn. Trees may fall, lightning may split the taller trees unlucky enough to become the equalizing point for the storm's electrical currents. And if you've ever been dangerously close to a lightning strike, then you know that Psalm 29's description of the ground shaking is no exaggeration. A tril-lion watts cannot discharge at 20,000 degrees without the surrounding air and ground rocking and reeling in response!

It's an awesome, often even a frightening, spectacle. But the real punch of this middle portion of Psalm 29 is not the tumultuous waves, the high-voltage lightning strikes, or the split oaks. More powerful than all of that is the conclusion of verse 9 when all who are in Yahweh's temple cry, "Glory!" It is an amazing feat of faith to be able to see a display like this storm but even so not be distracted from the Creator God whose glory the storm reveals. The response of this psalmist to this powerful storm is not, "Wow!" or "Awesome!" or "Cool!" or even "Yikes! Let's take shelter!" No, the response of the faithful is simply, "Glory to God in the highest! A sliver of God's nature just got paraded before our eyes!"

In verse 11 we are told that Yahweh gives strength to his people and this then leads to peace. A psalm that shook the foundations of the earth, a psalm that rattled the panes of our stained glass windows, a psalm that split oaks and caused us to plug our ears and cover our eyes from the noise and brightness of it all—this very psalm ends in peace. But this is not just the calm after the storm. This is not a depiction of that moment when suddenly the sun peeks back out and the only sound you can hear is the dripping of water from leaves.

No, the last Hebrew word of Psalm 29 is *shalom*. This is not "peace and quiet" but rather the peace that passes all understanding. This is the inner peace you get when you know that all is right with the world. This is the kind of peace that descends on your soul after a beautiful evening out with your family to celebrate a fiftieth anniversary—a peace that produces a deep sigh of satisfaction as you reflect on how much you love your children and grandchildren, how much they, blessedly enough, love you, and so how good it is to be alive in this particular moment.

Shalom is the sense that things are as they ought to be. In this case, it's the sense that things between you and the Almighty One of the cosmos are all right. And how do you get this peace, this sense that everything is plumb and in proper alignment? You get it, verse 11 says, because Yahweh gives strength to his people. And after all that we've seen in this psalm, that little line ought to deliver quite a few gigawatts of juice to your soul!

Because in this psalm the strength of God is what we've seen laying waste to forests, boiling up oceans, cracking the air with sound, frying the atmosphere with heat hotter than even the sun itself. And this, this is what gets hardwired into your soul! It's a wonder we don't disintegrate like a lightning-struck oak! Forget about Air Jordan or the Energizer bunny! We've got God's Holy Spirit connecting us to the Creator himself. It's like plugging your child's battery-operated toy train directly into a power company's substation.

It's a wonder we're not fried! But that was the fundamental mystery of Israel's existence in the Old Testament: God dwelled in the midst of her and yet she was not consumed. It's the mystery of the burning bush as Moses first saw it: the bush burned and burned and burned but never burned up! And so for us: the Holy Spirit of God himself glows within our hearts and yet we are not destroyed. The thunderstorm tells us that God's got vastly enough energy to wipe us off the face of the map if he wants to. Like moths that get too close to the flames of a bonfire, so we could easily just evaporate. But that doesn't happen. The God who roars and wheels his way through the thunderstorm uses his majestic power not to wipe us out but tenderly to give us shalom.

We have the blessing of peace because we know that what God wants more than anything is to use his power in the service of our salvation. How well we Christians know that, too. Whenever we see again that spectacle of God hanging limp on the cross, we see God's power in the service of securing our peace.

"He could have called ten thousand angels," the old hymn says of Jesus. Indeed! Anybody who in all of thirty microseconds can sizzle a trillion watts at a temperature three times that of the sun need not have let some Roman thugs spike nails through his hands and feet. But in order ultimately to channel his perfect power into our hearts, God put his power in service of our resurrection from the dead. He let his power drain out of Jesus so that at Pentecost the very power of God that leads to shalom could get funneled into us. In commenting on this psalm, James Mays noted that human beings seem to have an innate need for doxological experience. We yearn to be impressed by powerful people who possess qualities or skills we lack. We want to be invaded by their presence and then express our joy at the spectacle. We pine for such outlets for praise and doxology.

We need to worship something. We need to express doxological delight somewhere. Psalm 29, like the rest of Scripture, suggests that we look to the grandeur of creation for our first, primary source of awe-inspiring experiences. But on a deeper, vastly more profound level, Psalm 29 calls us to bring those experiences into conversation with the Bible's revelation that God loves us enough to want to save us by turning his strength loose in our souls. And it is that revelation that wrings from us the cry "Glory!"

As soon as we are able to utter our "Glory!" we find God coming right back at us with the blessing of peace—of shalom, of that deeply heaved sigh of contentment that comes when you know, you just know, that you are a walking miracle every bit as marvelous as a thunderstorm: for in your heart the very strength of God dwells and yet, far from being consumed by it, you are saved through it. For even now we begin to radiate that eternal light of the Lamb, in whose splendor we will live forever when we join our voices with all the saints in a chorus of "Glory" that will be louder than a thousand thunders as it rolls on and on across the crystal sea to the horizons of God's new creation. Amen.

Notes

Introduction

1. I first heard this couplet and the subsequent McGonagall couplet in a lecture given by Alvin Plantinga at Calvin College, titled "When Faith and Reason Clash: Evolution and the Bible." This lecture was later published in *Christian Scholars Review* 21, no. 1 (1991): 8–32.

2. J. Wentzel van Huyssteen, *Duet or Duel? Theology and Science in a Postmodern World* (Harrisburg, Pa.: Trinity, 1998), 131.

3. Paul Davies, *The Fifth Miracle: The Search for the Origin and Meaning of Life*, quoted in William A. Dembski, "The Unthinkable," *Books & Culture* 5, no. 5 (September/October 1999): 33.

4. Frederic Golden, "Albert Einstein: Person of the Century," *Time*, 31 December 1999, 64.

5. Anthony Lewis, "The Fault, Dear Brutus," *New York Times*, 31 December 1999, A-23.

6. Bob Herbert, "Miracles at Warp Speed," *New York Times*, 31 December 1999, A-23.

7. Keith Ward, *God, Faith, and the New Millennium: Christian Belief in an Age of Science* (Oxford: Oneworld, 1998), 14, 18.

8. Alan G. Padgett, "Creation by Design," *Books & Culture* 6, no. 4 (July/August 2000): 30.

9. Dava Sobel, *Galileo's Daughter: A Historical Memoir of Science, Faith, and Love* (New York: Penguin, 2000), 45–66.

10. We will return to a more expanded discussion of gospel content and gospel context in part 2 when we turn our attention more directly to how preachers can begin to utilize what we discuss in the first part of this book.

11. Roger Van Harn, *Pew Rights: For People Who Listen to Sermons* (Grand Rapids: Eerdmans, 1992), 18.

12. Barbara Brown Taylor, *The Luminous Web: Essays on Science and Religion* (Boston: Cowley, 2000), 6.

13. Ibid., 7–8.

Chapter 1: Biblical Authority in an Age of Science

1. Tom Beaudoin, *Virtual Faith: The Irreverent Spiritual Quest of Generation X* (San Francisco: Jossey-Bass, 1998), 126–27.

2. Ibid., 125.

3. Walter Brueggemann, *Finally Comes the Poet: Daring Speech for Proclamation* (Minneapolis: Augsburg, 1989), 82. Brueggemann adroitly outlines in this book some of the challenges that modern preachers face.

4. Indeed, this section of my book draws on a theological essay, "The Crisis of Biblical Authority in the Church," which I originally wrote as part of a yearlong study sponsored by the Center of Theological Inquiry in Princeton, New Jersey.

5. John Calvin, *Institutes of the Christian Religion* (Philadelphia: Westminster, 1960), 1.7.1.

6. Ibid., 1.7.4.

7. Ibid., 1.9.3.

8. Wolfhart Pannenberg, *Systematic Theology*, vol. 1, trans. Geoffrey W. Bromiley (Grand Rapids: Eerdmans, 1988), 224.

9. Langdon Gilkey, quoted in J. Christiaan Beker, "The Authority of Scripture: Normative or Incidental?" *Theology Today* 49, no. 3 (1992): 378.

10. Ibid., 380.

11. Richard B. Hays, "Salvation by Trust? Reading the Bible Faithfully," *Christian Century* 114, no. 7 (26 February 1997): 218.

12. Harry T. Cook, letter to the editor, *Christian Century* 114, no. 14 (23–30 April 1997): 426.

13. Ibid.

14. For a summary of Plantinga's and Wolterstorff's work, see Alvin Plantinga and Nicholas Wolterstorff, eds., *Faith and Rationality: Reason and Belief in God* (Notre Dame: University of Notre Dame Press, 1983), 16–93.

15. In *Return to Reason* (Grand Rapids: Eerdmans, 1990), 134–35, Kelly James Clark defines the criteria for classical foundationalism as follows: "Beliefs that are evident to the senses are *reports of immediate experience*—such as that there is a piece of paper before me, there is a tree before me, and the wall that I am looking at is yellow. Beliefs that are self-evident are those which *upon understanding them one sees them to be true*—such as that 2 + 2 = 4, all bachelors are unmarried males, and the whole is equal to the sum of its parts. And finally, beliefs that are incorrigible are *propositions about which one cannot be wrong*. These are usually reports of one's own immediate subjective states—much like the appearance beliefs discussed earlier—such as the beliefs that it seems to me that the wall in front of me is yellow, it appears to me that there is a tree before me" (italics in original). Basically, these are things about which you cannot be wrong. If you are sane, if your eyes and brain work at reasonably good levels, then you cannot be wrong about seeing a tree, tasting salt, or understanding that you cannot have a square circle or a married bachelor. In a sense, the beliefs that pass muster for classical foundationalism are what could be called "obvious," the kinds of things about which you could say to a skeptic, "Well, for heaven's sake! The tree is right there! Can't you see it?"

16. Clark defines a properly basic belief as a belief "one holds but not on the basis of other beliefs that one holds, that is, not inferentially" (ibid., 126). So, 2 + 2 = 4 is a properly basic belief because it is intuitively in the foundation of my most basic belief system, on which everything else is built. Of course, a person may hold many other beliefs, perhaps with great passion, that one would not regard as proper, basic, or even rational. If a man I meet is convinced that his next-door neighbor is Satan, I will have good cause to conclude that this is not a properly basic belief, inasmuch as such a conclusion would necessarily be

contingent upon, and inferred from, a pool of other propositions (at least some of which would doubtlessly prove to be suspect upon examination!).

17. Plantinga, in Plantinga and Wolterstorff, eds., *Faith and Rationality*, 80–81.

18. Pannenberg, *Systematic Theology*, 242.

19. Ibid.

20. Beker, "Authority of Scripture," 77.

21. Plantinga has recently extended his work in this area into a specifically Christian context with his book *Warranted Christian Belief* (New York: Oxford University Press, 2000). I will draw on this work in coming pages when countering the naturalism of Richard Dawkins and others.

22. Hays, "Salvation by Trust?" 221.

23. Plantinga, *Warranted Christian Belief*, 175–76.

Chapter 2: Holy Curiosity and Science

1. Robert MacNeil, *Wordstruck: A Memoir* (New York: Viking, 1989), 67.

2. Richard Dawkins, quoted in "Is Science Killing the Soul?" *Edge*, <http://www.edge.org/documents/archive/edge53.html>.

3. Diogenes Allen, *Christian Belief in a Postmodern World: The Full Wealth of Conviction* (Louisville: Westminster/John Knox, 1989), 23.

4. Although even here one needs to be a bit cautious. Historian Jacques Barzun recently noted, "When we speak of [seventeenth-century] science and scientists we are committing an anachronism. At that time the word science had not been narrowed down to one kind of knowledge; it meant whatever is known, and men of learning were still able to possess most of it." Barzun then goes on to point out that "scientist" as we use the term today was not coined until about 1840. When that which eventually became "science" as we now define the enterprise was born in the sixteenth and seventeenth centuries, it actually still drew from and in some sense included a great many fields of inquiry, including alchemy, magic, and astrology—fields we would no longer regard as very scientific in the contemporary meaning of the word but which at that time were believed to have validity in making sense of reality. See Barzun's *From Dawn to Decadence: 1500 to the Present: 500 Years of Western Cultural Life* (New York: HarperCollins, 2000), 191–93.

5. Allen, *Christian Belief in a Postmodern World*, 24–27.

6. I draw fairly extensively here from material I covered in *Remember Creation: God's World of Wonder and Delight* (Grand Rapids: Eerdmans, 1998).

7. Ian Barbour, *When Science Meets Religion: Enemies, Strangers, or Partners?* (San Francisco: HarperCollins, 2000), 124–26.

8. Unfortunately, even within largely Christian circles the desire to know at times transmuted into a desire for mastery and control over nature. It would, therefore, be a bit simplistic to claim that even at its inception science was only driven by childlike curiosity or a desire to praise God through taking note of God's creation gifts. Still, my point here is that it is possible to perceive science, and for Christians to practice science, in a context of faith seeking understanding that in turn can indeed become cause for still greater praise of God.

9. Sallie McFague, *The Body of God: An Ecological Theology* (Minneapolis: Augsburg Fortress, 1993), 50ff. See also her work *Super, Natural Christians: How We Should Love Nature* (Minneapolis: Augsburg Fortress, 1997), 26ff.

Chapter 3: Where Faith and Science Disagree

1. Even today, when almost everyone knows better, we still use the traditional language of the sun moving, even though we are aware it is the earth's rotation that creates the illusion of the sun in motion. There is a difference between how we speak of our observations and what we intend to teach (or even what we already know to be true).

2. Allen, *Christian Belief in a Postmodern World*, 31.

3. Sobel, *Galileo's Daughter*, 53–54.

4. Quoted in Allen, *Christian Belief in a Postmodern World*, 47.

5. Carl Sagan, introduction to *A Brief History of Time: From the Big Bang to Black Holes*, by Stephen W. Hawking (New York: Bantam, 1988), x. A more scientific treatment of Hawking's notion that the universe may have no edge and no beginning will be taken up later.

6. Quoted in Barbour, *When Science Meets Religion*, 154–55.

7. Ibid., 155. Of course, one could question the poetic value of blind happenstance and cosmic quirks that just coincidentally but for no apparent purpose yielded humanity. One could ask how much beauty there is in a universe doomed to destruction, with no God even to remember it, much less to preserve even the merest bit of anything we now regard as noble or lovely. There may well be more beauty and poetry in a mother's lovingly mixing pancake batter to prepare her children a Saturday morning breakfast treat than there is in the rather bleak and pointless picture of an entropic universe hurtling toward ultimate destruction. But let us not quibble over poetry!

8. Keith Ward, *God, Chance, and Necessity* (Oxford: Oneworld, 1996), 11–12.

9. Richard Dawkins, quoted in Barbour, *When Science Meets Religion*, 155.

10. Chris Floyd, "Daniel Dennett's Darwinian Mind: An Interview with a 'Dangerous' Man," *Science & Spirit* 11, no. 2 (May/June 2000): 19.

11. Richard Dawkins, quoted in "Is Science Killing the Soul?" 7.

12. Some of Plantinga's thinking on this subject is summarized in Willem Drees, *Religion, Science, and Naturalism* (Cambridge: Cambridge University Press, 1996), 159ff.

13. John Polkinghorne, *Belief in God in an Age of Science* (New Haven: Yale University Press, 1998), 80.

14. Ibid., 83.

15. A more recent attempt to grant both evolutionary science and biblical theology their due is the Intelligent Design movement led by writers such as Michael Behe and William Dembski. These writers are willing to grant the broad sweep, as well as many of the finer points, of evolutionary development both in the universe and on this planet. They insist, however, that the odds of blind chance actually yielding beings as complex and self-aware as humanity are so infinitesimally remote that it requires the reality of a designer. They also point to things like the human eye as well as to vastly smaller units at the subcellular level that are, in Behe's terminology, "irreducibly complex"—so complex, in fact, that taken individually, much less taken all together, their development and combination in just the right forms at just the right times are impossible if left to chance and coincidence. These are serious arguments that quickly become very complicated. They may also prove to be correct. As some have pointed out, however, the argument for design based on inexplicable complexity is balanced on the same razor's edge as other arguments like that of the "God of the gaps"; namely, it is possible that what seems irreducibly complex today will seem less complex a hundred years from now, depending on how science advances. For all its cleverness and savvy, the argument for intelligent design based on the unlikelihood of certain combinations happening at certain times will not stand if science one day uncovers some mechanism in nature that makes certain combinations at certain times inevitable (or much more likely) in ways that are wholly explicable in scientific terms after all. It may well be that such a discovery will never be

made, but the viability of God as both the designer and the mover of the entire process of universal history and creation needs to be more broadly and comprehensively grounded, being free (on the basis of faith alone) from any constraints in the physical world. As it is, Daniel Dennett has in recent years promoted what he calls "Darwin's dangerous idea," whereby he claims that Christians who have blithely adopted evolutionary theory as "just God's way of doing things" have failed to grasp what subsequent evolutionary theory has "proven." Dennett contends that evolution necessarily eliminates God because we can now see that cells can and do evolve completely on their own. Scientists have, so to speak, found the magic "switch" or mechanism (natural selection operating over a long period of time) that drives the process. Dennett, however, is moving rather quickly from a possible physical finding of how things work—natural selection over eons of time—to an unwarranted elision of this belief with his conviction that there is no God. It is not at all clear that discovering how something works eliminates the possibility of an outside party who designed or observed the workings of the entity in question. Such physical findings do not lead naturally to any metaphysical or spiritual insights, unless one is looking for corroborating evidence for a belief one held in the first place (in this case, the belief that there is no God).

16. Scientists, of course, are aware of this argument and realize the potential limitation it could place on their work, which is perhaps why someone like Stephen Hawking has sought to shut down the very possibility of there being anything "beyond" the universe. By suggesting that the universe has no edge or boundary in space, and by further conjecturing that the universe may well have had no "beginning" in any sense, Hawking has attempted to chase God out of his last remaining potential hiding places. But as Keith Ward has so adroitly said, Hawking's perspective, in addition to being its own form of a leap of faith, naively ignores the fact that for religious believers the question is not whether (or how) God may or may not have gotten the entire process "started" but rather whether the entire cosmos, as it now exists, has a meaningful purpose and destiny. It is not a matter of whether or not we can "find" God hiding in some nook of reality to which science has actual or theoretical access but whether the whole shebang is held in the loving hands of a purposive Creator.

17. See John Polkinghorne and Michael Welker, eds., *The End of the World and the Ends of God: Science and Theology on Eschatology* (Harrisburg, Pa.: Trinity, 2000), 5.

18. Polkinghorne, *Belief in God in an Age of Science*, 100.

19. Van Huyssteen, *Duet or Duel?* 3.

20. All of the above summarizes Barbour, *When Science Meets Religion*, 1–38.

21. Van Huyssteen, *Duet or Duel?* xv.

22. Ibid., 21–22, 26.

23. Of course, it could be asserted that my suggestion to combine Independence and Integration really amounts to no more than the category of Dialogue. But because I wish to maintain the epistemic separateness of each field's specific way of discovering truth (the Independence model) while trying genuinely to arrive at a coherent and more comprehensive world-and-life view, I think a hybrid of these two is significantly different and, I would argue, stronger than the Dialogue category, in which conversation and selective borrowing takes place only now and again. I am seeking an approach that is more comprehensive and ongoing than just occasional dialogue.

24. In fact, when discussing this play with John Polkinghorne, I discovered that Stoppard had once contacted him. As part of Stoppard's larger research on contemporary physics, he had read one of Polkinghorne's books on the quantum world.

25. Tom Stoppard, *Hapgood* (London: Faber & Faber, 1988), 40–41.

Chapter 4: Learning from Science

1. Here, however, I begin to feel a bit nervous about some of the claims made by process theology as well as by other similarly minded theologians. Classically, it has been claimed that the omniscience of God means that God knows every truth that is knowable. Process theology, however, points out that since the future does not yet exist at any given moment in our history, even God cannot know the future—even God cannot know what is not yet real but only everything that is *currently* real. Of course, issues having to do with the temporal and the eternal quickly become very snarled. It is by no means clear to me, however, that the future would perforce be off limits to God's reality just because it is for us finite human beings. And surely there are at least *some* facts about the future that God can, does, and must know, not the least of which is the fact that he will one day fully establish an eternal kingdom of *shalom* through Jesus the Son. It may well be, as we will explore later in this book, that God has built in some free play of events in ways that may mean even God will not fully know how every detail will play out. I hesitate, however, to go too far in the direction of limiting God's foreknowledge of future events and continue to hold out for the traditional idea that foreknowledge need not mean foreordained in the sense of being predetermined.

2. Just because *God* knows every true proposition, however, does not indicate that we do. Even Christians who try to base their knowledge and worldview on Scripture have been known to misapprehend matters, including in areas where it was once believed the Bible definitively taught *x* or *y* regarding the physical universe. Science cannot discover anything that God does not already know. True enough. However, science can discover and has discovered things that *Christians* do not already know, sometimes even causing Christians to revise what they once thought to be true about matters related to the layout, makeup, and origins of the physical universe. In this sense, it should not be forgotten that science can and sometimes does help believers to read the Bible more accurately.

3. Nicholas Wolterstorff, "Tertullian's Enduring Question," quoted in *Books & Culture* 5, no. 5 (September/October 1999): 3.

4. Pope John Paul II, quoted in Sobel, *Galileo's Daughter,* 11.

5. It should be noted, however, that smart refutations of Hume's argument were made long before the Newtonian view of the world was undercut. Theologians did not need Einstein to mount a good defense against Hume's antimiracle argumentation!

6. Hawking, *A Brief History of Time,* 175.

7. Of course, were a grand unification theory or anything remotely approaching such a theory ever achieved, it would be a remarkable grasp of creation's blueprint and perhaps as fine a demonstration as imaginable that humanity does indeed contain a spark of the divine (which Christians call the image of God). It would not be the equivalent of knowing the mind of God, but even accessing God's blueprint for this creation—similar to the discovery and now the writing out of DNA in the human genome project—is a stellar achievement and one which Christians could not but applaud and support as evidence of God's gift of rationality to us. Still, it would not exhaust "the mind of God."

8. It should be noted that not all cosmologists and physicists agree on the existence of the singularity. Certain aspects of quantum theory may eliminate the need to posit a singular point of cosmic origin. My summary reflects the work of those whose theories are based on the likelihood of some kind of singularity having once existed.

9. Van Huyssteen, *Duet or Duel?* 51. This is the case, however, even if there once was a singularity. More uncertain is whether any form of singularity ever existed in an absolute sense. Either way, van Huyssteen's comment that we eventually reach the limits of scientific rationality remains valid.

10. It should be clear, however, that although I believe the Genesis text reflects this ancient folk cosmology, that is a very different matter from saying that Genesis teaches

this cosmology in ways that would require people of faith to embrace precisely this view. Any Christian who believes that the earth is round, that the earth orbits the sun—and not the other way around—and that this planet is *not* bounded by a glass firmament clearly has a very different view of the universe than the one reflected in basically the whole of the Bible. But, as was stated earlier, the Bible's *reflecting* a set of background beliefs about cosmology is different in important ways from *teaching* that cosmology as the way every subsequent reader of the Bible must envision the universe.

11. It should be noted, however, that many physicists and cosmologists have no difficulty in claiming that the singularity did not have to *be* anywhere; it just was. Even if one factors in the existence of God, it still could be possible to say that the singularity or the infant universe would not need a location in the sense of other dimensions or of somehow being contained by something else. My argument here is more for the existence of God in dimensions or realms beyond the merely physical and is only partially for a larger location in a strictly spatial sense.

12. Bertrand Russell, quoted in Taylor, *The Luminous Web*, 31.

13. Barbour, *When Science Meets Religion*, 62. The precise numbers here depend on how one counts possible neural connections in the brain. The number of atoms in the universe is estimated to be somewhere around 10^{18}, whereas, by some estimates at least, the number of neural connections in a single human brain is approximately 10^{14}. Regardless of the precise number, it is a staggering number of connections. The brain remains the single most complex phenomenon we are aware of in the cosmos.

14. Taylor, *The Luminous Web*, 35, 43.

15. Barbour, *When Science Meets Religion*, 58.

16. It should be noted, however, that discoveries made in the spring of 2001 indicate that this universe is unlikely ever to collapse on itself in a "big crunch." Recent evidence from the Hubble space telescope indicates that the universe's rate of expansion is faster the farther out one goes into space, likely indicating that Einstein's belief (which was eventually discarded by Einstein as his worst blunder) in a cosmological constant that counteracts gravity's tendency to pull things back toward the center is correct after all. Hence, any theory of "cosmic promiscuity" that depends on a long series of explosion-expansion-collapse-reexplosion may now be undermined.

17. Fred Hoyle and Chandra Wickramasinghe, quoted in Barbour, *When Science Meets Religion*, 112.

18. Fred Hoyle, "The Universe: Past and Present Reflections," *Engineering and Science* (November 1981): 12. Owen Gingerich's comments are from a public lecture at the Center of Theological Inquiry, Princeton, New Jersey, on 14 November 1991.

19. Ward, *God, Chance, and Necessity*, 116–17.

20. John F. Haught, *God After Darwin: A Theology of Evolution* (Boulder, Colo.: Westview, 2000), 99.

21. Polkinghorne, *Belief in God in an Age of Science*, 6–7.

22. Alvin Plantinga, "Dennett's Dangerous Idea: Darwin, Mind, and Meaning," *Books & Culture* 2, no. 3 (May/June 1996): 17.

23. I have drawn much of this material from Albert Einstein, *Relativity: The Special and the General Theory: A Clear Explanation That Anyone Can Understand*, trans. Robert W. Lawson (New York: Crown, 1961), mcmlxi. Additional explanatory help (since upon reading Einstein's "explanation that anyone can understand," I determined that I most definitely am *not* anyone) was drawn from Stephen Hawking's *A Brief History of Time*.

24. John Polkinghorne, *Science and Theology: An Introduction* (London: SPCK, 1998), 40–41.

Chapter 5: Science's Story in Theological Conversation

1. See Plantinga's *God, Freedom, and Evil* (Grand Rapids: Eerdmans, 1977).
2. William Schweiker, "Time as a Moral Space," in *The End of the World and the Ends of God: Science and Theology on Eschatology,* ed. John Polkinghorne and Michael Welker (Harrisburg, Pa.: Trinity, 2000), 129–30.
3. Ibid., 136.
4. Haught, *God After Darwin,* 97.
5. Ibid., 98.
6. Van Huyssteen, *Duet or Duel?* 135–47.
7. Natalie Angier, "On Human Nature and the Evolution of Culture: A Conversation with Paul Ehrlich," *New York Times,* 10 October 2000, F1–F2.
8. Warren S. Brown, "Cognitive Contributions to the Soul," in *Whatever Happened to the Soul? Scientific and Theological Portraits of Human Nature,* ed. Warren S. Brown, Nancey Murphy, and H. Newton Malony (Minneapolis: Augsburg Fortress, 1998), 104–8.
9. Albert Einstein, quoted in Thomas Torrance, "Einstein and God," in *Reflections: Center of Theological Inquiry Public Lecture Series 1997* (newsletter), 19.
10. Taylor, *The Luminous Web,* 68.

Chapter 6: The Gospel's Content in a Cosmic Context

1. Herbert O'Driscoll's comments were delivered in a lecture presented at Princeton Theological Seminary's Institute of Theology, June 1992.

Chapter 7: As It Was in the Beginning . . .

1. Richard Lischer, "A Sense of Calling," *Christian Century* 116, no. 8 (10 March 1999): 277.
2. Phillip Pullman, as quoted in Sarah Lyall, "The Man Who Dared to Make Religion the Villain," *New York Times,* 7 November 2000.
3. See the introduction by Walter Hooper in the 1980 edition of C. S. Lewis, *The Weight of Glory and Other Addresses* (New York: Macmillan, 1980), xxii.
4. C. S. Lewis, "Transposition," in *The Weight of Glory and Other Addresses* (New York: Macmillan, 1980), 69. In general, all of the material in this section summarizing Lewis's essay came from this edition of the work, 54–73.

Select Bibliography

Achtemeier, Elizabeth. *Nature, God, and Pulpit*. Grand Rapids: Eerdmans, 1992.

Allen, Diogenes. *Christian Belief in a Postmodern World: The Full Wealth of Conviction*. Louisville: Westminster/John Knox, 1989.

Barbour, Ian. *When Science Meets Religion: Enemies, Strangers, or Partners?* San Francisco: HarperSanFrancisco, 2000.

Beaudoin, Tom. *Virtual Faith: The Irreverent Spiritual Quest of Generation X*. San Francisco: Jossey-Bass, 1998.

Brown Taylor, Barbara. *The Luminous Web: Essays on Science and Religion*. Boston: Cowley, 2000.

Brown, Warren S., Nancey Murphy, and H. Newton Malony, eds. *Whatever Happened to the Soul? Scientific and Theological Portraits of Human Nature*. Minneapolis: Fortress, 1998.

Brueggemann, Walter. *Finally Comes the Poet: Daring Speech for Proclamation*. Minneapolis: Fortress, 1989.

Clark, Kelly James. *Return to Reason: A Critique of Enlightenment Evidentialism and a Defense of Reason and Belief in God*. Grand Rapids: Eerdmans, 1990.

Dawkins, Richard. *The Blind Watchmaker*. New York: W. W. Norton, 1986.

Dennett, Daniel. *Darwin's Dangerous Idea*. New York: Simon and Schuster, 1995.

Einstein, Albert. *Relativity: The Special and the General Theory: A Clear Explanation That Anyone Can Understand*. New York: Crown, 1961.

Hawking, Stephen W. *A Brief History of Time: From the Big Bang to Black Holes*. New York: Bantam, 1988.

Lewis, C. S. *The Weight of Glory and Other Addresses*. New York: Macmillan, 1980.

McFague, Sallie. *The Body of God: An Ecological Theology*. Minneapolis: Fortress, 1993.

———. *Super, Natural Christians: How We Should Love Nature*. Minneapolis: Fortress Press, 1997.

McGrath, Alister E. *A Scientific Theology*. Vol. 1, *Nature*. Grand Rapids: Eerdmans, 2001.

Pannenberg, Wolfhart. *Systematic Theology*. Vol. 1. Trans. Geoffrey W. Bromiley. Grand Rapids: Eerdmans, 1988.

Plantinga, Alvin. *God, Freedom, and Evil*. Grand Rapids: Eerdmans, 1977.

———. *Warranted Christian Belief*. New York: Oxford University Press, 2000.

Plantinga, Alvin, and Nicholas Wolterstorff, eds. *Faith and Rationality: Reason and Belief in God*. Notre Dame: University of Notre Dame Press, 1983.

Polkinghorne, John. *Belief in God in an Age of Science*. New Haven: Yale University Press, 1998.

———. *The Faith of a Physicist: Reflections of a Bottom-Up Thinker*. Minneapolis: Fortress, 1996.

———. *Science and Theology: An Introduction*. London: SPCK, Minneapolis: Fortress, 1998.

Polkinghorne, John, and Michael Welker, eds. *The End of the World and the Ends of God: Science and Theology on Eschatology*. Harrisburg, Pa.: Trinity, 2000.

Sobel, Dava. *Galileo's Daughter: A Historical Memoir of Science, Faith, and Love*. New York: Penguin, 2000.

Stoppard, Tom. *Hapgood*. London: Faber and Faber, 1988.

Van Harn, Roger. *Pew Rights: For People Who Listen to Sermons*. Grand Rapids: Eerdmans, 1992.

van Huyssteen, J. Wentzel. *Duet or Duel? Theology and Science in a Postmodern World*. Harrisburg, Pa.: Trinity, 1998.

Ward, Keith. *God, Chance, and Necessity*. Oxford: Oneworld, 1996.

———. *God, Faith, and the New Millennium: Christian Belief in an Age of Science*. Oxford: Oneworld, 1998.

Index

Scott E. Hoezee has been minister of preaching and administration at Calvin Christian Reformed Church in Grand Rapids since 1993. He is the author of five books and is a regular book reviewer. He has served as book review editor for *Perspectives: A Journal of Reformed Thought* since 2000.

Printed in July 2019
by Rotomail Italia S.p.A., Vignate (MI) - Italy